Order this book online at www.trafford.com
or email orders@trafford.com

Most Trafford titles are also available at major online book retailers.

Printed in Victoria, BC, Canada.

ISBN: 978-1-4120-8083-5

*Our mission is to efficiently provide the world's finest, most comprehensive book publishing
service, enabling every author to experience success. To find out how to publish your book, your
way, and have it available worldwide, visit us online at www.trafford.com*

Trafford rev. 1/20/2010

 www.trafford.com

North America & international
toll-free: 1 888 232 4444 (USA & Canada)
phone: 250 383 6864 ♦ fax: 812 355 4082

CONTENTS

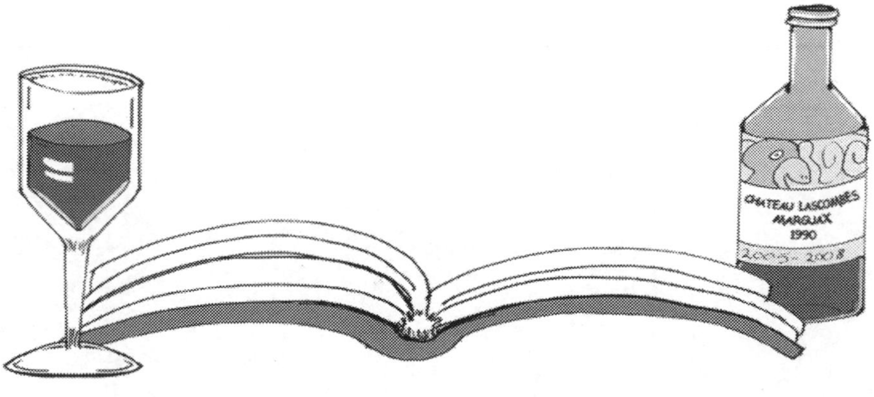

CHATEAU LASCOMBES
MARGAUX
1990
2005-2008

CHAPTER ONE

"Where's the babysitter?"

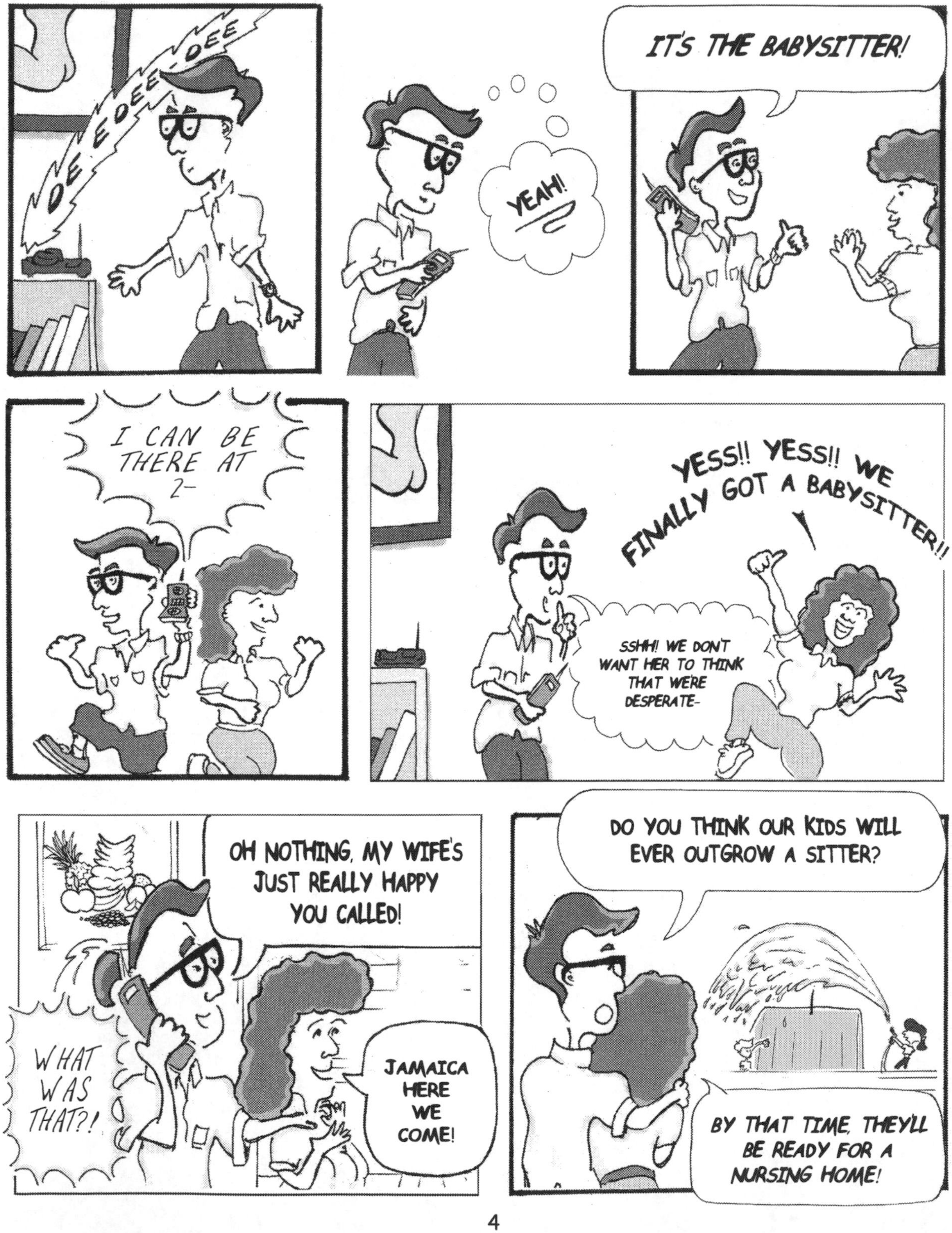

DE EDEE-DEE
YEAH!
IT'S THE BABYSITTER!
I CAN BE THERE AT 2-
YESS!! YESS!! WE FINALLY GOT A BABYSITTER!!
SSHH! WE DON'T WANT HER TO THINK THAT WE'RE DESPERATE-
WHAT WAS THAT?!
OH NOTHING, MY WIFE'S JUST REALLY HAPPY YOU CALLED!
JAMAICA HERE WE COME!
DO YOU THINK OUR KIDS WILL EVER OUTGROW A SITTER?
BY THAT TIME, THEY'LL BE READY FOR A NURSING HOME!

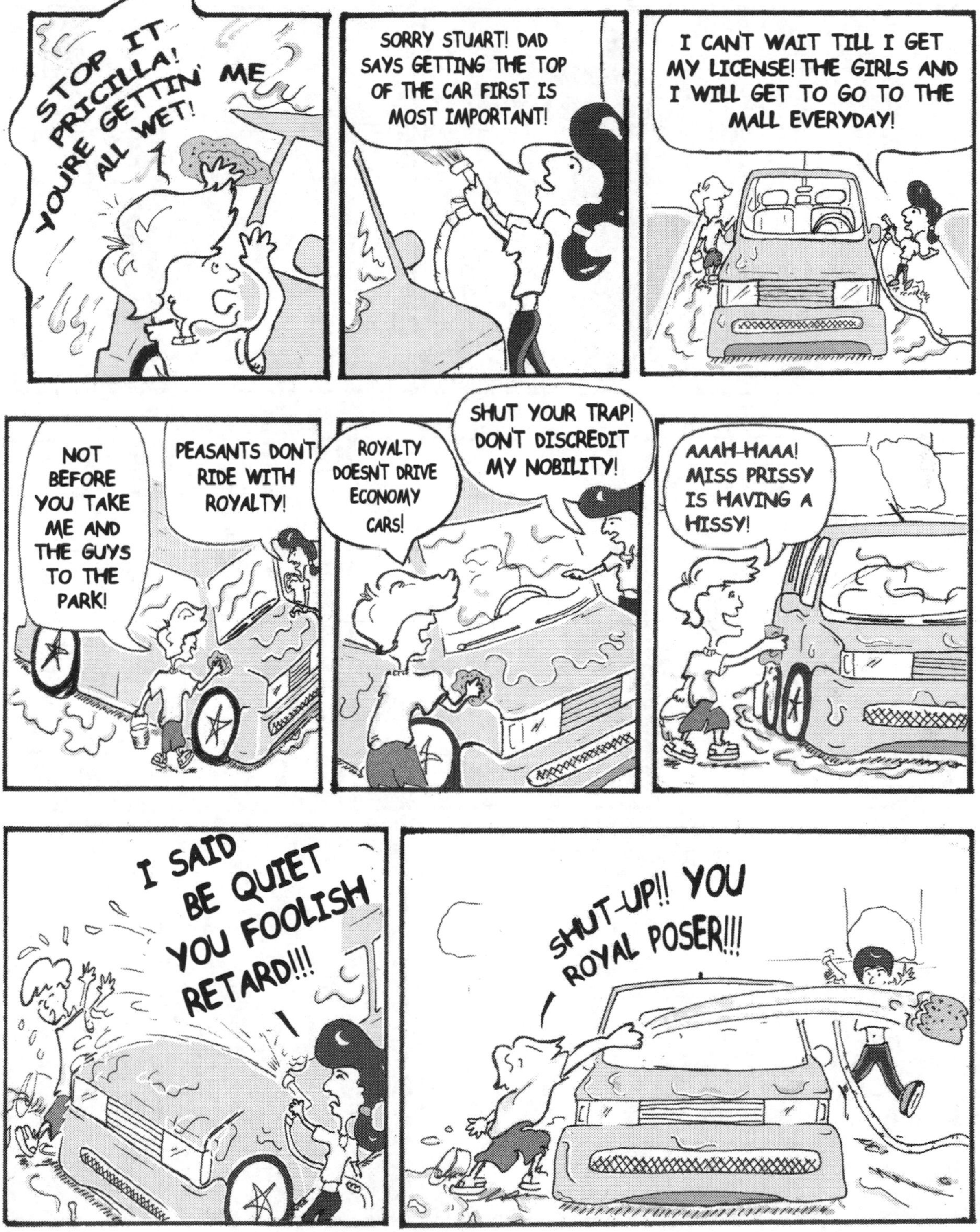
STOP IT PRICILLA! YOU'RE GETTIN' ME ALL WET!
SORRY STUART! DAD SAYS GETTING THE TOP OF THE CAR FIRST IS MOST IMPORTANT!
I CAN'T WAIT TILL I GET MY LICENSE! THE GIRLS AND I WILL GET TO GO TO THE MALL EVERYDAY!
NOT BEFORE YOU TAKE ME AND THE GUYS TO THE PARK!
PEASANTS DON'T RIDE WITH ROYALTY!
ROYALTY DOESN'T DRIVE ECONOMY CARS!
SHUT YOUR TRAP! DON'T DISCREDIT MY NOBILITY!
AAAH-HAAA! MISS PRISSY IS HAVING A HISSY!
I SAID BE QUIET YOU FOOLISH RETARD!!!
SHUT-UP!! YOU ROYAL POSER!!!

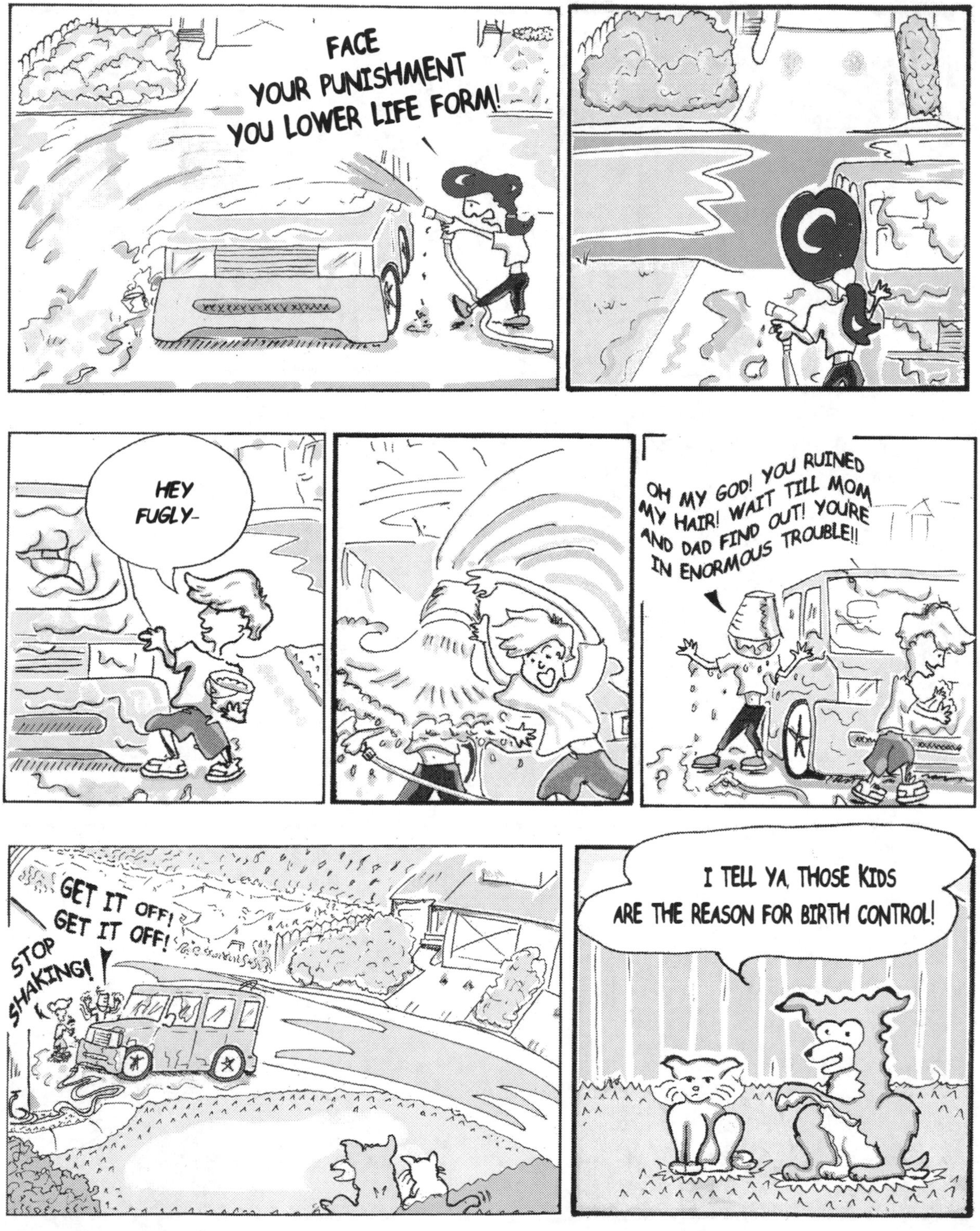
FACE YOUR PUNISHMENT YOU LOWER LIFE FORM!
HEY FUGLY-
OH MY GOD! YOU RUINED MY HAIR! WAIT TILL MOM AND DAD FIND OUT! YOU'RE IN ENORMOUS TROUBLE!!
GET IT OFF! GET IT OFF!
STOP SHAKING!
I TELL YA, THOSE KIDS ARE THE REASON FOR BIRTH CONTROL!

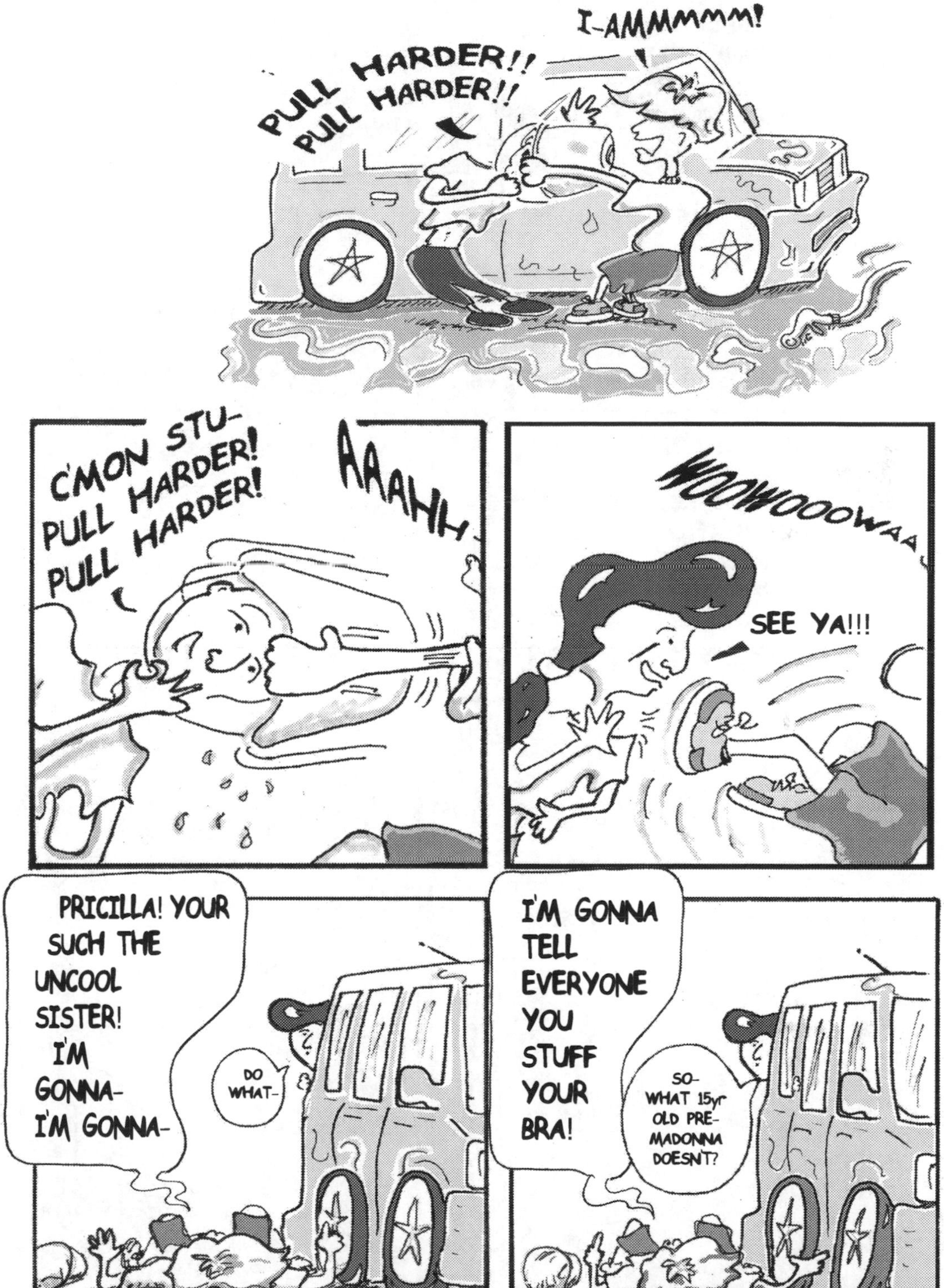
I-AMMMMM!
PULL HARDER!!
PULL HARDER!!
C'MON STU-
PULL HARDER!
PULL HARDER!
AAAHH
WOOWOOOOWAA
SEE YA!!!
PRICILLA! YOUR SUCH THE UNCOOL SISTER! I'M GONNA- I'M GONNA-
DO WHAT-
I'M GONNA TELL EVERYONE YOU STUFF YOUR BRA!
SO- WHAT 15yr OLD PRE-MADONNA DOESN'T?

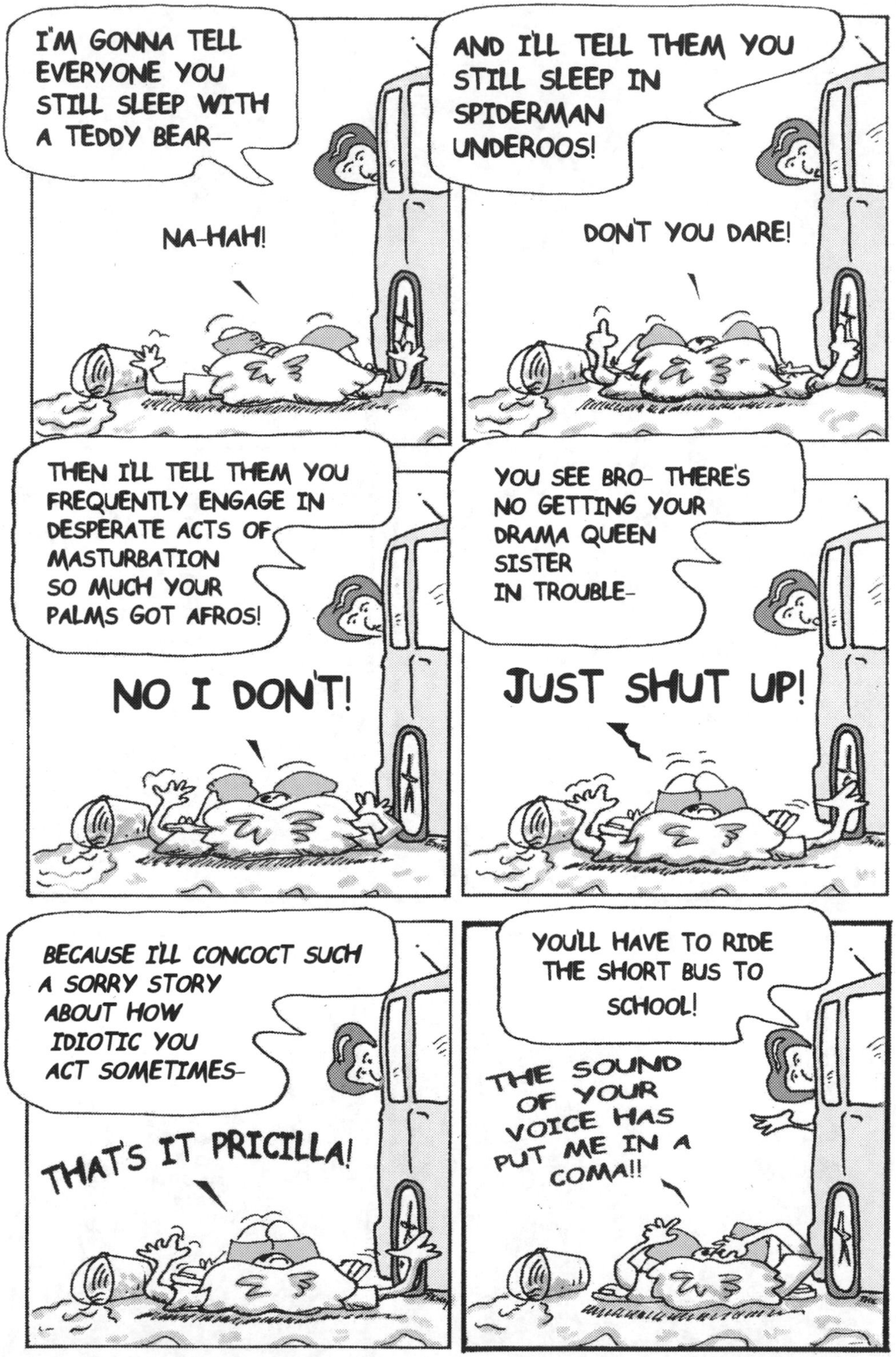
I'M GONNA TELL EVERYONE YOU STILL SLEEP WITH A TEDDY BEAR—
NA-HAH!
AND I'LL TELL THEM YOU STILL SLEEP IN SPIDERMAN UNDEROOS!
DON'T YOU DARE!
THEN I'LL TELL THEM YOU FREQUENTLY ENGAGE IN DESPERATE ACTS OF MASTURBATION SO MUCH YOUR PALMS GOT AFROS!
NO I DON'T!
YOU SEE BRO- THERE'S NO GETTING YOUR DRAMA QUEEN SISTER IN TROUBLE-
JUST SHUT UP!
BECAUSE I'LL CONCOCT SUCH A SORRY STORY ABOUT HOW IDIOTIC YOU ACT SOMETIMES-
THAT'S IT PRICILLA!
YOU'LL HAVE TO RIDE THE SHORT BUS TO SCHOOL!
THE SOUND OF YOUR VOICE HAS PUT ME IN A COMA!!

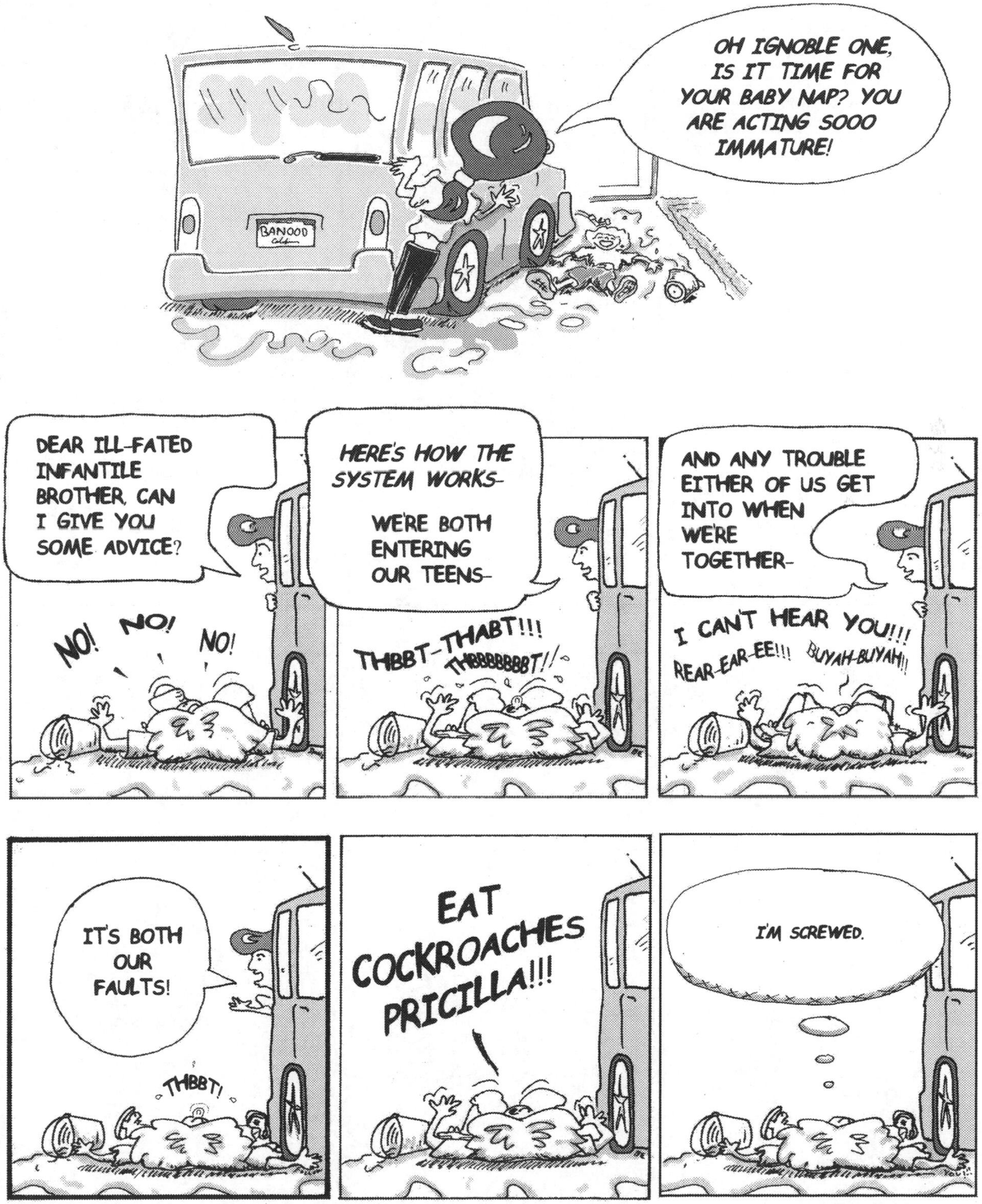

OH IGNOBLE ONE, IS IT TIME FOR YOUR BABY NAP? YOU ARE ACTING SOOO IMMATURE!
BANOOD
DEAR ILL-FATED INFANTILE BROTHER, CAN I GIVE YOU SOME ADVICE?
NO! NO! NO!
HERE'S HOW THE SYSTEM WORKS-
WE'RE BOTH ENTERING OUR TEENS-
THBBT-THABT!!! THBBBBBBBT!!
AND ANY TROUBLE EITHER OF US GET INTO WHEN WE'RE TOGETHER-
I CAN'T HEAR YOU!!! REAR-EAR-EE!!! BUYAH-BUYAH!!
IT'S BOTH OUR FAULTS!
THBBT!
EAT COCKROACHES PRICILLA!!!
I'M SCREWED.

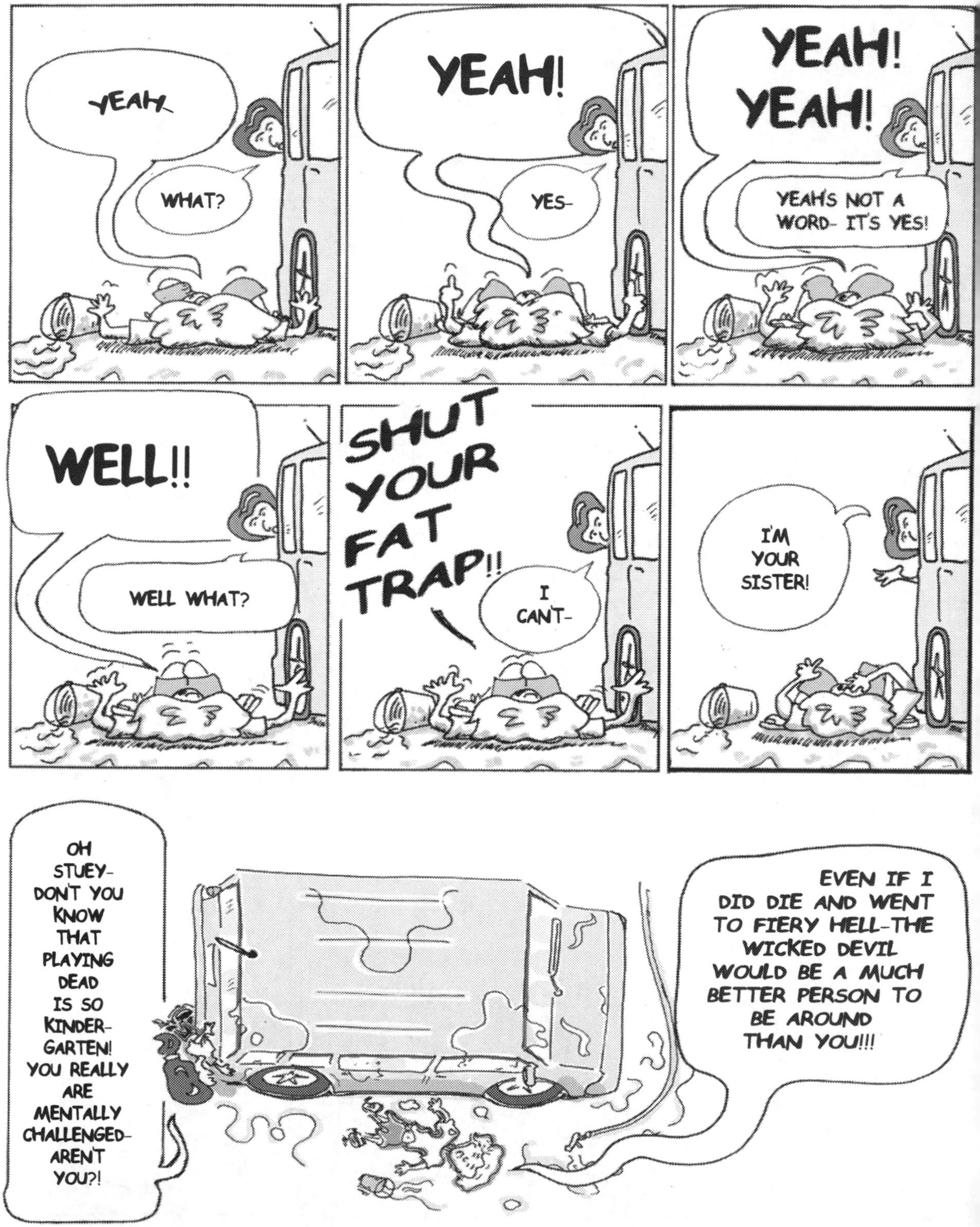
YEAH-
WHAT?
YEAH!
YES-
YEAH! YEAH!
YEAH'S NOT A WORD- IT'S YES!
WELL!!
WELL WHAT?
SHUT YOUR FAT TRAP!!
I CAN'T-
I'M YOUR SISTER!
OH STUEY- DON'T YOU KNOW THAT PLAYING DEAD IS SO KINDER-GARTEN! YOU REALLY ARE MENTALLY CHALLENGED- AREN'T YOU?!
EVEN IF I DID DIE AND WENT TO FIERY HELL-THE WICKED DEVIL WOULD BE A MUCH BETTER PERSON TO BE AROUND THAN YOU!!!

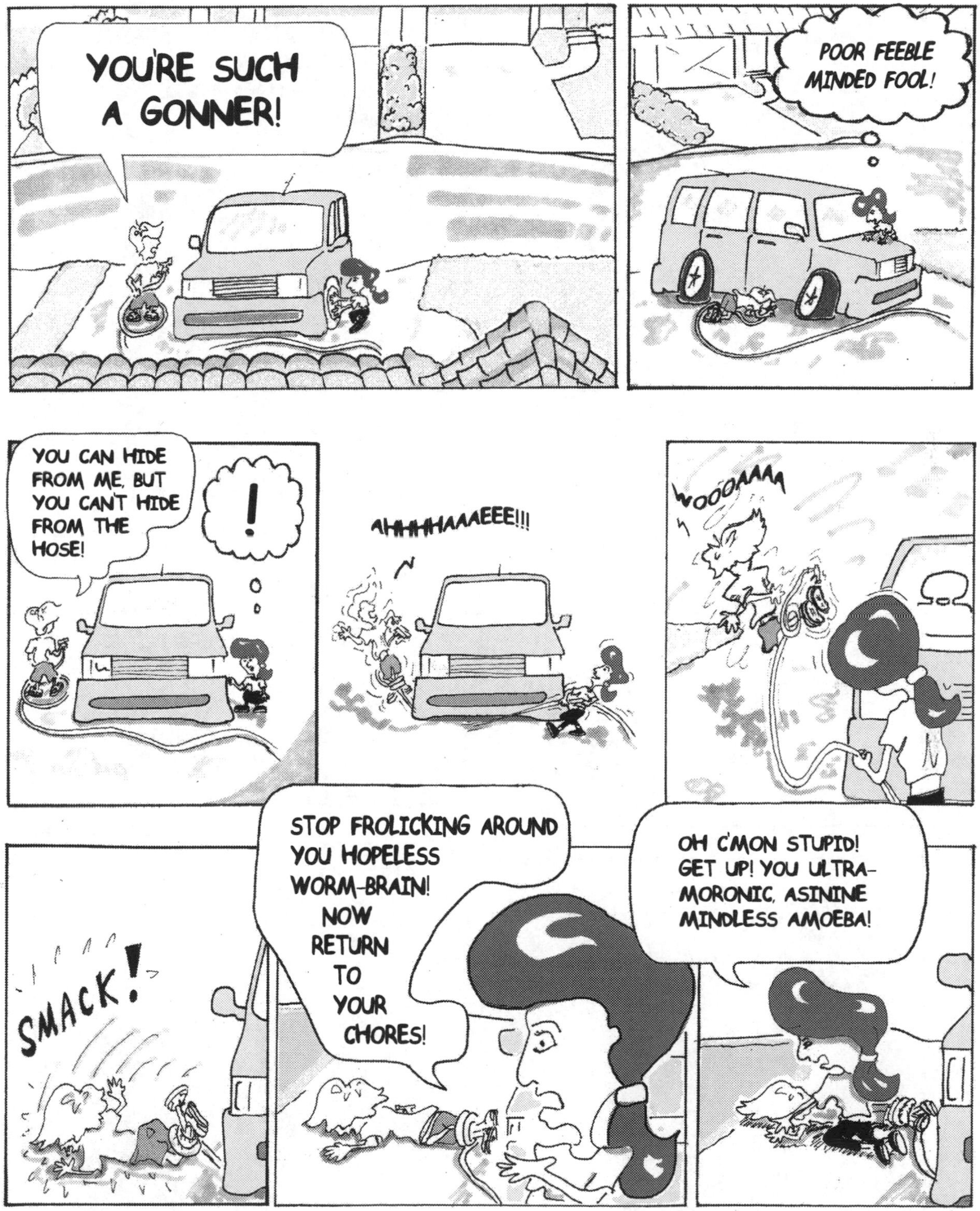
YOU'RE SUCH A GONNER!
POOR FEEBLE MINDED FOOL!
YOU CAN HIDE FROM ME, BUT YOU CAN'T HIDE FROM THE HOSE!
!
AHHHHHAAAEEE!!!
WOOOAAAA
SMACK!
STOP FROLICKING AROUND YOU HOPELESS WORM-BRAIN! NOW RETURN TO YOUR CHORES!
OH C'MON STUPID! GET UP! YOU ULTRA-MORONIC, ASININE MINDLESS AMOEBA!

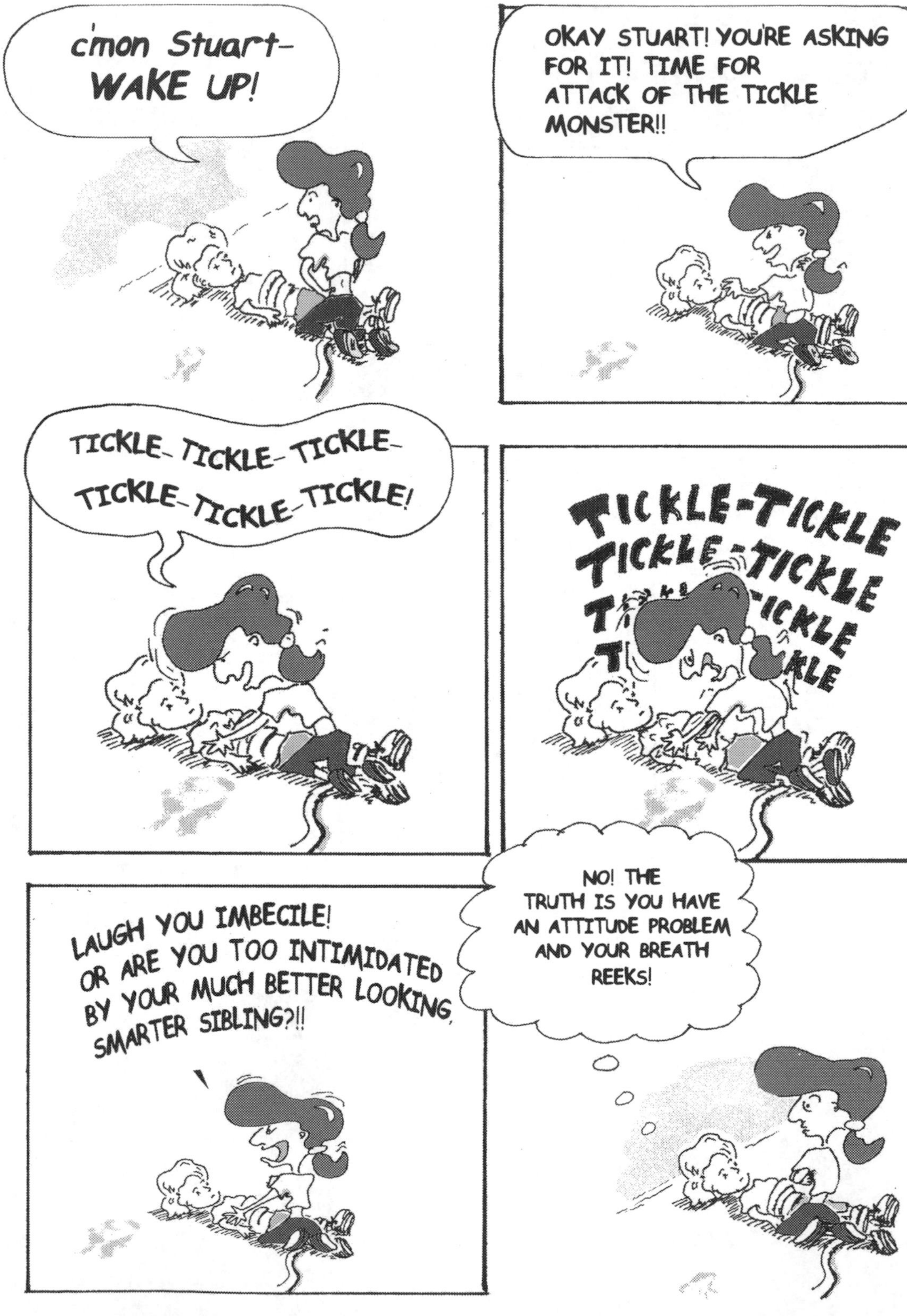
c'mon Stuart-
WAKE UP!
OKAY STUART! YOU'RE ASKING FOR IT! TIME FOR ATTACK OF THE TICKLE MONSTER!!
TICKLE-TICKLE-TICKLE-TICKLE-TICKLE-TICKLE!
TICKLE-TICKLE
TICKLE-TICKLE
LAUGH YOU IMBECILE! OR ARE YOU TOO INTIMIDATED BY YOUR MUCH BETTER LOOKING, SMARTER SIBLING?!!
NO! THE TRUTH IS YOU HAVE AN ATTITUDE PROBLEM AND YOUR BREATH REEKS!

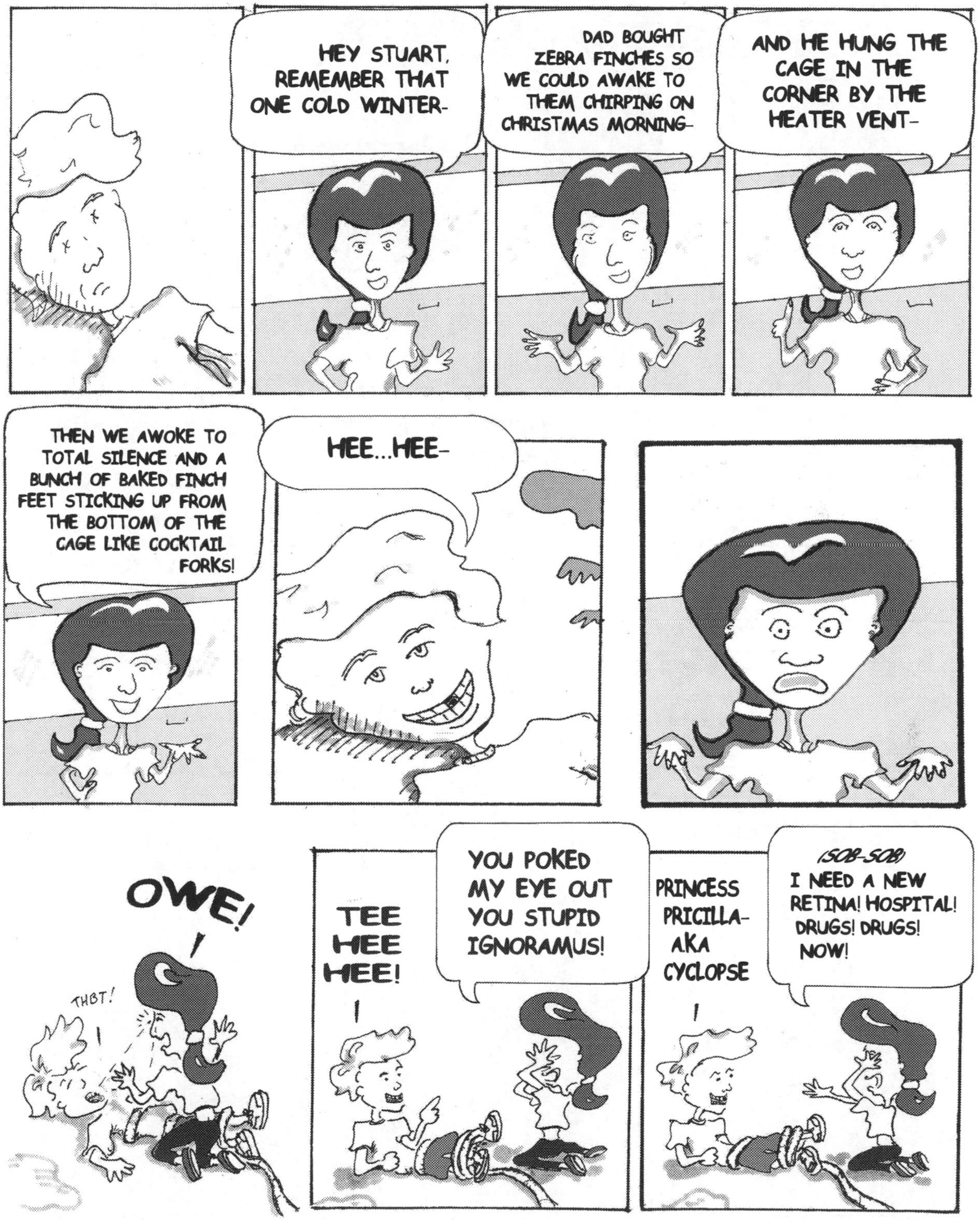
HEY STUART, REMEMBER THAT ONE COLD WINTER-
DAD BOUGHT ZEBRA FINCHES SO WE COULD AWAKE TO THEM CHIRPING ON CHRISTMAS MORNING-
AND HE HUNG THE CAGE IN THE CORNER BY THE HEATER VENT-
THEN WE AWOKE TO TOTAL SILENCE AND A BUNCH OF BAKED FINCH FEET STICKING UP FROM THE BOTTOM OF THE CAGE LIKE COCKTAIL FORKS!
HEE...HEE-
OWE!
THBT!
TEE HEE HEE!
YOU POKED MY EYE OUT YOU STUPID IGNORAMUS!
PRINCESS PRICILLA- AKA CYCLOPSE
(SOB-SOB) I NEED A NEW RETINA! HOSPITAL! DRUGS! DRUGS! NOW!

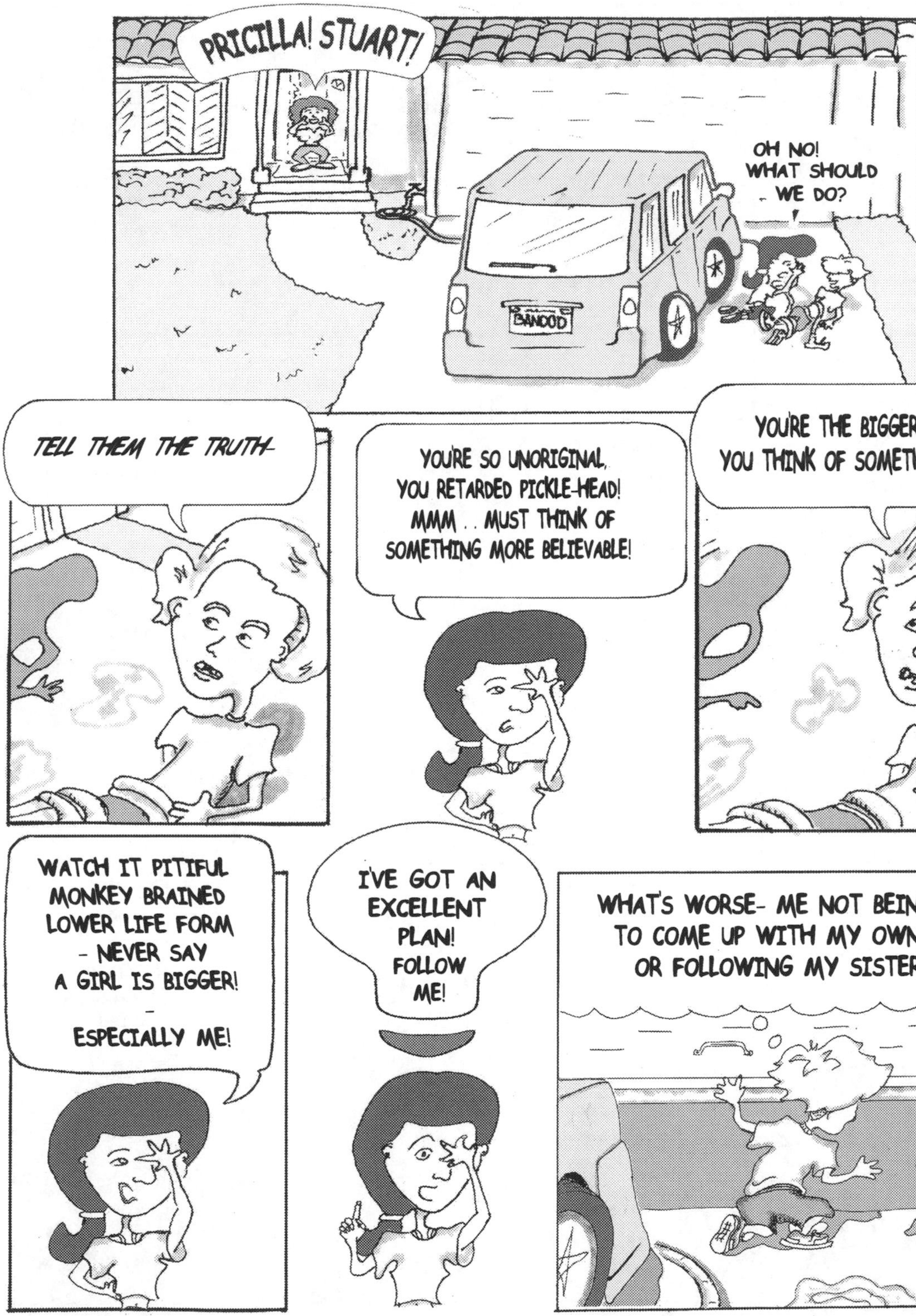
PRICILLA! STUART!
OH NO! WHAT SHOULD WE DO?
BANOOD
TELL THEM THE TRUTH-
YOU'RE SO UNORIGINAL, YOU RETARDED PICKLE-HEAD! MMM . . MUST THINK OF SOMETHING MORE BELIEVABLE!
YOU'RE THE BIGGER SUB-LINK, YOU THINK OF SOMETHING!
WATCH IT PITIFUL MONKEY BRAINED LOWER LIFE FORM - NEVER SAY A GIRL IS BIGGER! - ESPECIALLY ME!
I'VE GOT AN EXCELLENT PLAN! FOLLOW ME!
WHAT'S WORSE- ME NOT BEING ABLE TO COME UP WITH MY OWN LIE- OR FOLLOWING MY SISTERS'!?

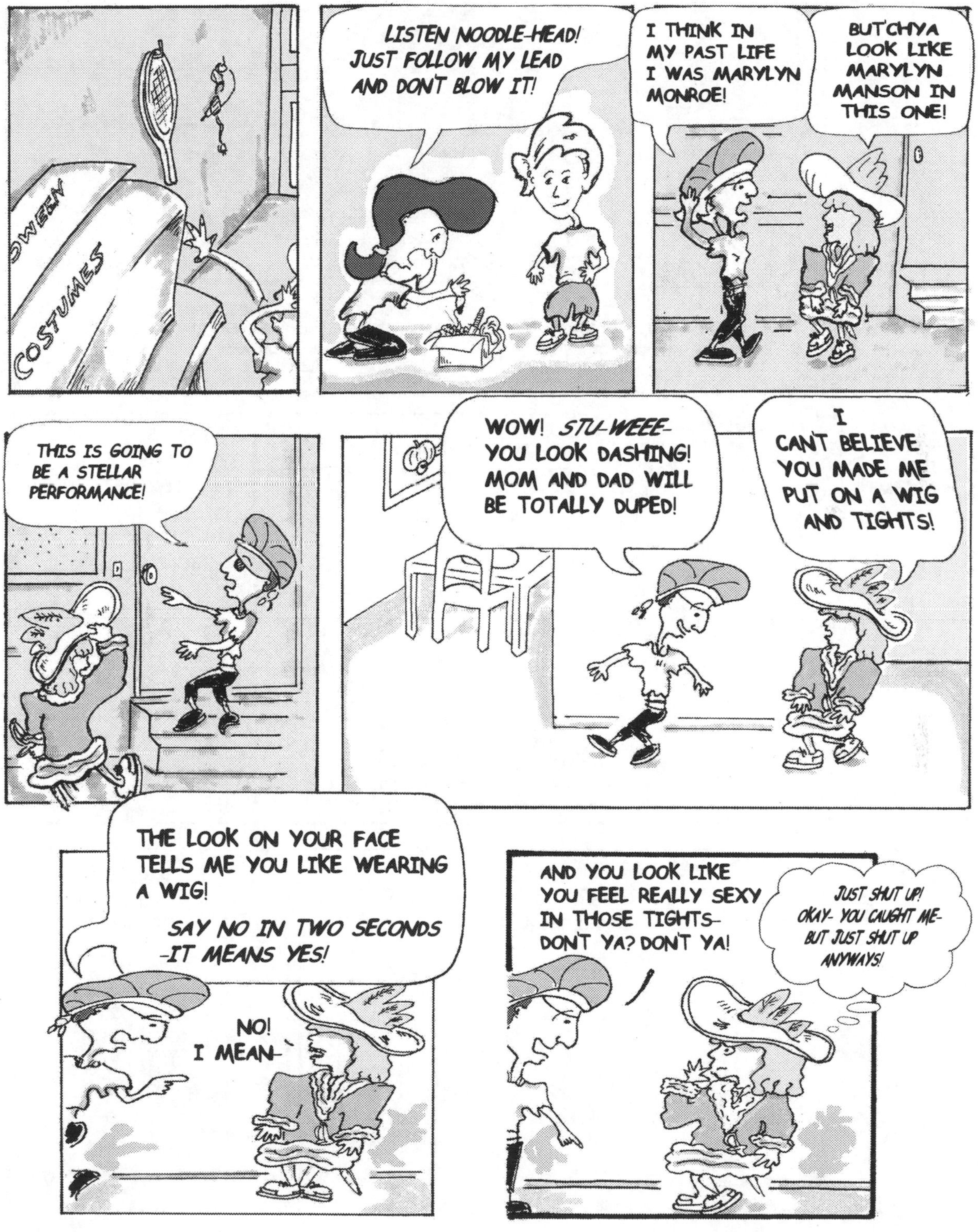
OWEEN
COSTUMES
LISTEN NOODLE-HEAD! JUST FOLLOW MY LEAD AND DON'T BLOW IT!
I THINK IN MY PAST LIFE I WAS MARYLYN MONROE!
BUT'CHYA LOOK LIKE MARYLYN MANSON IN THIS ONE!
THIS IS GOING TO BE A STELLAR PERFORMANCE!
WOW! STU-WEEE- YOU LOOK DASHING! MOM AND DAD WILL BE TOTALLY DUPED!
I CAN'T BELIEVE YOU MADE ME PUT ON A WIG AND TIGHTS!
THE LOOK ON YOUR FACE TELLS ME YOU LIKE WEARING A WIG!
SAY NO IN TWO SECONDS -IT MEANS YES!
NO! I MEAN-
AND YOU LOOK LIKE YOU FEEL REALLY SEXY IN THOSE TIGHTS- DON'T YA? DON'T YA!
JUST SHUT UP! OKAY- YOU CAUGHT ME- BUT JUST SHUT UP ANYWAYS!

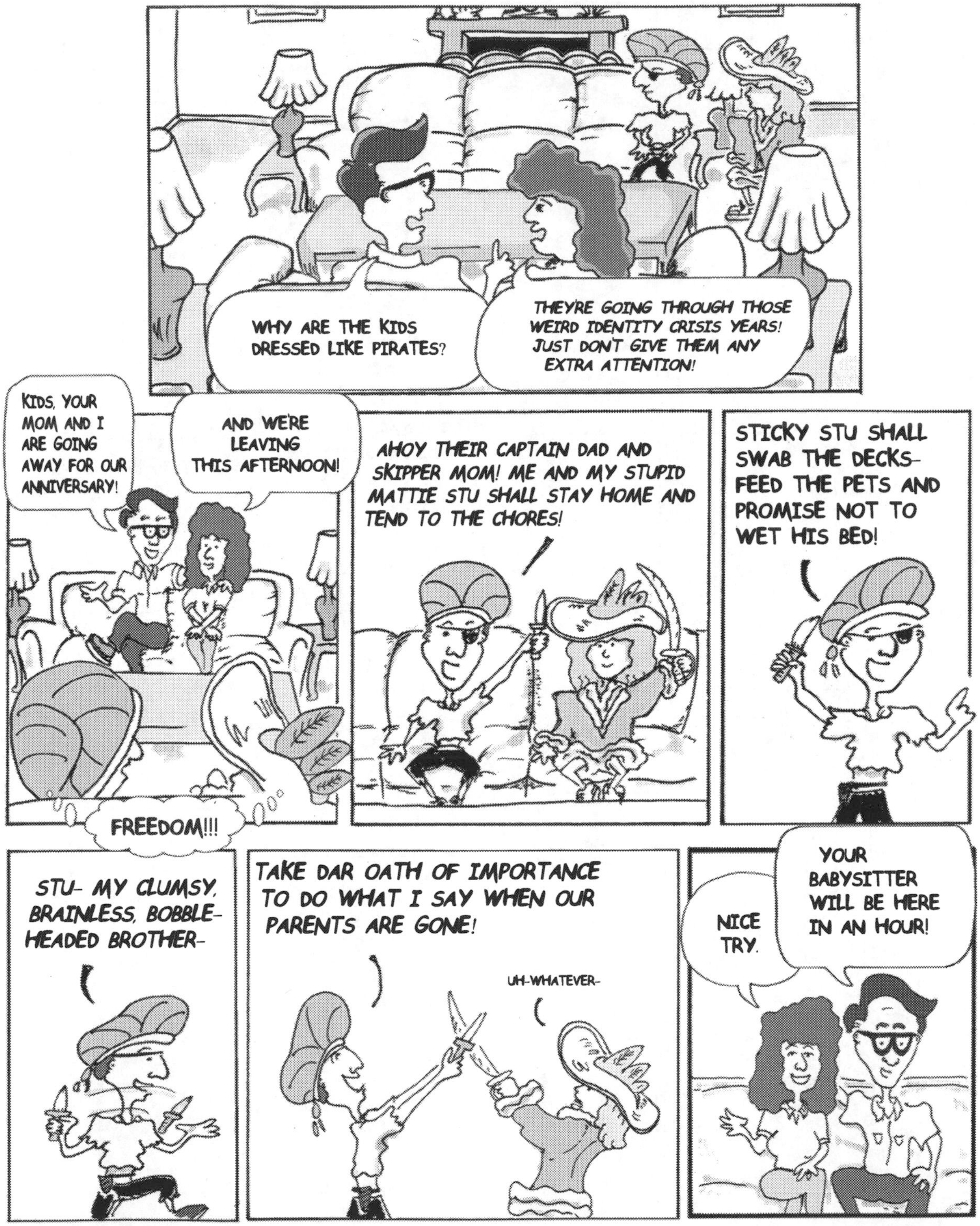
WHY ARE THE KIDS DRESSED LIKE PIRATES?
THEY'RE GOING THROUGH THOSE WEIRD IDENTITY CRISIS YEARS! JUST DON'T GIVE THEM ANY EXTRA ATTENTION!
KIDS, YOUR MOM AND I ARE GOING AWAY FOR OUR ANNIVERSARY!
AND WE'RE LEAVING THIS AFTERNOON!
FREEDOM!!!
AHOY THEIR CAPTAIN DAD AND SKIPPER MOM! ME AND MY STUPID MATTIE STU SHALL STAY HOME AND TEND TO THE CHORES!
STICKY STU SHALL SWAB THE DECKS- FEED THE PETS AND PROMISE NOT TO WET HIS BED!
STU- MY CLUMSY, BRAINLESS, BOBBLE-HEADED BROTHER-
TAKE DAR OATH OF IMPORTANCE TO DO WHAT I SAY WHEN OUR PARENTS ARE GONE!
UH-WHATEVER-
NICE TRY.
YOUR BABYSITTER WILL BE HERE IN AN HOUR!

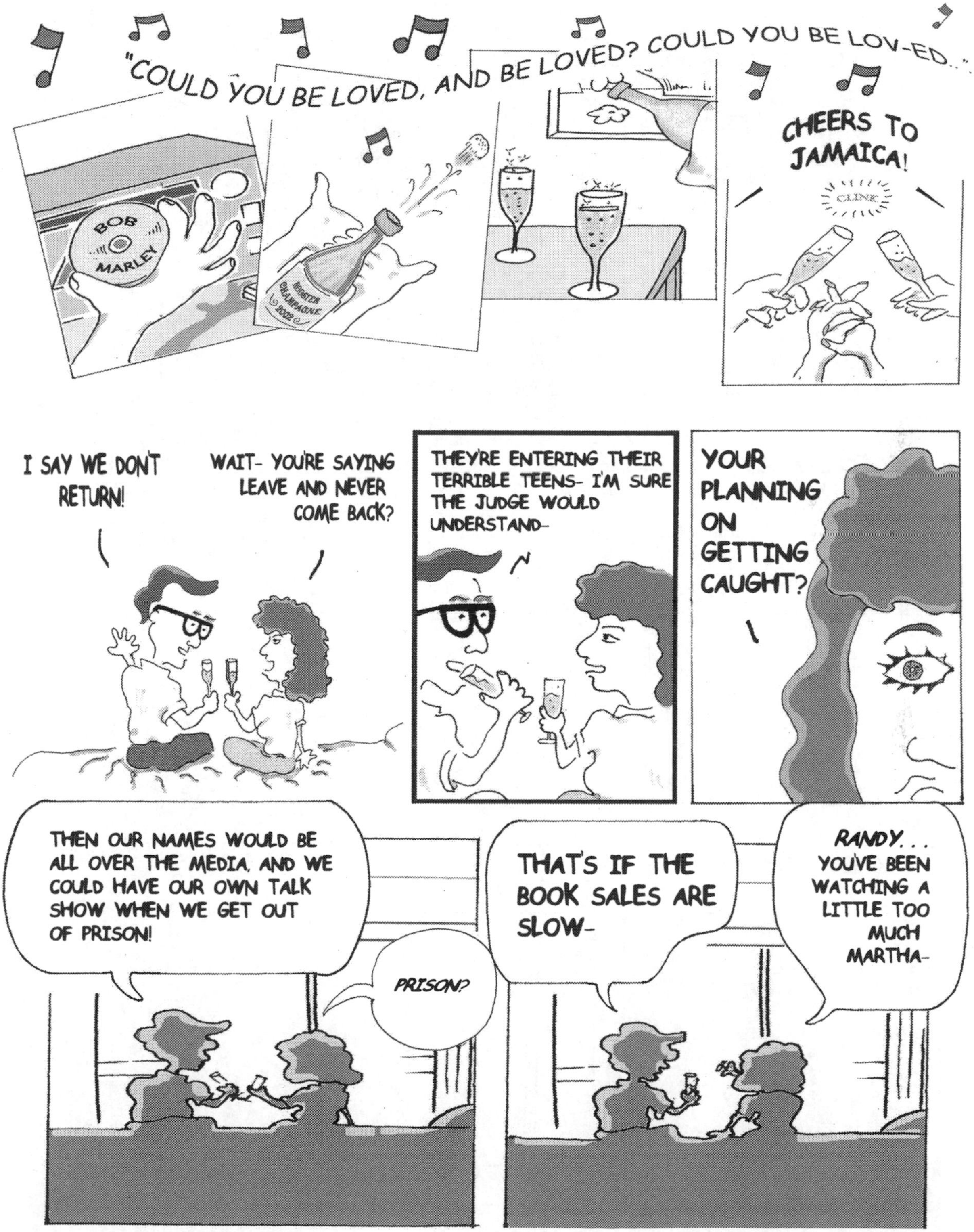
"COULD YOU BE LOVED, AND BE LOVED? COULD YOU BE LOV-ED..."
BOB MARLEY
ROOSTER CHAMPAGNE 2002
CHEERS TO JAMAICA!
CLINK
I SAY WE DON'T RETURN!
WAIT- YOU'RE SAYING LEAVE AND NEVER COME BACK?
THEY'RE ENTERING THEIR TERRIBLE TEENS- I'M SURE THE JUDGE WOULD UNDERSTAND-
YOUR PLANNING ON GETTING CAUGHT?
THEN OUR NAMES WOULD BE ALL OVER THE MEDIA, AND WE COULD HAVE OUR OWN TALK SHOW WHEN WE GET OUT OF PRISON!
PRISON?
THAT'S IF THE BOOK SALES ARE SLOW-
RANDY... YOU'VE BEEN WATCHING A LITTLE TOO MUCH MARTHA-

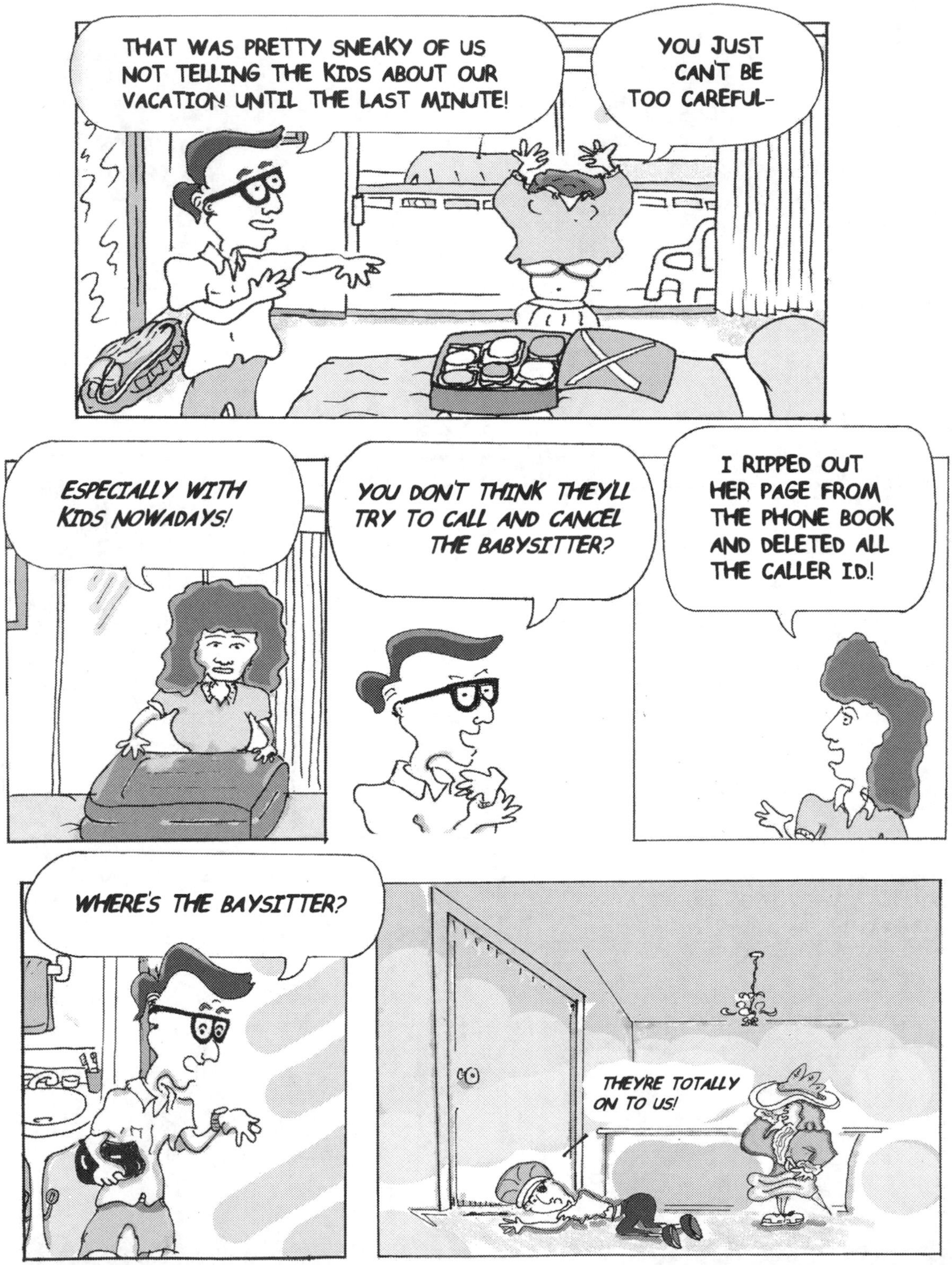
THAT WAS PRETTY SNEAKY OF US NOT TELLING THE KIDS ABOUT OUR VACATION UNTIL THE LAST MINUTE!
YOU JUST CAN'T BE TOO CAREFUL-
ESPECIALLY WITH KIDS NOWADAYS!
YOU DON'T THINK THEY'LL TRY TO CALL AND CANCEL THE BABYSITTER?
I RIPPED OUT HER PAGE FROM THE PHONE BOOK AND DELETED ALL THE CALLER I.D.!
WHERE'S THE BAYSITTER?
THEY'RE TOTALLY ON TO US!

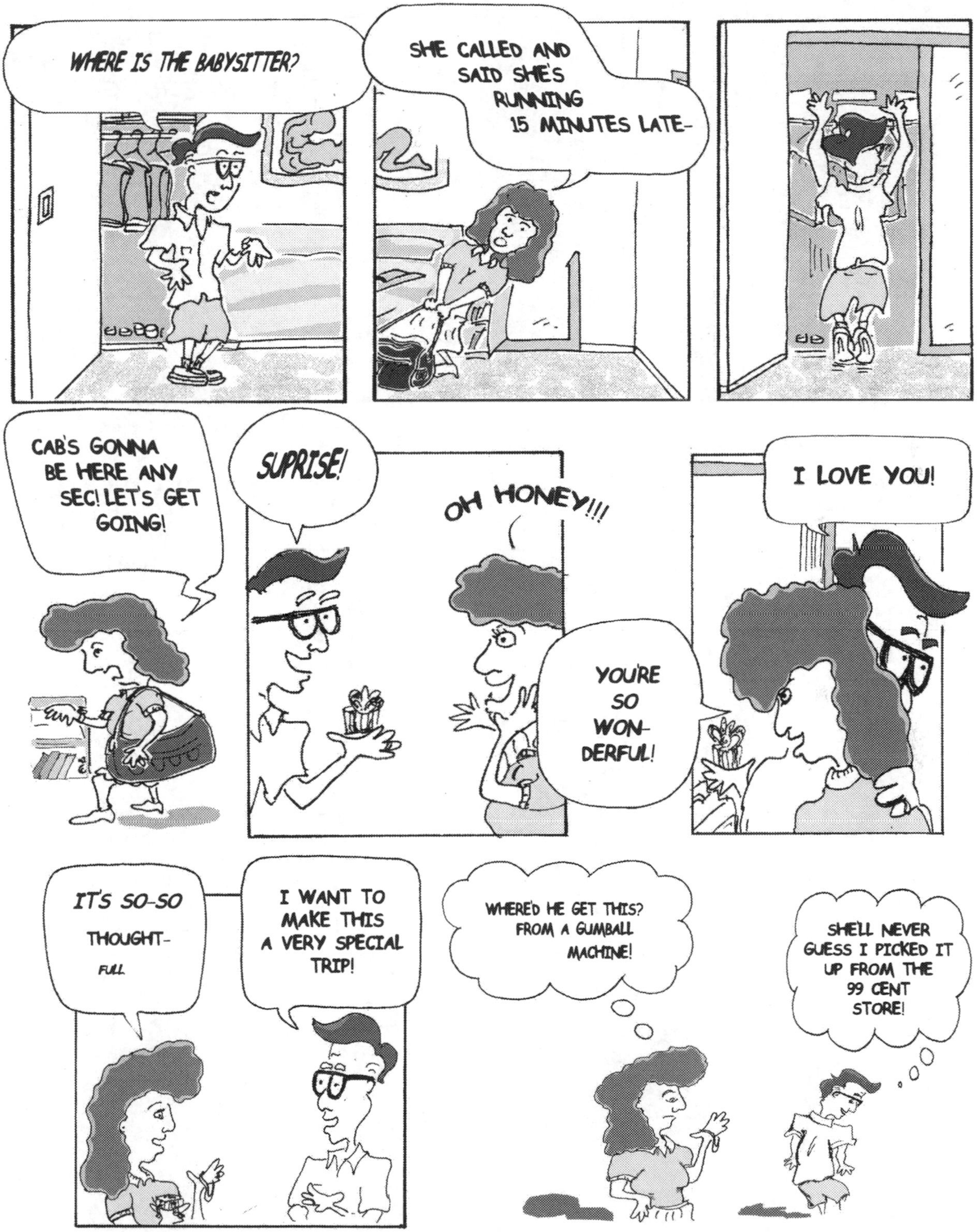
WHERE IS THE BABYSITTER?
SHE CALLED AND SAID SHE'S RUNNING 15 MINUTES LATE-
CAB'S GONNA BE HERE ANY SEC! LET'S GET GOING!
SUPRISE!
OH HONEY!!!
YOU'RE SO WON-DERFUL!
I LOVE YOU!
IT'S SO-SO THOUGHT-FULL
I WANT TO MAKE THIS A VERY SPECIAL TRIP!
WHERE'D HE GET THIS? FROM A GUMBALL MACHINE!
SHE'LL NEVER GUESS I PICKED IT UP FROM THE 99 CENT STORE!

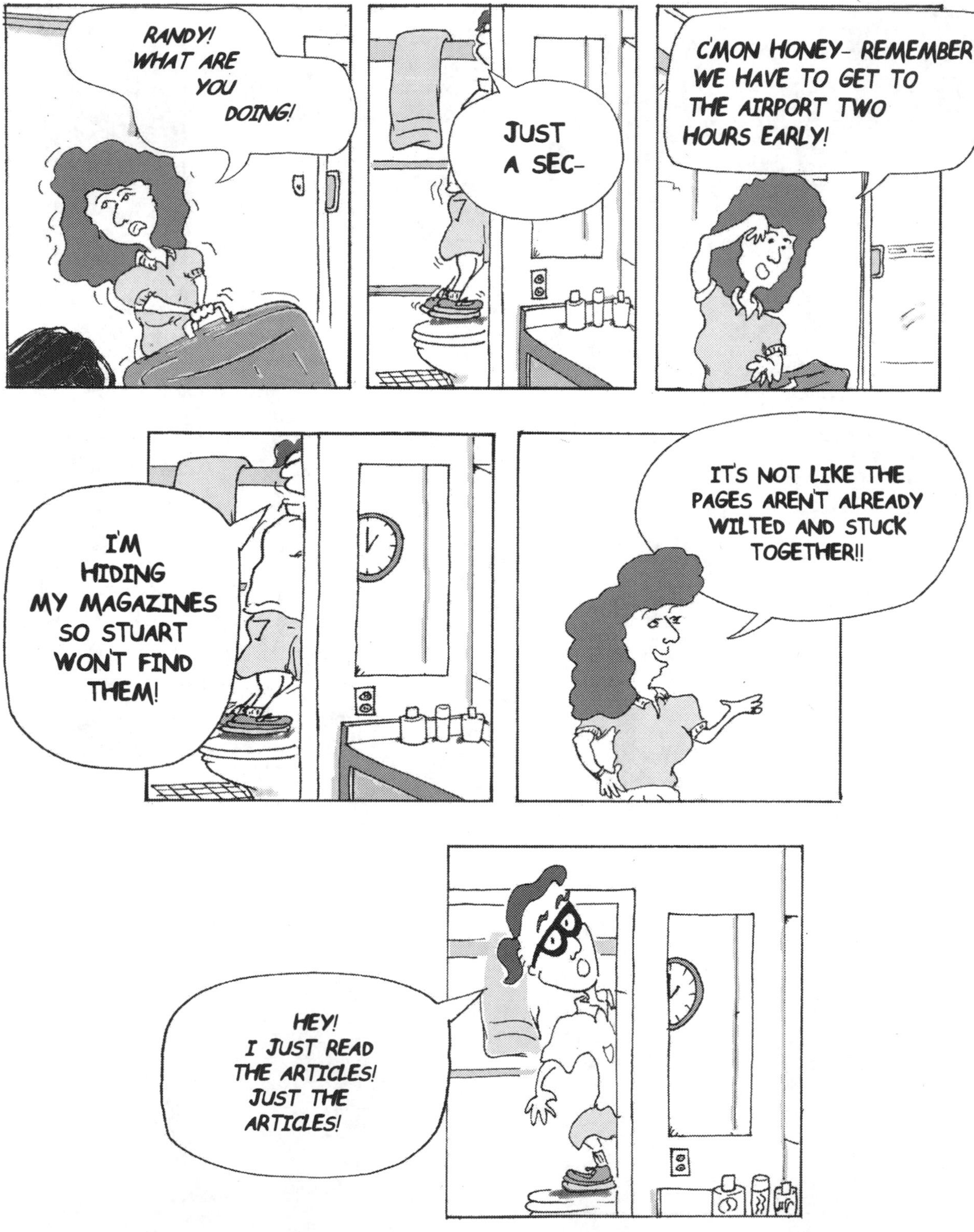
RANDY! WHAT ARE YOU DOING!
JUST A SEC-
C'MON HONEY- REMEMBER WE HAVE TO GET TO THE AIRPORT TWO HOURS EARLY!
I'M HIDING MY MAGAZINES SO STUART WON'T FIND THEM!
IT'S NOT LIKE THE PAGES AREN'T ALREADY WILTED AND STUCK TOGETHER!!
HEY! I JUST READ THE ARTICLES! JUST THE ARTICLES!

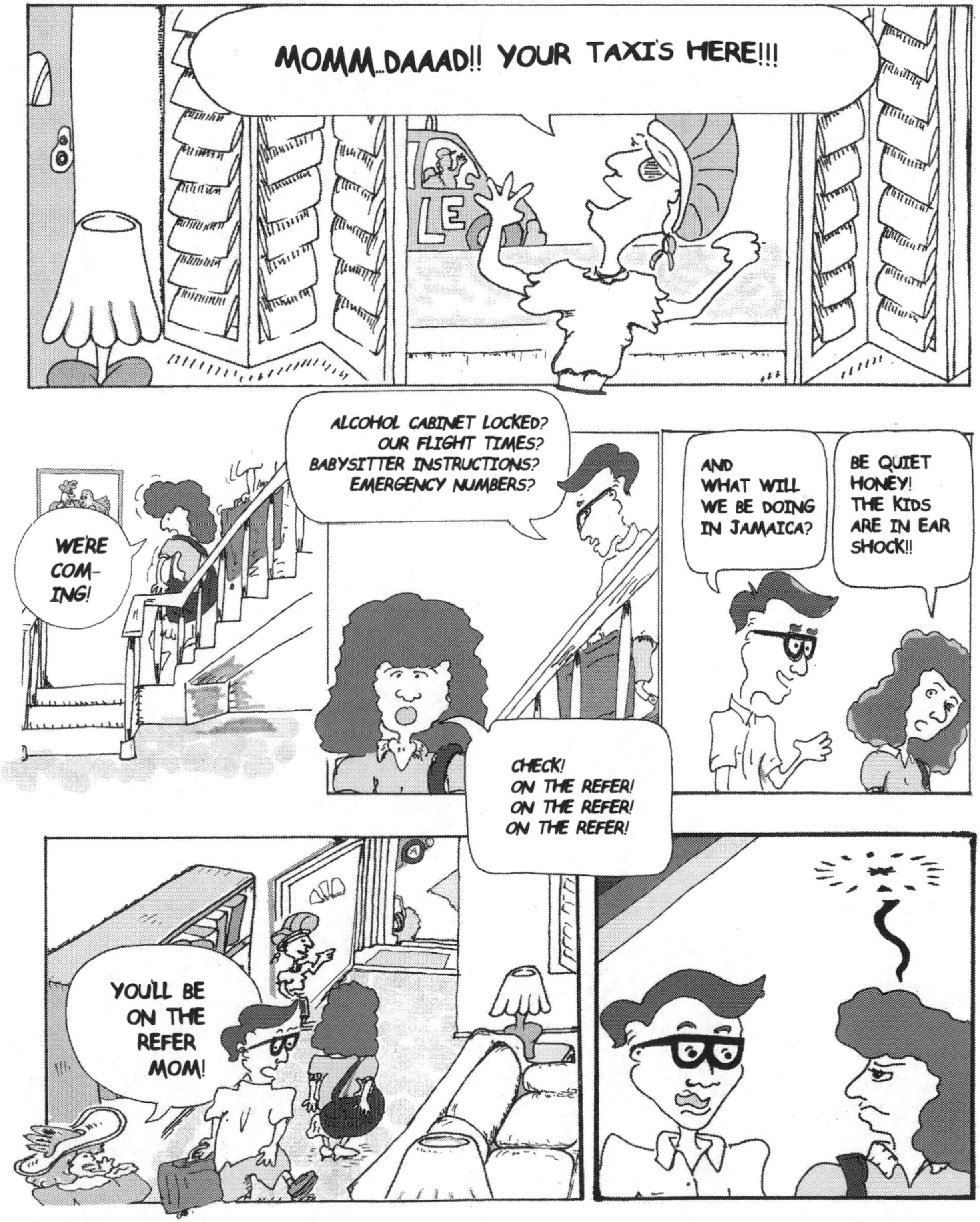
MOMM...DAAAD!! YOUR TAXI'S HERE!!!
WE'RE COM-ING!
ALCOHOL CABINET LOCKED? OUR FLIGHT TIMES? BABYSITTER INSTRUCTIONS? EMERGENCY NUMBERS?
CHECK! ON THE REFER! ON THE REFER! ON THE REFER!
AND WHAT WILL WE BE DOING IN JAMAICA?
BE QUIET HONEY! THE KIDS ARE IN EAR SHOCK!!
YOU'LL BE ON THE REFER MOM!

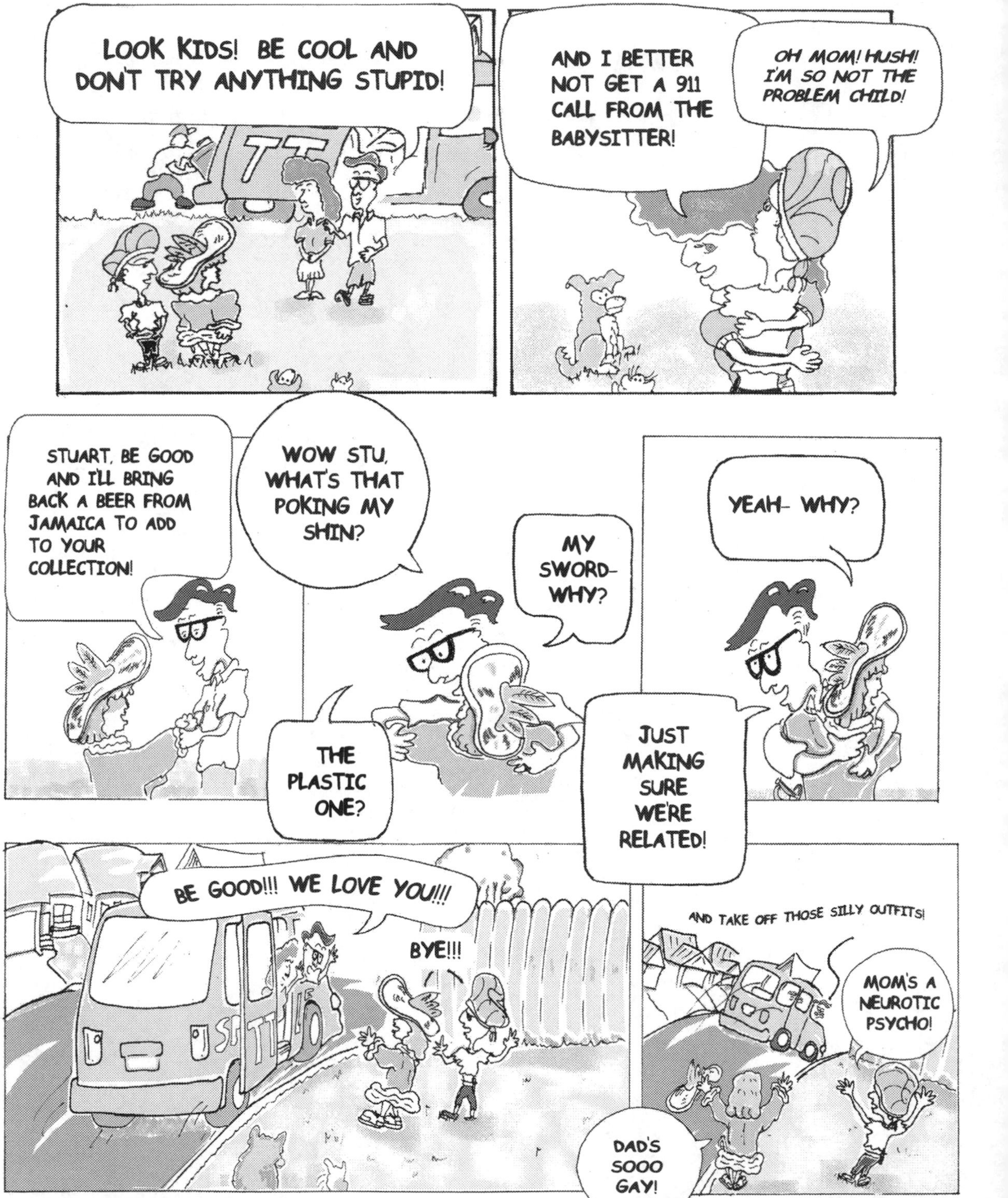
LOOK KIDS! BE COOL AND DON'T TRY ANYTHING STUPID!
AND I BETTER NOT GET A 911 CALL FROM THE BABYSITTER!
OH MOM! HUSH! I'M SO NOT THE PROBLEM CHILD!
STUART, BE GOOD AND I'LL BRING BACK A BEER FROM JAMAICA TO ADD TO YOUR COLLECTION!
WOW STU, WHAT'S THAT POKING MY SHIN?
MY SWORD- WHY?
THE PLASTIC ONE?
YEAH- WHY?
JUST MAKING SURE WE'RE RELATED!
BE GOOD!!! WE LOVE YOU!!!
BYE!!!
AND TAKE OFF THOSE SILLY OUTFITS!
MOM'S A NEUROTIC PSYCHO!
DAD'S SOOO GAY!

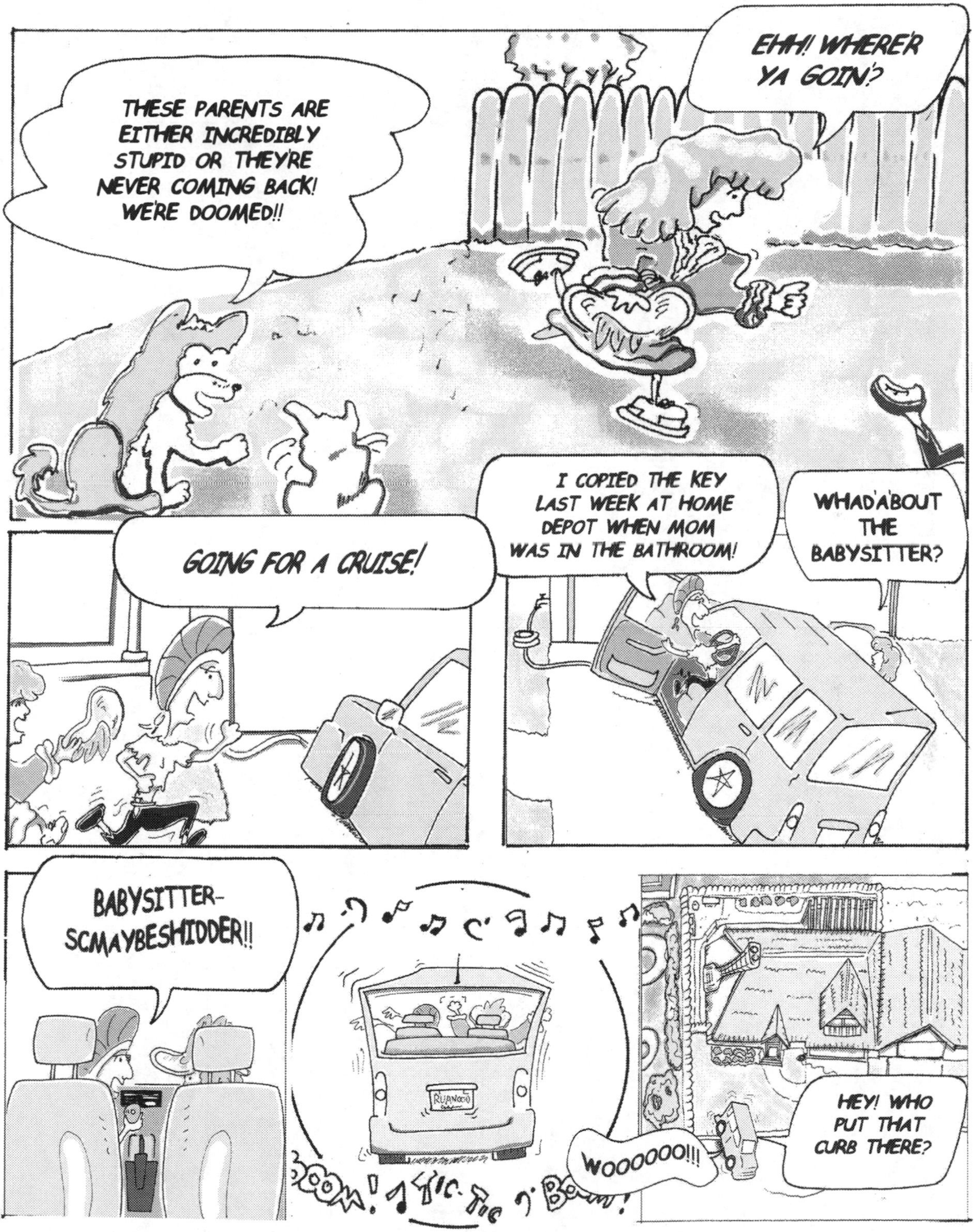
THESE PARENTS ARE EITHER INCREDIBLY STUPID OR THEY'RE NEVER COMING BACK! WE'RE DOOMED!!
EHH! WHERE'R YA GOIN'?
GOING FOR A CRUISE!
I COPIED THE KEY LAST WEEK AT HOME DEPOT WHEN MOM WAS IN THE BATHROOM!
WHAD'ABOUT THE BABYSITTER?
BABYSITTER-SCMAYBESHIDDER!!
WOOOOOO!!!
HEY! WHO PUT THAT CURB THERE?

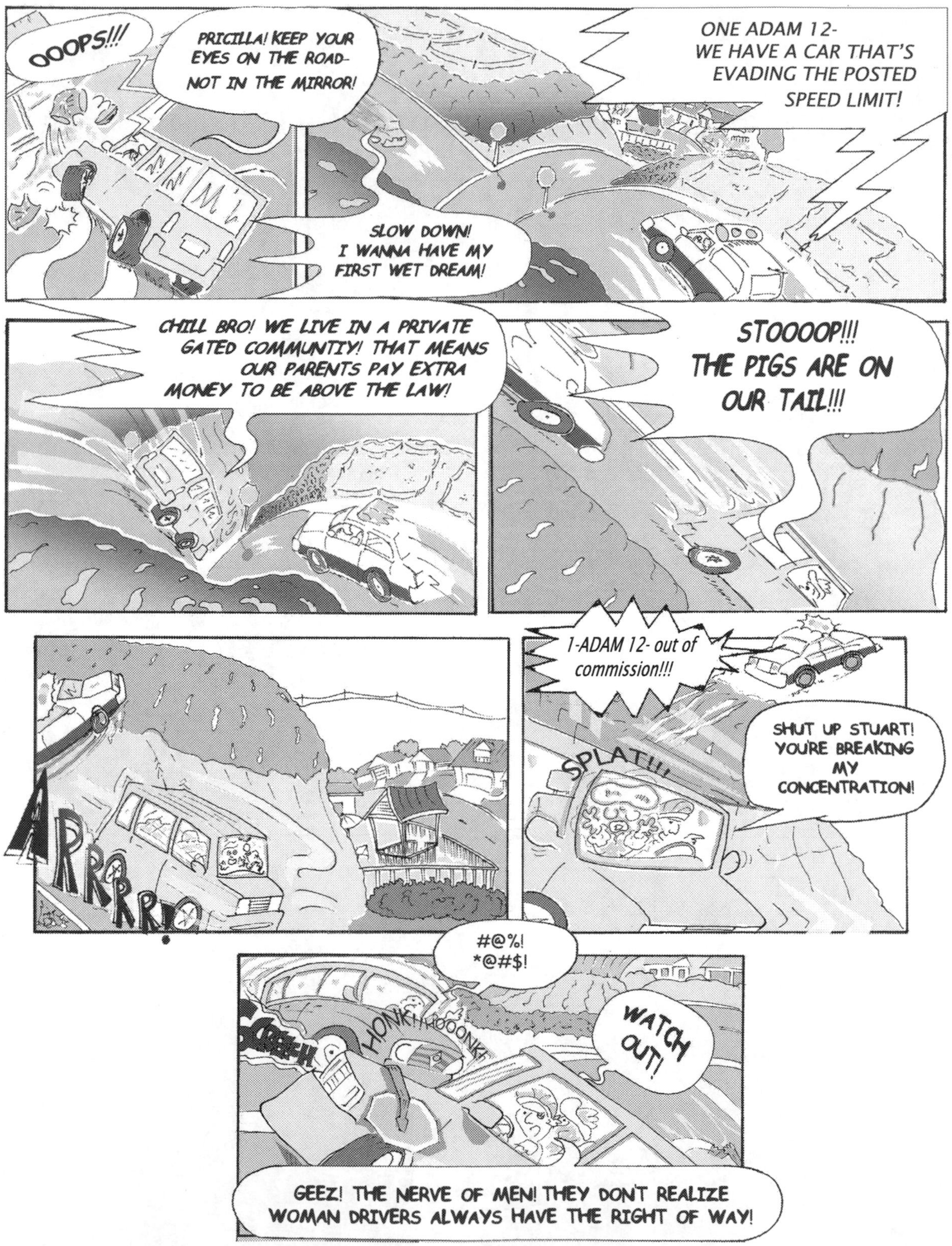
OOOPS!!!
PRICILLA! KEEP YOUR EYES ON THE ROAD- NOT IN THE MIRROR!
ONE ADAM 12- WE HAVE A CAR THAT'S EVADING THE POSTED SPEED LIMIT!
SLOW DOWN! I WANNA HAVE MY FIRST WET DREAM!
CHILL BRO! WE LIVE IN A PRIVATE GATED COMMUNTIY! THAT MEANS OUR PARENTS PAY EXTRA MONEY TO BE ABOVE THE LAW!
STOOOOP!!! THE PIGS ARE ON OUR TAIL!!!
1-ADAM 12- out of commission!!!
SPLAT!!!
SHUT UP STUART! YOU'RE BREAKING MY CONCENTRATION!
#@%! *@#$!
HONK! HOOONK!
WATCH OUT!
GEEZ! THE NERVE OF MEN! THEY DON'T REALIZE WOMAN DRIVERS ALWAYS HAVE THE RIGHT OF WAY!

CHAPTER TWO

VACATION CANCELLED

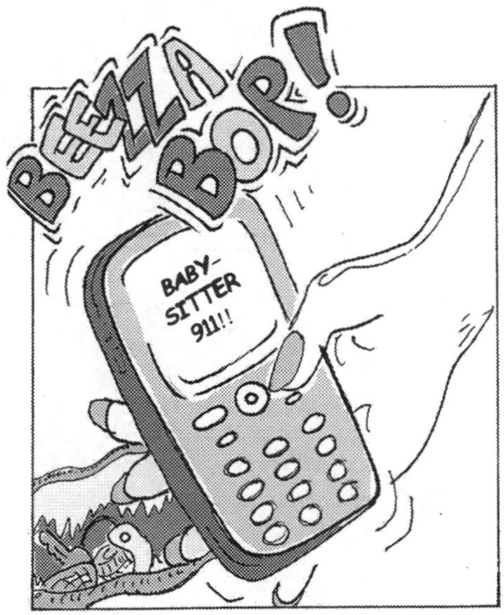
BEEZZA BOP!
BABY-SITTER 911!!

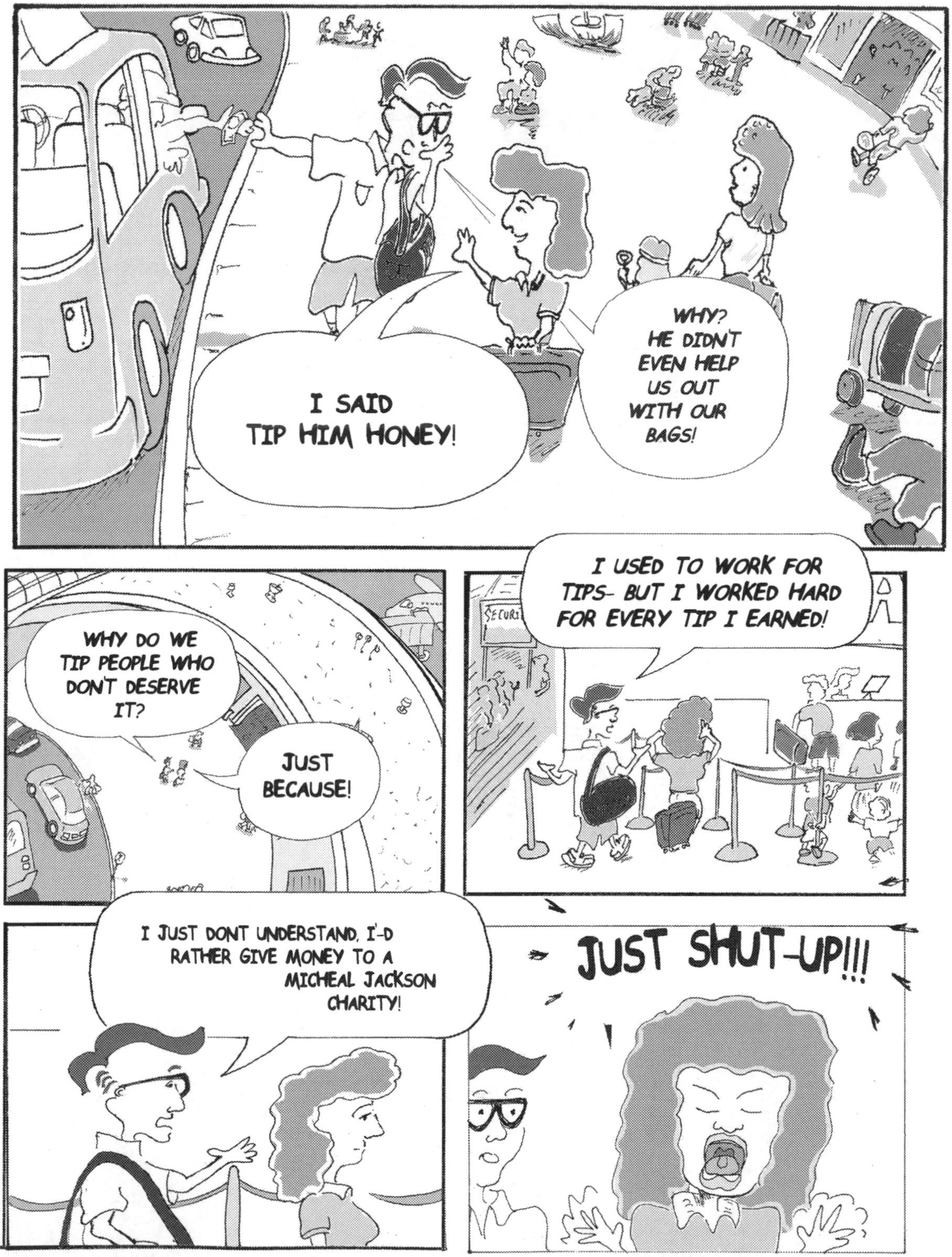
I SAID TIP HIM HONEY!
WHY? HE DIDN'T EVEN HELP US OUT WITH OUR BAGS!
WHY DO WE TIP PEOPLE WHO DON'T DESERVE IT?
JUST BECAUSE!
I USED TO WORK FOR TIPS- BUT I WORKED HARD FOR EVERY TIP I EARNED!
I JUST DONT UNDERSTAND, I'-D RATHER GIVE MONEY TO A MICHEAL JACKSON CHARITY!
JUST SHUT-UP!!!

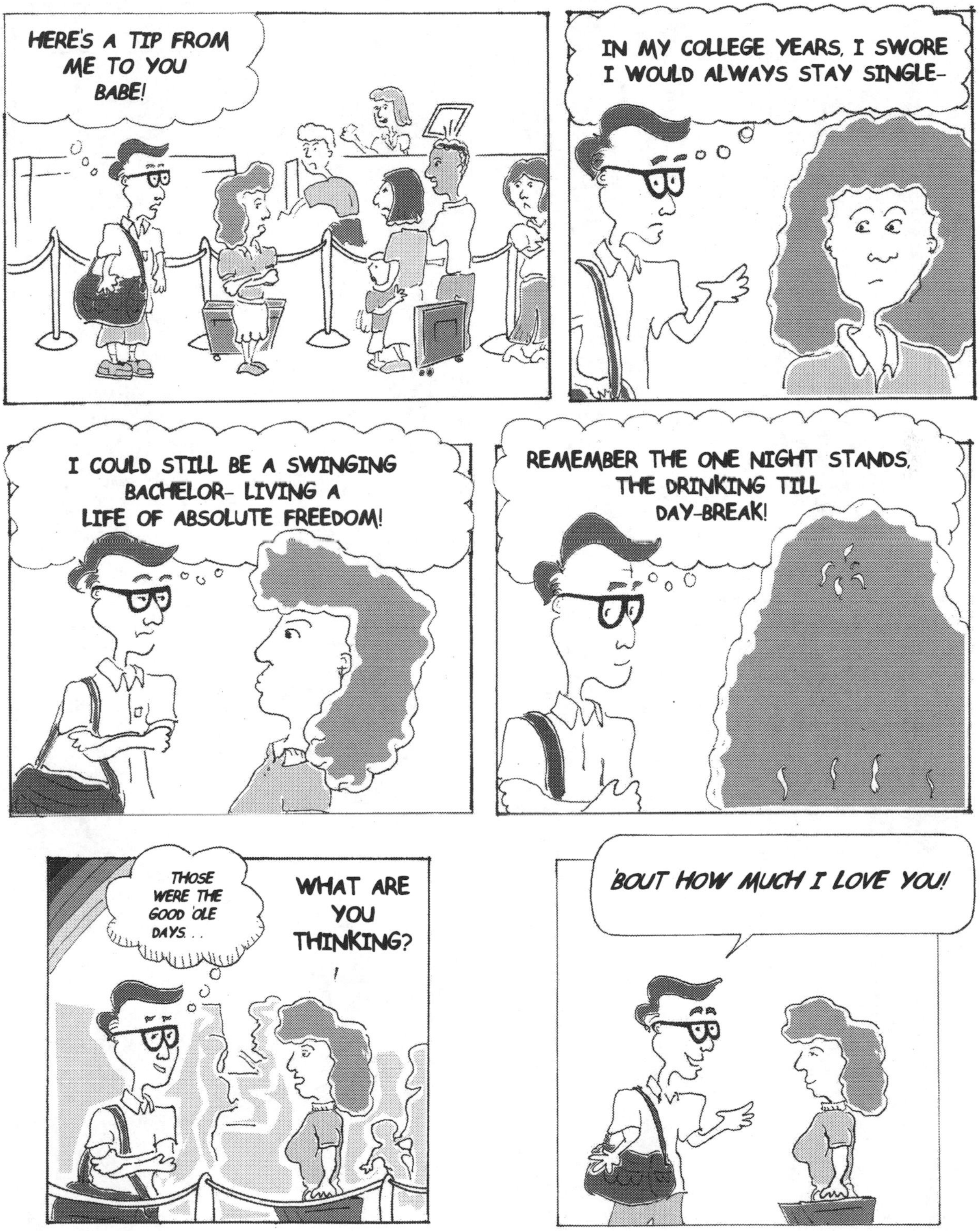
HERE'S A TIP FROM ME TO YOU BABE!
IN MY COLLEGE YEARS, I SWORE I WOULD ALWAYS STAY SINGLE-
I COULD STILL BE A SWINGING BACHELOR- LIVING A LIFE OF ABSOLUTE FREEDOM!
REMEMBER THE ONE NIGHT STANDS, THE DRINKING TILL DAY-BREAK!
THOSE WERE THE GOOD 'OLE DAYS . . .
WHAT ARE YOU THINKING?
'BOUT HOW MUCH I LOVE YOU!

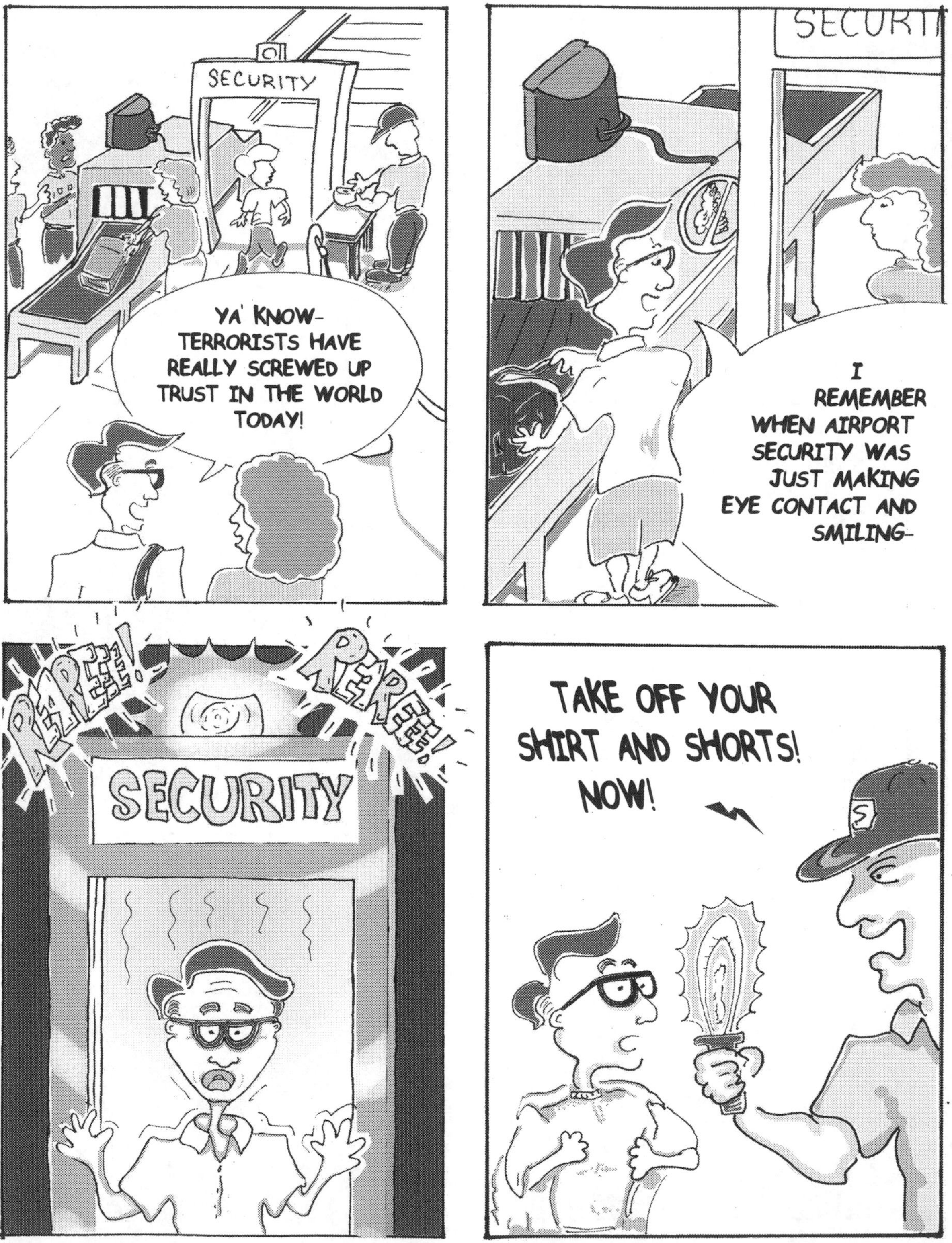
SECURITY
YA' KNOW- TERRORISTS HAVE REALLY SCREWED UP TRUST IN THE WORLD TODAY!
SECURI
I REMEMBER WHEN AIRPORT SECURITY WAS JUST MAKING EYE CONTACT AND SMILING-
SECURITY
TAKE OFF YOUR SHIRT AND SHORTS! NOW!

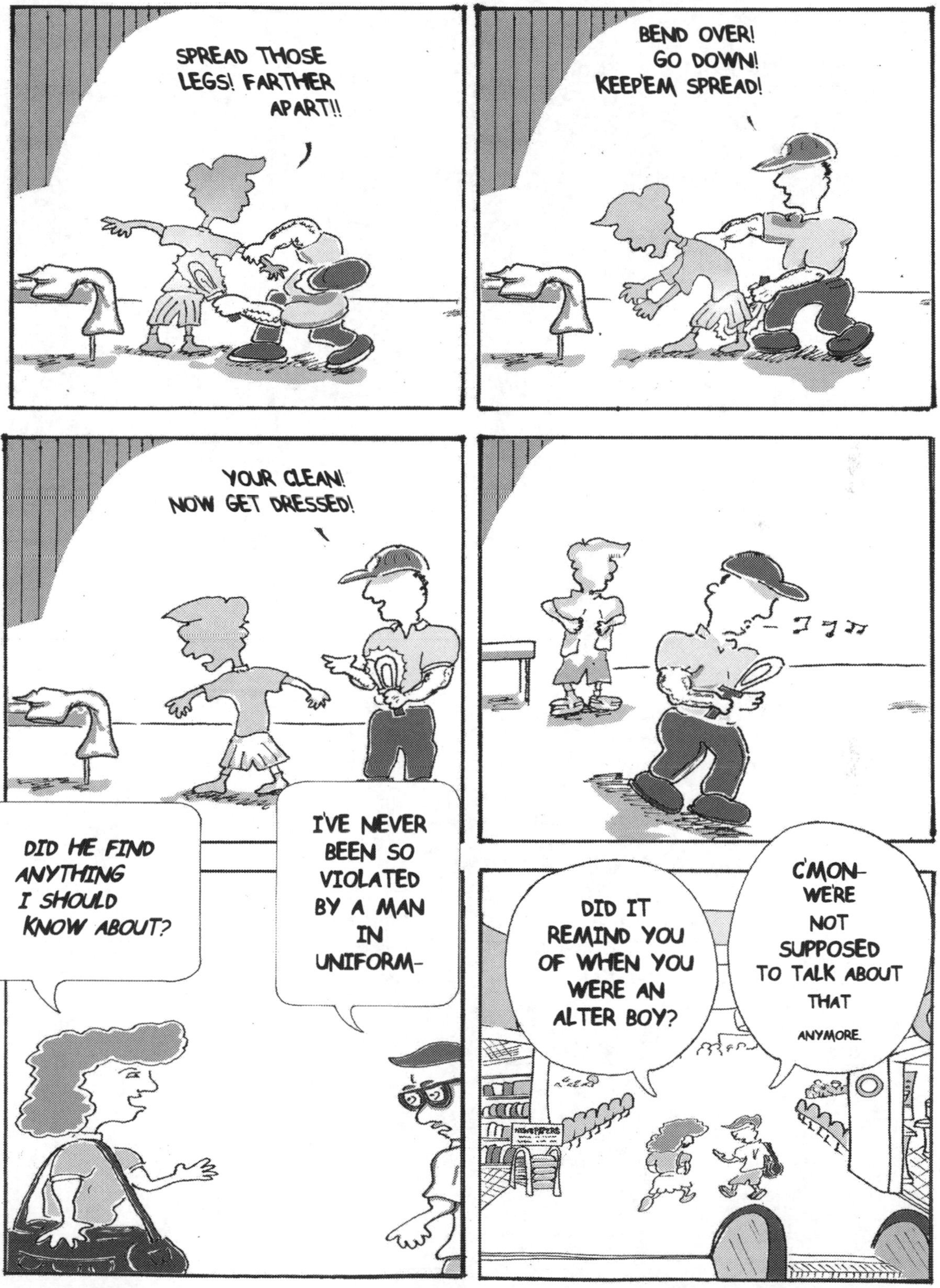
SPREAD THOSE LEGS! FARTHER APART!!
BEND OVER! GO DOWN! KEEP'EM SPREAD!
YOUR CLEAN! NOW GET DRESSED!
DID HE FIND ANYTHING I SHOULD KNOW ABOUT?
I'VE NEVER BEEN SO VIOLATED BY A MAN IN UNIFORM-
DID IT REMIND YOU OF WHEN YOU WERE AN ALTER BOY?
C'MON- WE'RE NOT SUPPOSED TO TALK ABOUT THAT ANYMORE.
NEWSPAPERS

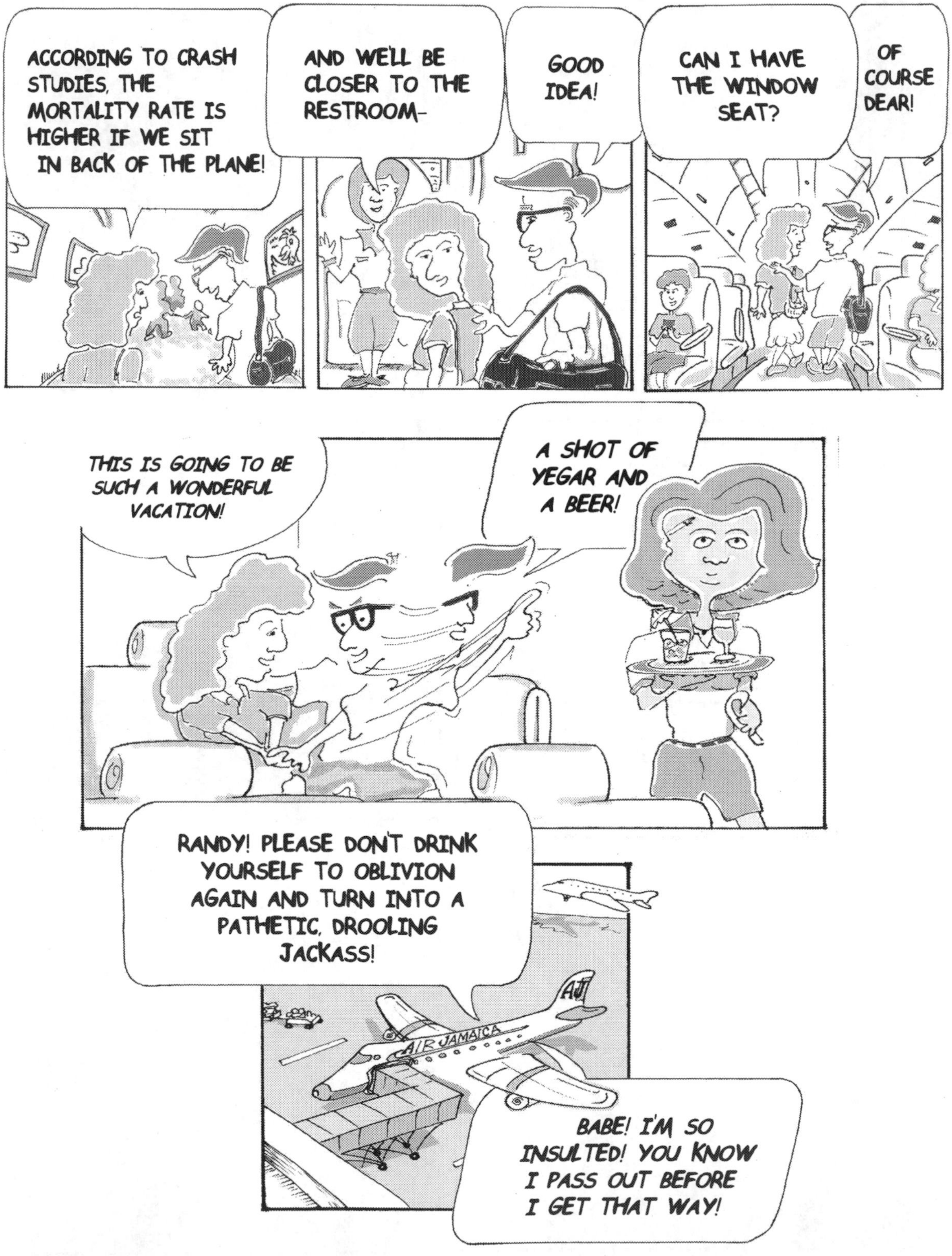
ACCORDING TO CRASH STUDIES, THE MORTALITY RATE IS HIGHER IF WE SIT IN BACK OF THE PLANE!
AND WE'LL BE CLOSER TO THE RESTROOM-
GOOD IDEA!
CAN I HAVE THE WINDOW SEAT?
OF COURSE DEAR!
THIS IS GOING TO BE SUCH A WONDERFUL VACATION!
A SHOT OF YEGAR AND A BEER!
RANDY! PLEASE DON'T DRINK YOURSELF TO OBLIVION AGAIN AND TURN INTO A PATHETIC, DROOLING JACKASS!
AIR JAMAICA
AJ
BABE! I'M SO INSULTED! YOU KNOW I PASS OUT BEFORE I GET THAT WAY!

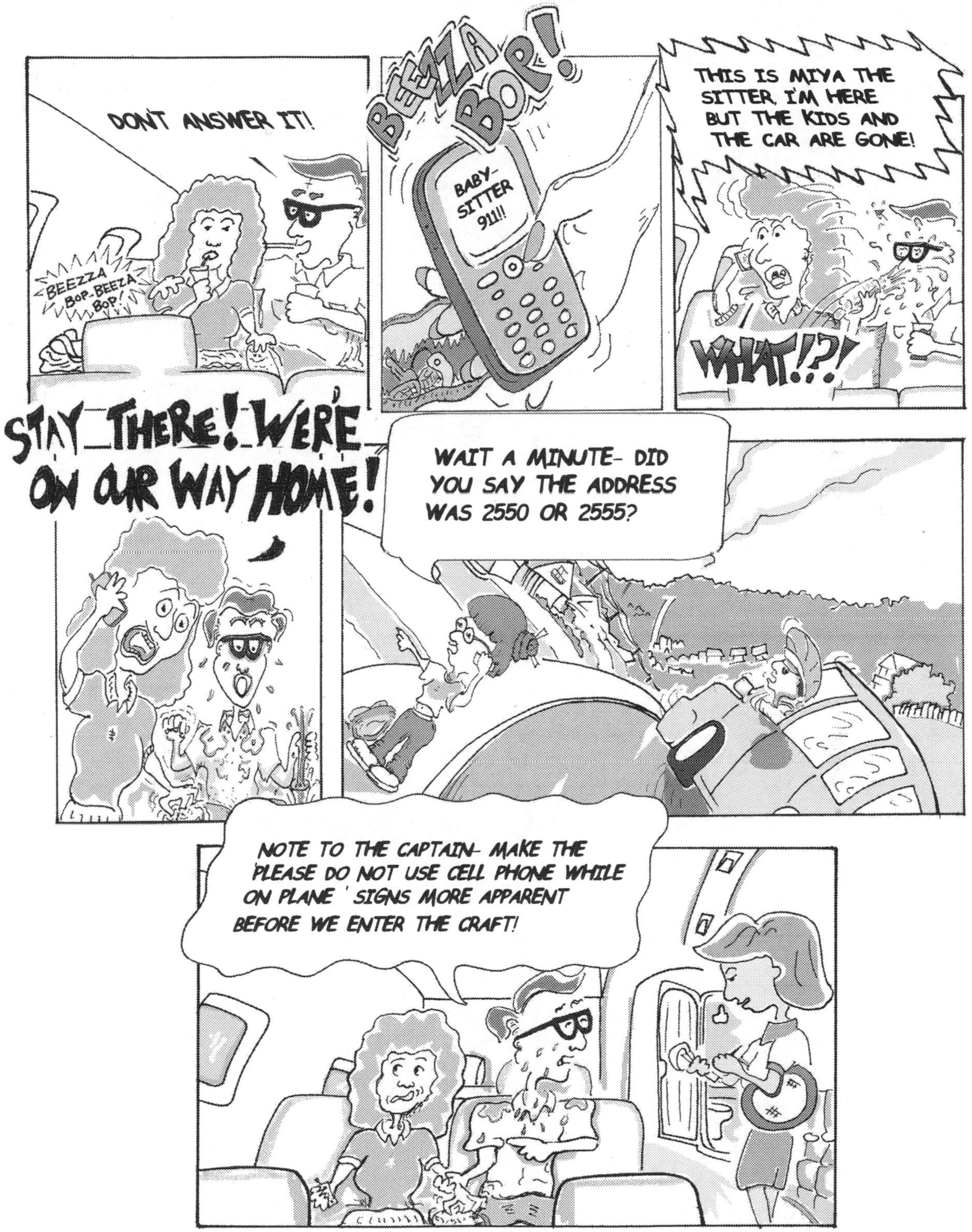

DON'T ANSWER IT!
BEEZZA BOP-BEEZA BOP!
BEEZZA BOP!
BABY-SITTER 911!!
THIS IS MIYA THE SITTER, I'M HERE BUT THE KIDS AND THE CAR ARE GONE!
WHAT!?!
STAY THERE! WE'RE ON OUR WAY HOME!
WAIT A MINUTE- DID YOU SAY THE ADDRESS WAS 2550 OR 2555?
NOTE TO THE CAPTAIN- MAKE THE 'PLEASE DO NOT USE CELL PHONE WHILE ON PLANE' SIGNS MORE APPARENT BEFORE WE ENTER THE CRAFT!

CHAPTER
THREE

PROPER SUPERVISION

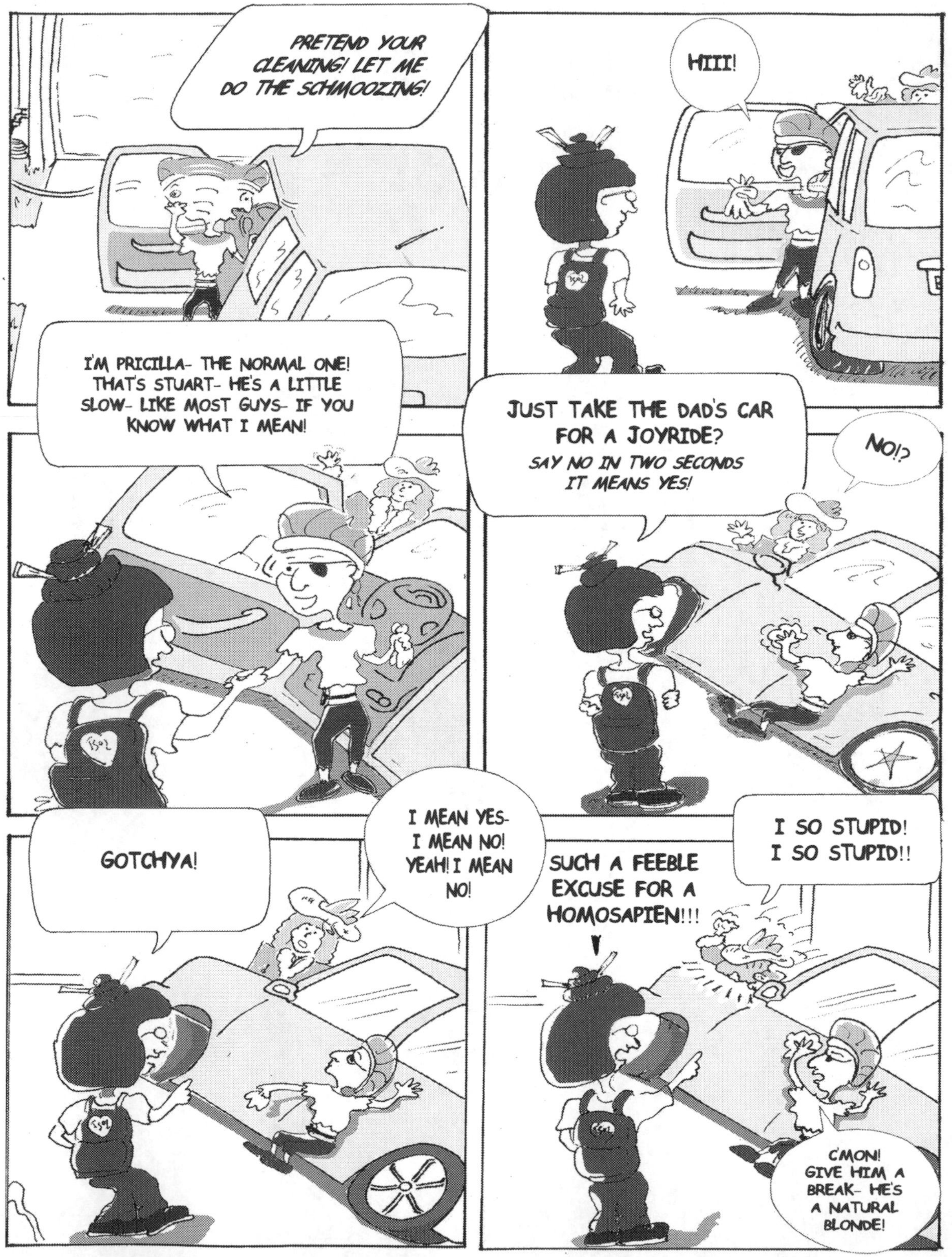

PRETEND YOUR CLEANING! LET ME DO THE SCHMOOZING!
HIII!
I'M PRICILLA- THE NORMAL ONE! THAT'S STUART- HE'S A LITTLE SLOW- LIKE MOST GUYS- IF YOU KNOW WHAT I MEAN!
JUST TAKE THE DAD'S CAR FOR A JOYRIDE?
SAY NO IN TWO SECONDS IT MEANS YES!
NO!?
GOTCHYA!
I MEAN YES- I MEAN NO! YEAH! I MEAN NO!
SUCH A FEEBLE EXCUSE FOR A HOMOSAPIEN!!!
I SO STUPID! I SO STUPID!!
C'MON! GIVE HIM A BREAK- HE'S A NATURAL BLONDE!

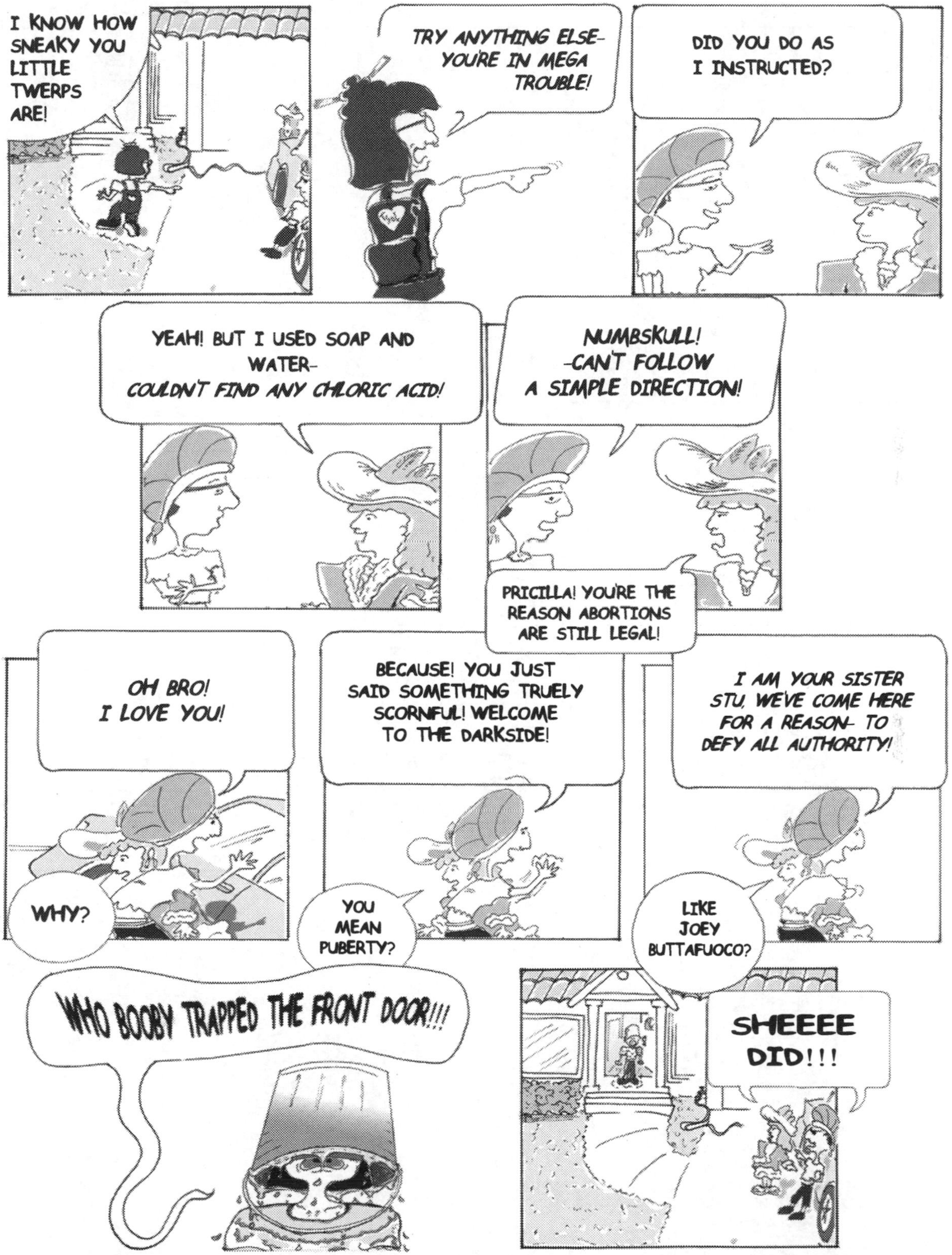
I KNOW HOW SNEAKY YOU LITTLE TWERPS ARE!
TRY ANYTHING ELSE- YOU'RE IN MEGA TROUBLE!
DID YOU DO AS I INSTRUCTED?
YEAH! BUT I USED SOAP AND WATER- COULDN'T FIND ANY CHLORIC ACID!
NUMBSKULL! -CAN'T FOLLOW A SIMPLE DIRECTION!
PRICILLA! YOU'RE THE REASON ABORTIONS ARE STILL LEGAL!
OH BRO! I LOVE YOU!
WHY?
BECAUSE! YOU JUST SAID SOMETHING TRUELY SCORNFUL! WELCOME TO THE DARKSIDE!
YOU MEAN PUBERTY?
I AM YOUR SISTER STU, WE'VE COME HERE FOR A REASON- TO DEFY ALL AUTHORITY!
LIKE JOEY BUTTAFUOCO?
WHO BOOBY TRAPPED THE FRONT DOOR!!!
SHEEEE DID!!!

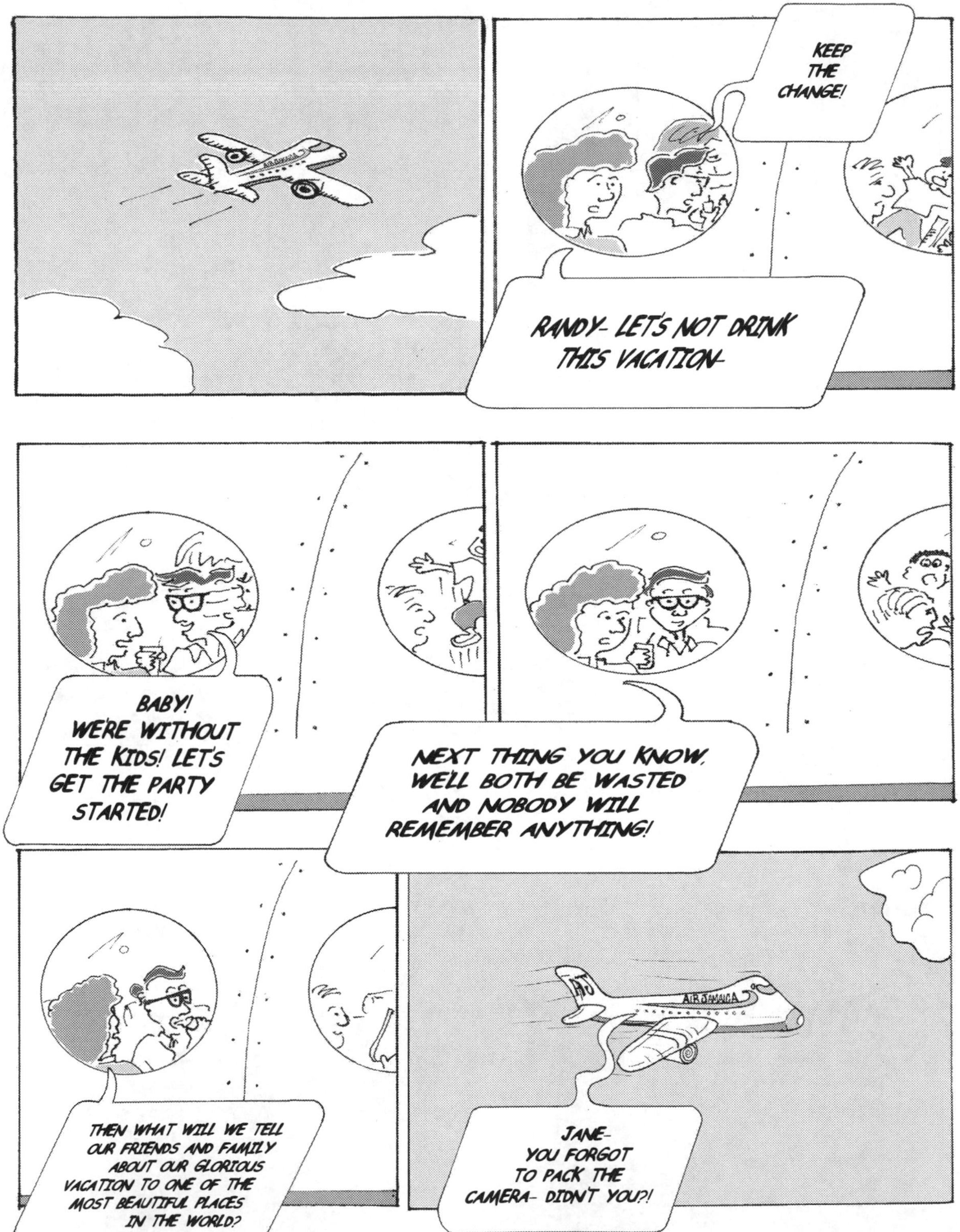

KEEP THE CHANGE!
RANDY- LET'S NOT DRINK THIS VACATION-
BABY! WE'RE WITHOUT THE KIDS! LET'S GET THE PARTY STARTED!
NEXT THING YOU KNOW, WE'LL BOTH BE WASTED AND NOBODY WILL REMEMBER ANYTHING!
THEN WHAT WILL WE TELL OUR FRIENDS AND FAMILY ABOUT OUR GLORIOUS VACATION TO ONE OF THE MOST BEAUTIFUL PLACES IN THE WORLD?
JANE- YOU FORGOT TO PACK THE CAMERA- DIDN'T YOU?!

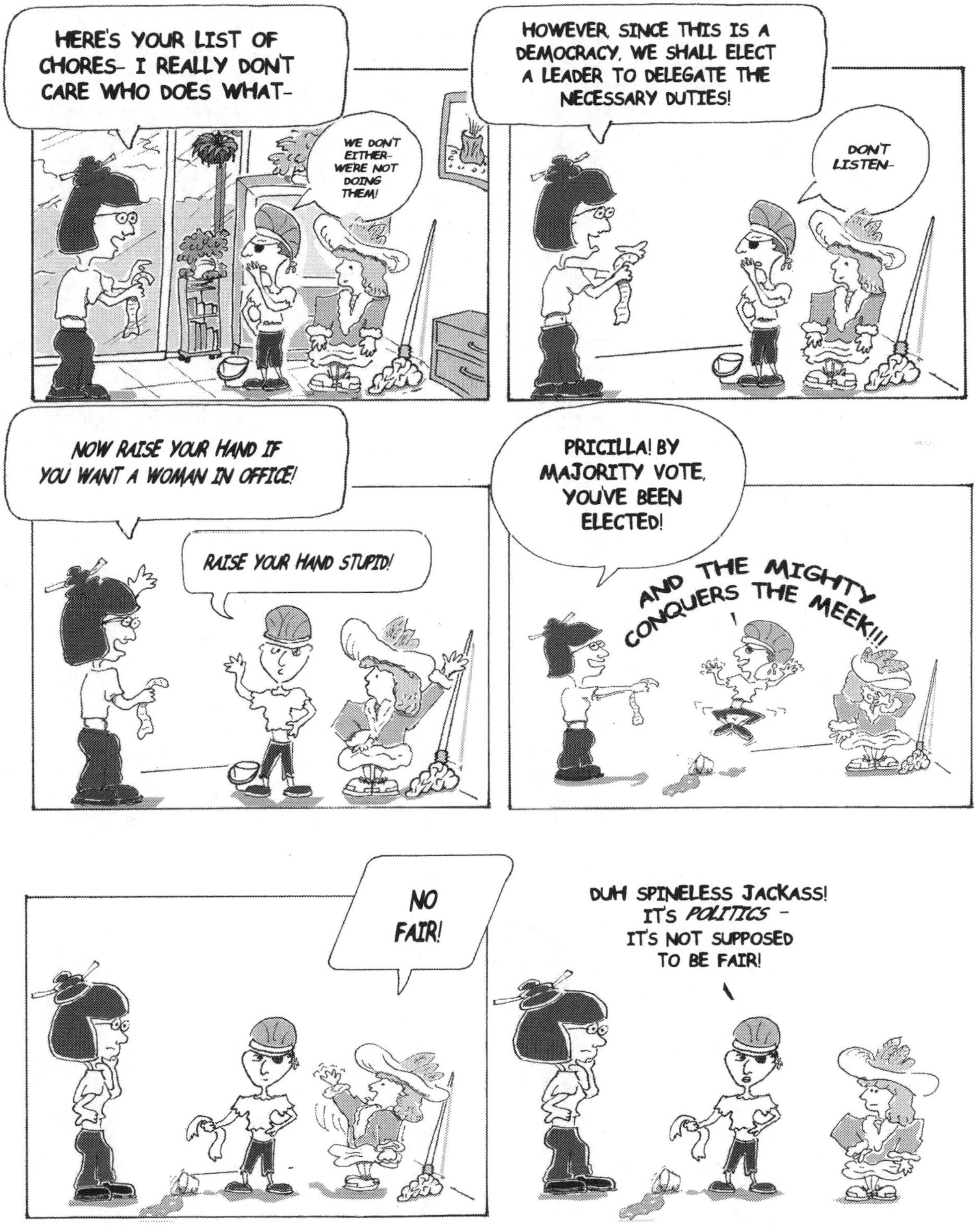
HERE'S YOUR LIST OF CHORES- I REALLY DON'T CARE WHO DOES WHAT-
WE DON'T EITHER- WERE NOT DOING THEM!
HOWEVER, SINCE THIS IS A DEMOCRACY, WE SHALL ELECT A LEADER TO DELEGATE THE NECESSARY DUTIES!
DON'T LISTEN-
NOW RAISE YOUR HAND IF YOU WANT A WOMAN IN OFFICE!
RAISE YOUR HAND STUPID!
PRICILLA! BY MAJORITY VOTE, YOU'VE BEEN ELECTED!
AND THE MIGHTY CONQUERS THE MEEK!!!
NO FAIR!
DUH SPINELESS JACKASS! IT'S POLITICS - IT'S NOT SUPPOSED TO BE FAIR!

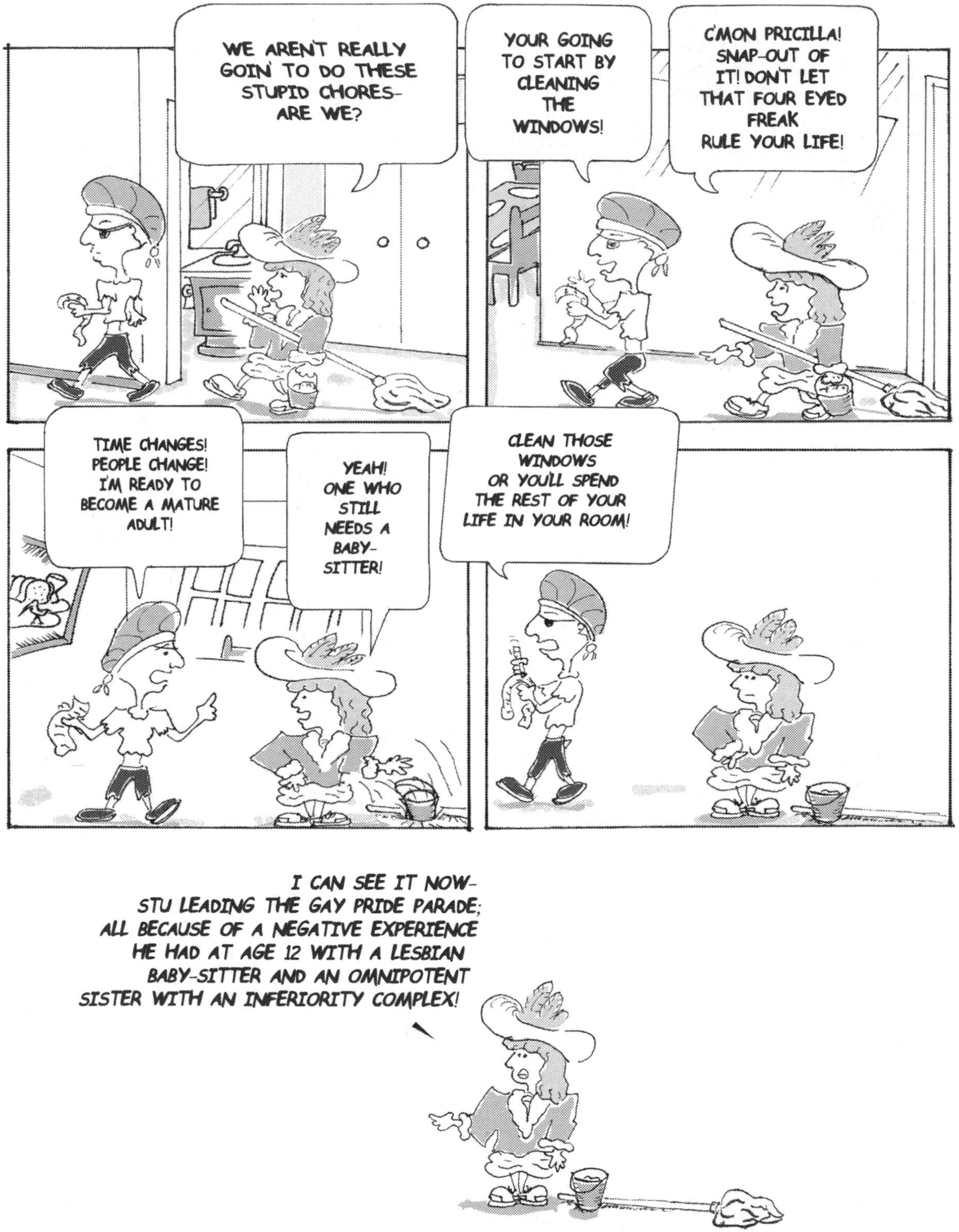
WE AREN'T REALLY GOIN' TO DO THESE STUPID CHORES- ARE WE?
YOUR GOING TO START BY CLEANING THE WINDOWS!
C'MON PRICILLA! SNAP-OUT OF IT! DON'T LET THAT FOUR EYED FREAK RULE YOUR LIFE!
TIME CHANGES! PEOPLE CHANGE! I'M READY TO BECOME A MATURE ADULT!
YEAH! ONE WHO STILL NEEDS A BABY-SITTER!
CLEAN THOSE WINDOWS OR YOU'LL SPEND THE REST OF YOUR LIFE IN YOUR ROOM!
I CAN SEE IT NOW- STU LEADING THE GAY PRIDE PARADE; ALL BECAUSE OF A NEGATIVE EXPERIENCE HE HAD AT AGE 12 WITH A LESBIAN BABY-SITTER AND AN OMNIPOTENT SISTER WITH AN INFERIORITY COMPLEX!

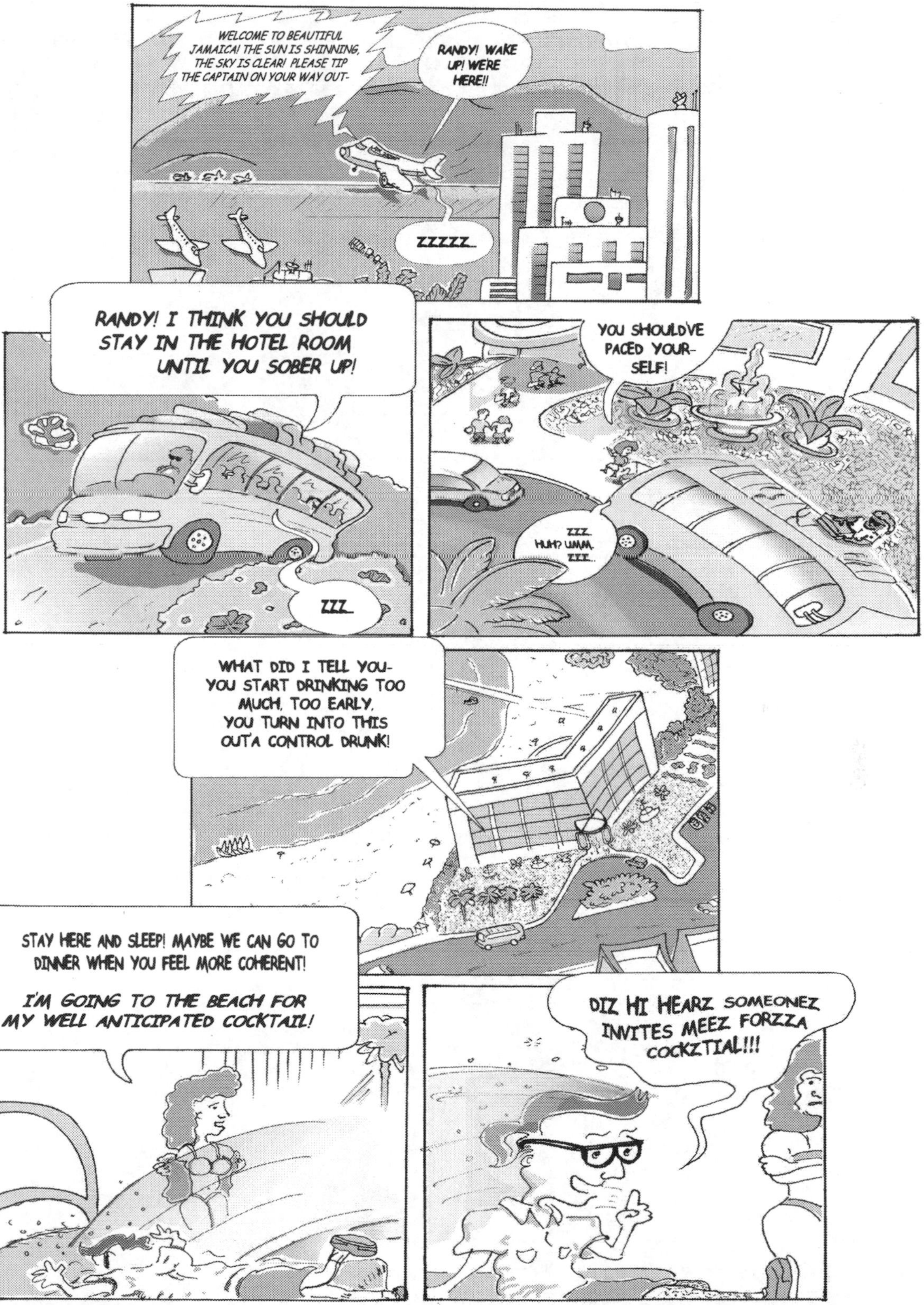
WELCOME TO BEAUTIFUL JAMAICA! THE SUN IS SHINNING, THE SKY IS CLEAR! PLEASE TIP THE CAPTAIN ON YOUR WAY OUT-
RANDY! WAKE UP! WERE HERE!!
ZZZZZ
RANDY! I THINK YOU SHOULD STAY IN THE HOTEL ROOM UNTIL YOU SOBER UP!
ZZZ
YOU SHOULD'VE PACED YOUR-SELF!
ZZZ. HUH? UMM. ZZZ..
WHAT DID I TELL YOU- YOU START DRINKING TOO MUCH, TOO EARLY, YOU TURN INTO THIS OUT'A CONTROL DRUNK!
STAY HERE AND SLEEP! MAYBE WE CAN GO TO DINNER WHEN YOU FEEL MORE COHERENT!
I'M GOING TO THE BEACH FOR MY WELL ANTICIPATED COCKTAIL!
DIZ HI HEARZ SOMEONEZ INVITES MEEZ FORZZA COCKZTIAL!!!

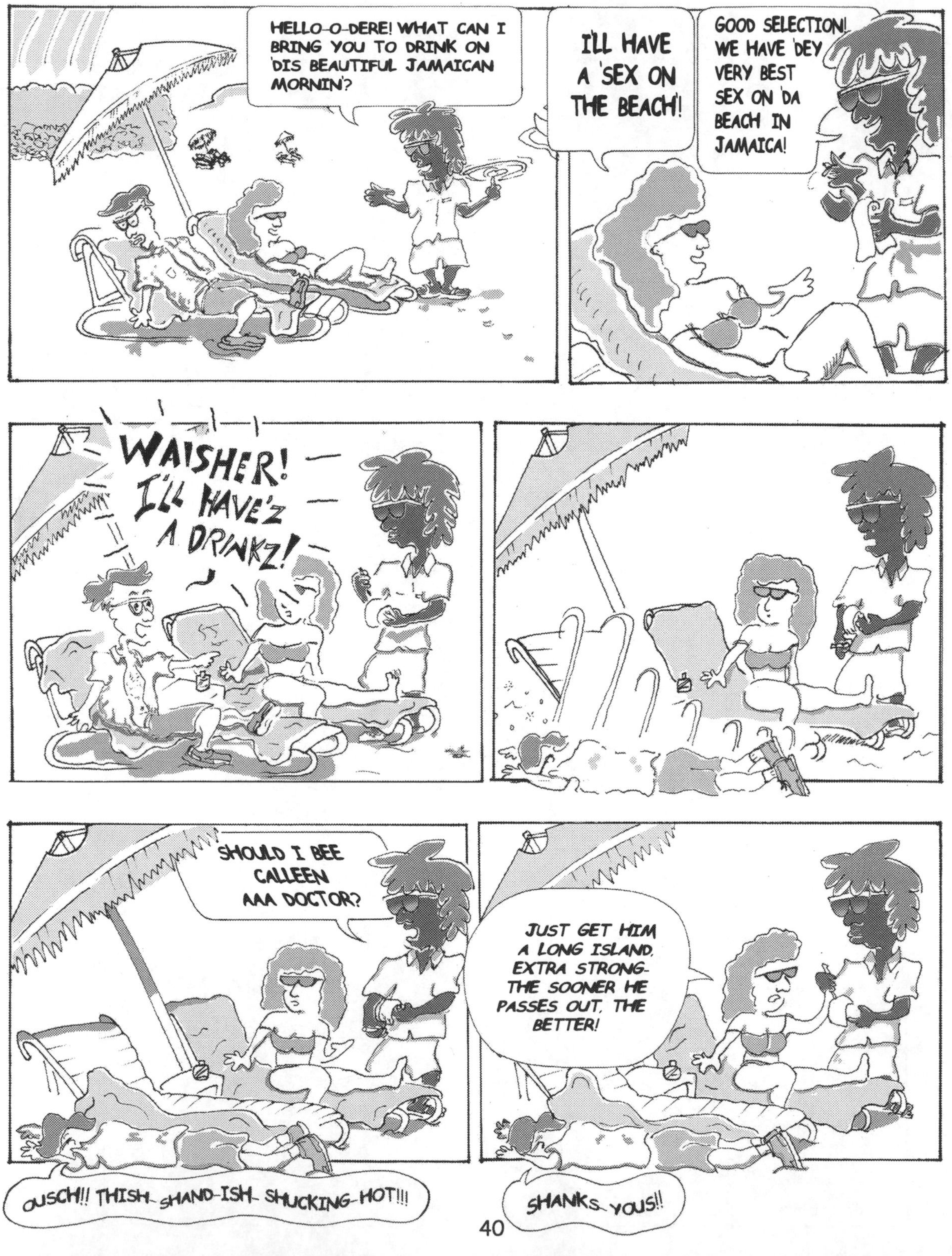
HELLO-O-DERE! WHAT CAN I BRING YOU TO DRINK ON 'DIS BEAUTIFUL JAMAICAN MORNIN'?
I'LL HAVE A 'SEX ON THE BEACH'!
GOOD SELECTION! WE HAVE 'DEY VERY BEST SEX ON 'DA BEACH IN JAMAICA!
WAISHER! I'LL HAVE'Z A DRINKZ!
SHOULD I BEE CALLEEN AAA DOCTOR?
OUSCH!! THISH-SHAND-ISH-SHUCKING-HOT!!!
JUST GET HIM A LONG ISLAND, EXTRA STRONG-THE SOONER HE PASSES OUT, THE BETTER!
SHANKS-YOUS!!

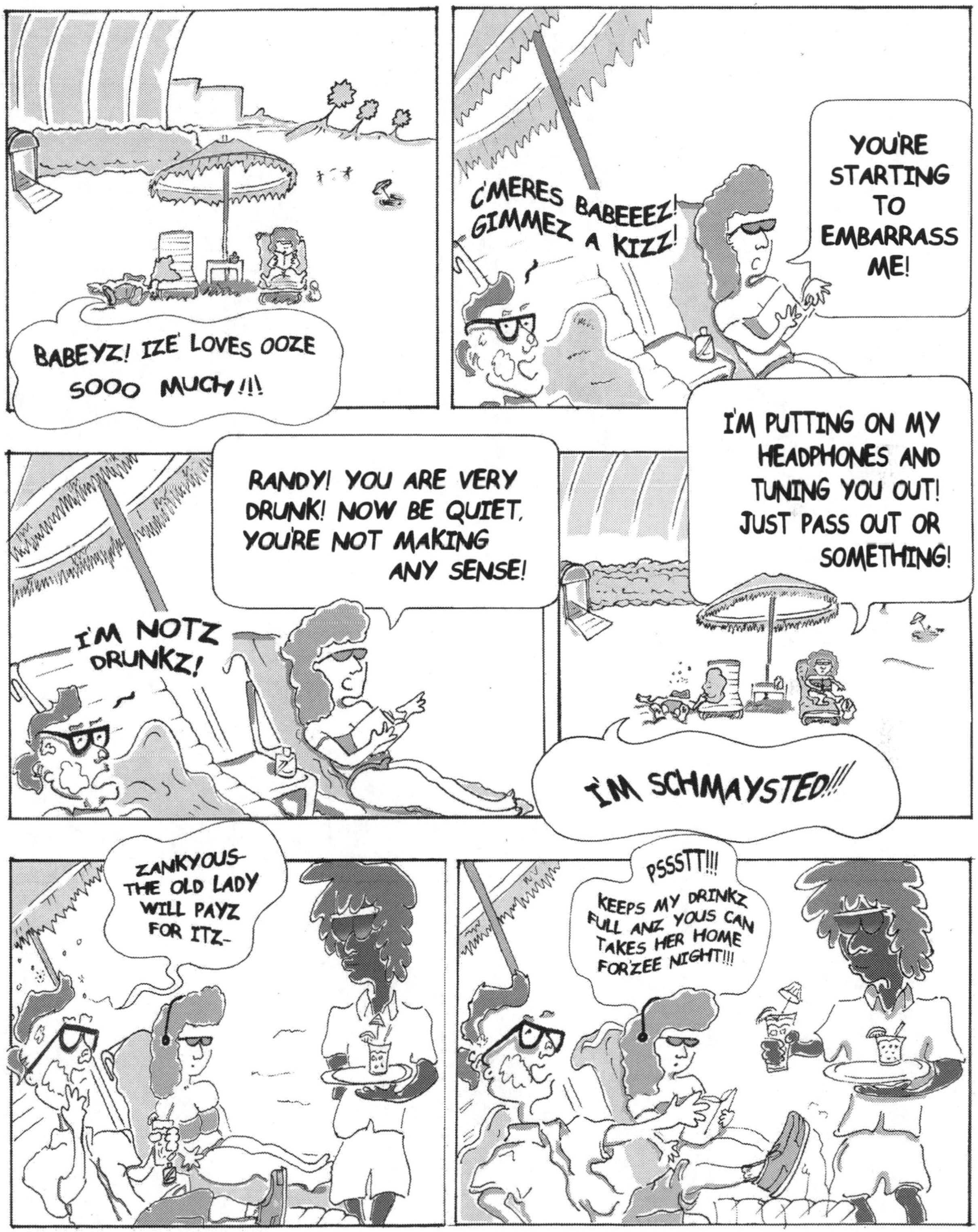
BABEYZ! IZE' LOVES OOZE SOOO MUCH!!!
C'MERES BABEEEZ! GIMMEZ A KIZZ!
YOU'RE STARTING TO EMBARRASS ME!
I'M NOTZ DRUNKZ!
RANDY! YOU ARE VERY DRUNK! NOW BE QUIET, YOU'RE NOT MAKING ANY SENSE!
I'M PUTTING ON MY HEADPHONES AND TUNING YOU OUT! JUST PASS OUT OR SOMETHING!
I'M SCHMAYSTED!!!
ZANKYOUS-THE OLD LADY WILL PAYZ FOR ITZ-
PSSSTT!!!
KEEPS MY DRINKZ FULL ANZ YOUS CAN TAKES HER HOME FOR'ZEE NIGHT!!!

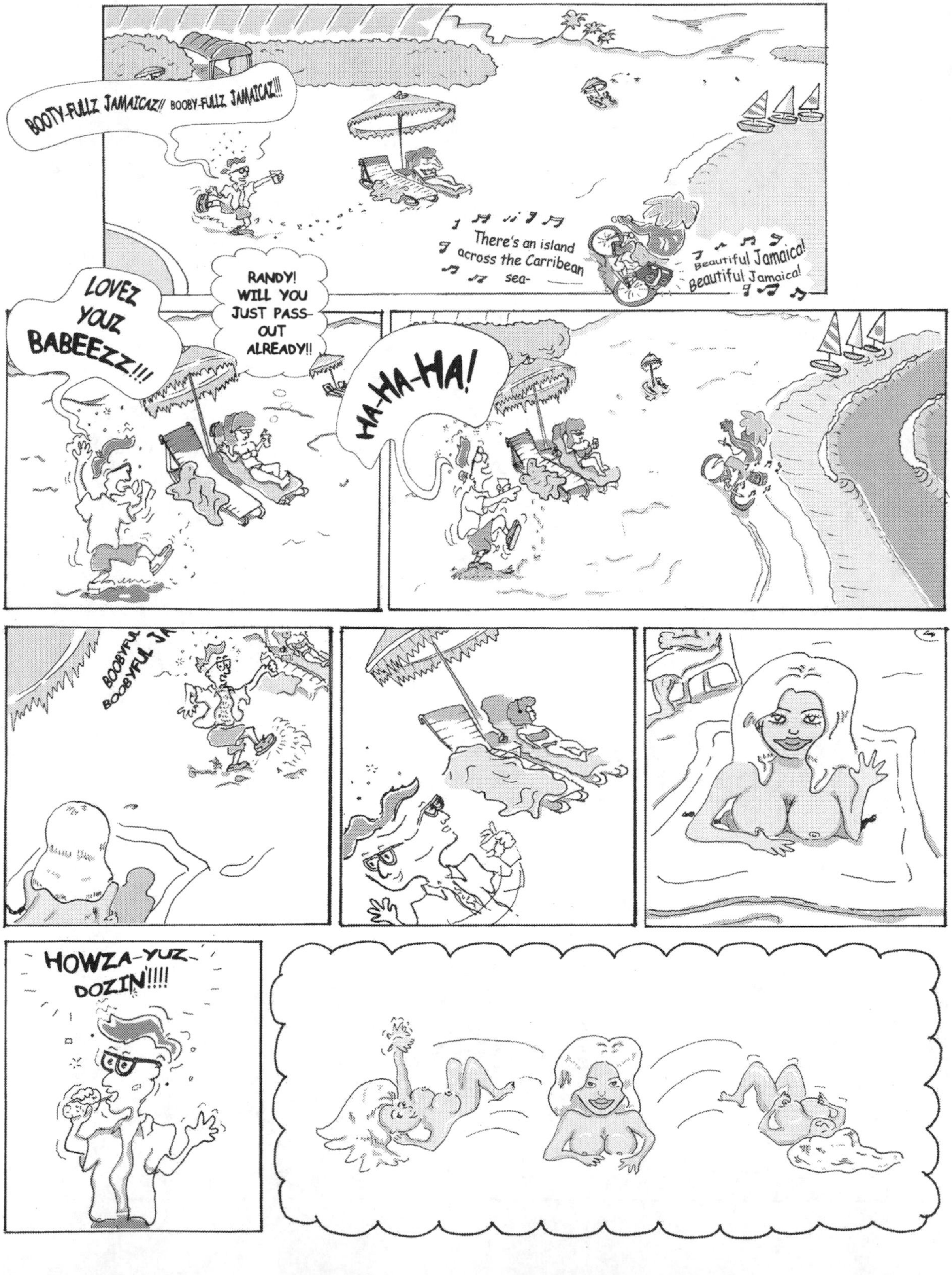
BOOTY-FULLZ JAMAICAZ!! BOOBY-FULLZ JAMAICAZ!!!
There's an island across the Carribean sea-
Beautiful Jamaica! Beautiful Jamaica!
LOVEZ YOUZ BABEEZZ!!!
RANDY! WILL YOU JUST PASS-OUT ALREADY!!
HA-HA-HA!
BOOBYFUL JA
BOOBYFUL
HOWZA-YUZ-DOZIN!!!!

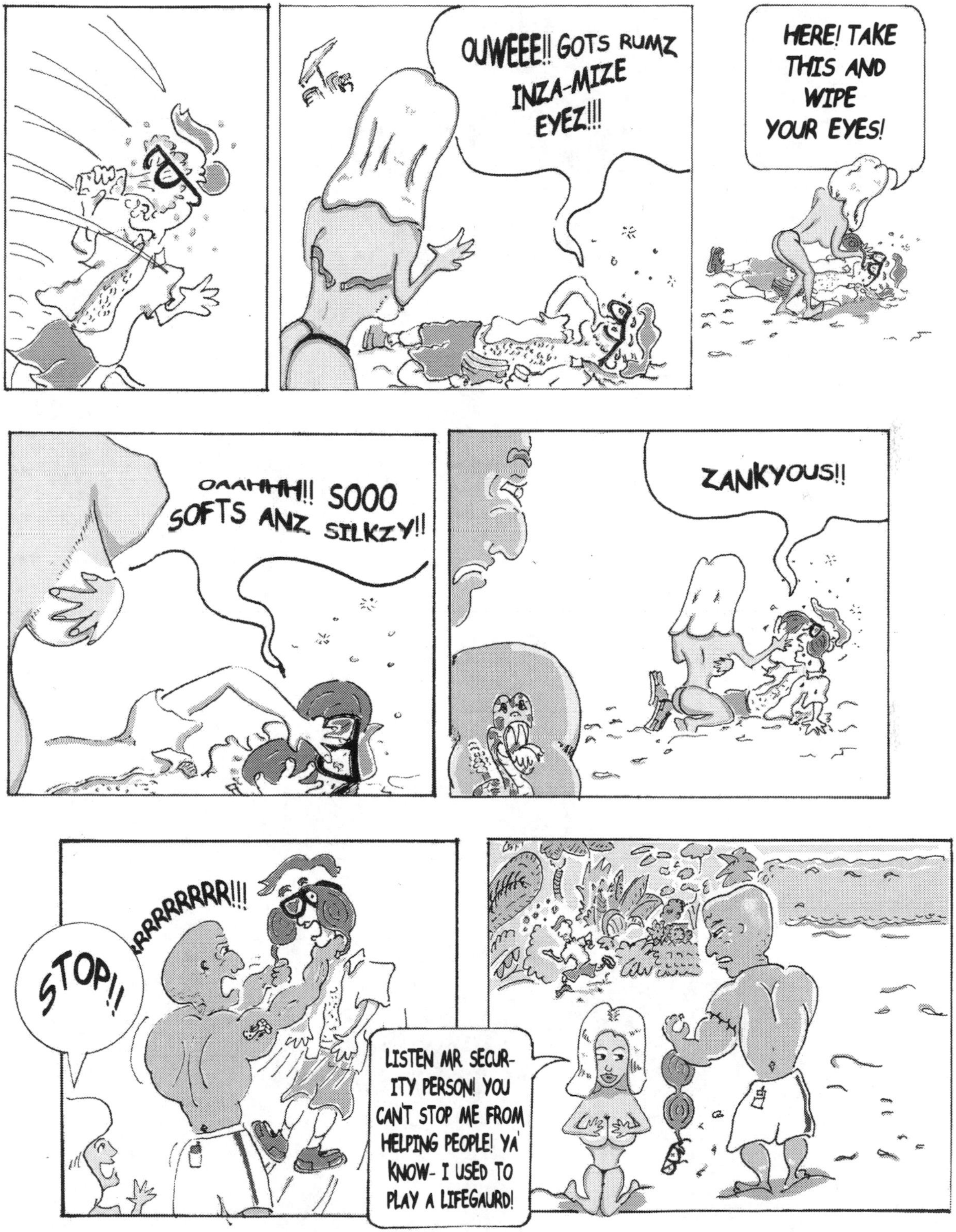
OUWEEE!! GOTS RUMZ INZA-MIZE EYEZ!!!
HERE! TAKE THIS AND WIPE YOUR EYES!
OAAHHHH!! SOOO SOFTS ANZ SILKZY!!
ZANKYOUS!!
STOP!!
RRRRRRRRR!!!
LISTEN MR SECUR-ITY PERSON! YOU CAN'T STOP ME FROM HELPING PEOPLE! YA' KNOW- I USED TO PLAY A LIFEGAURD!

CHAPTER FOUR

KABLOOM!!!

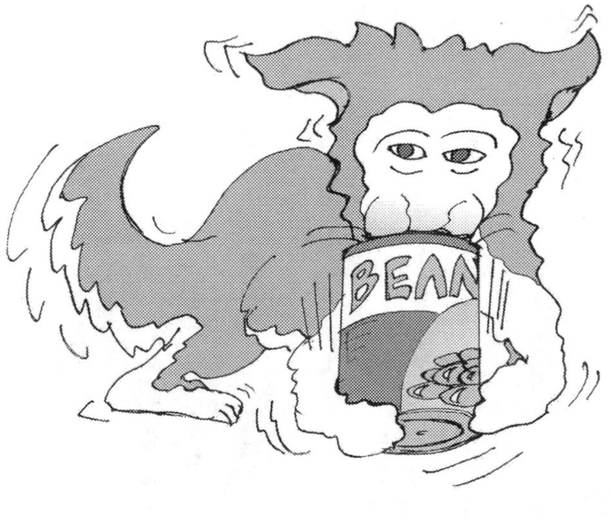
BEAN

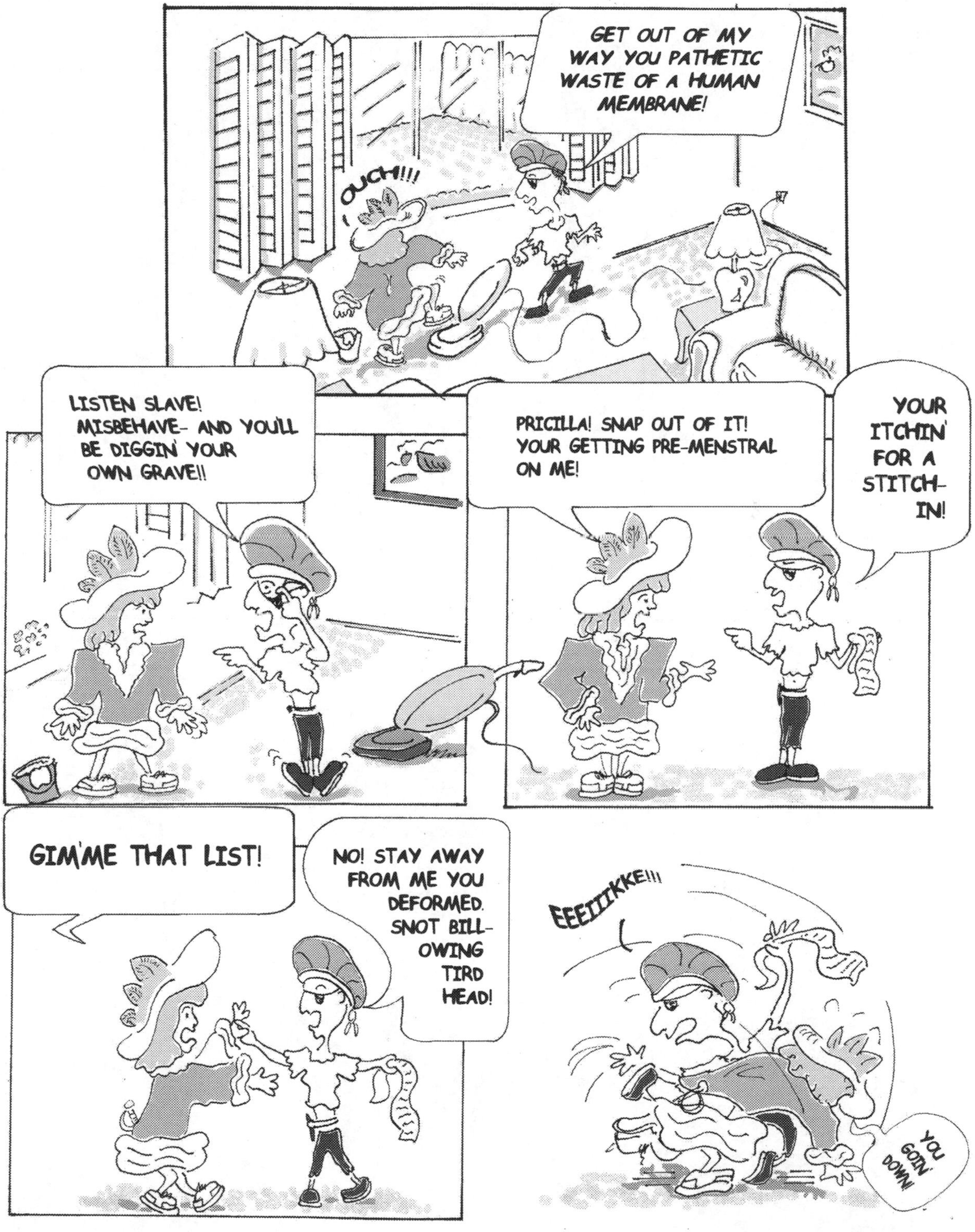
GET OUT OF MY WAY YOU PATHETIC WASTE OF A HUMAN MEMBRANE!
OUCH!!!!
LISTEN SLAVE! MISBEHAVE- AND YOU'LL BE DIGGIN' YOUR OWN GRAVE!!
PRICILLA! SNAP OUT OF IT! YOUR GETTING PRE-MENSTRAL ON ME!
YOUR ITCHIN' FOR A STITCH-IN!
GIM'ME THAT LIST!
NO! STAY AWAY FROM ME YOU DEFORMED. SNOT BILL-OWING TIRD HEAD!
EEEIIIKKE!!!
YOU GOIN' DOWN!

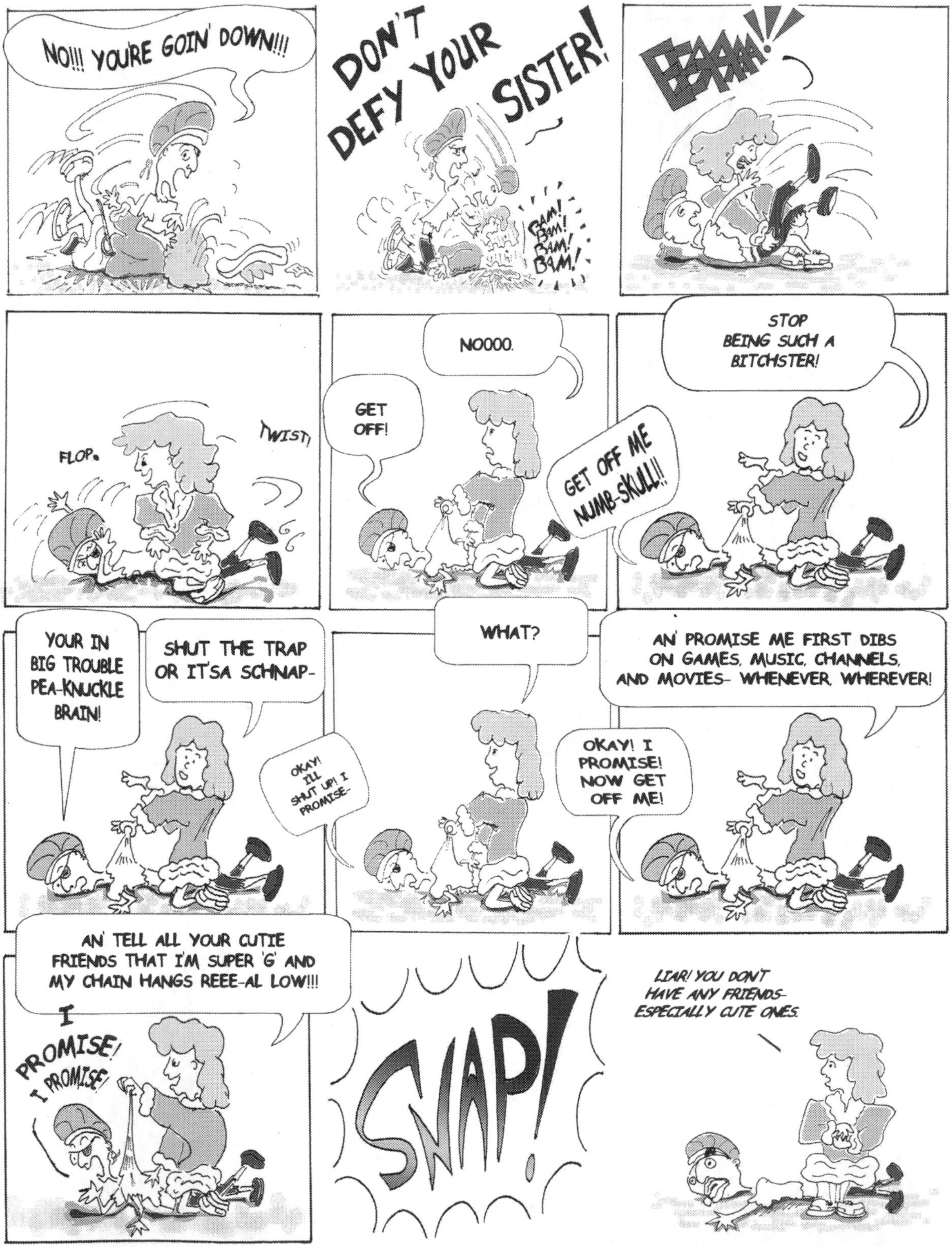
NO!!! YOU'RE GOIN' DOWN!!!
DON'T DEFY YOUR SISTER!
BAM! BAM! BAM! BAM!
FLOP.
TWIST!
NOOOO.
GET OFF!
GET OFF ME NUMB-SKULL!!
STOP BEING SUCH A BITCHSTER!
YOUR IN BIG TROUBLE PEA-KNUCKLE BRAIN!
SHUT THE TRAP OR IT'SA SCHNAP-
WHAT?
OKAY! I'LL SHUT UP! I PROMISE-
AN' PROMISE ME FIRST DIBS ON GAMES, MUSIC, CHANNELS, AND MOVIES- WHENEVER, WHEREVER!
OKAY! I PROMISE! NOW GET OFF ME!
AN' TELL ALL YOUR CUTIE FRIENDS THAT I'M SUPER 'G' AND MY CHAIN HANGS REEE-AL LOW!!!
I PROMISE! I PROMISE!
SNAP!
LIAR! YOU DON'T HAVE ANY FRIENDS- ESPECIALLY CUTE ONES.

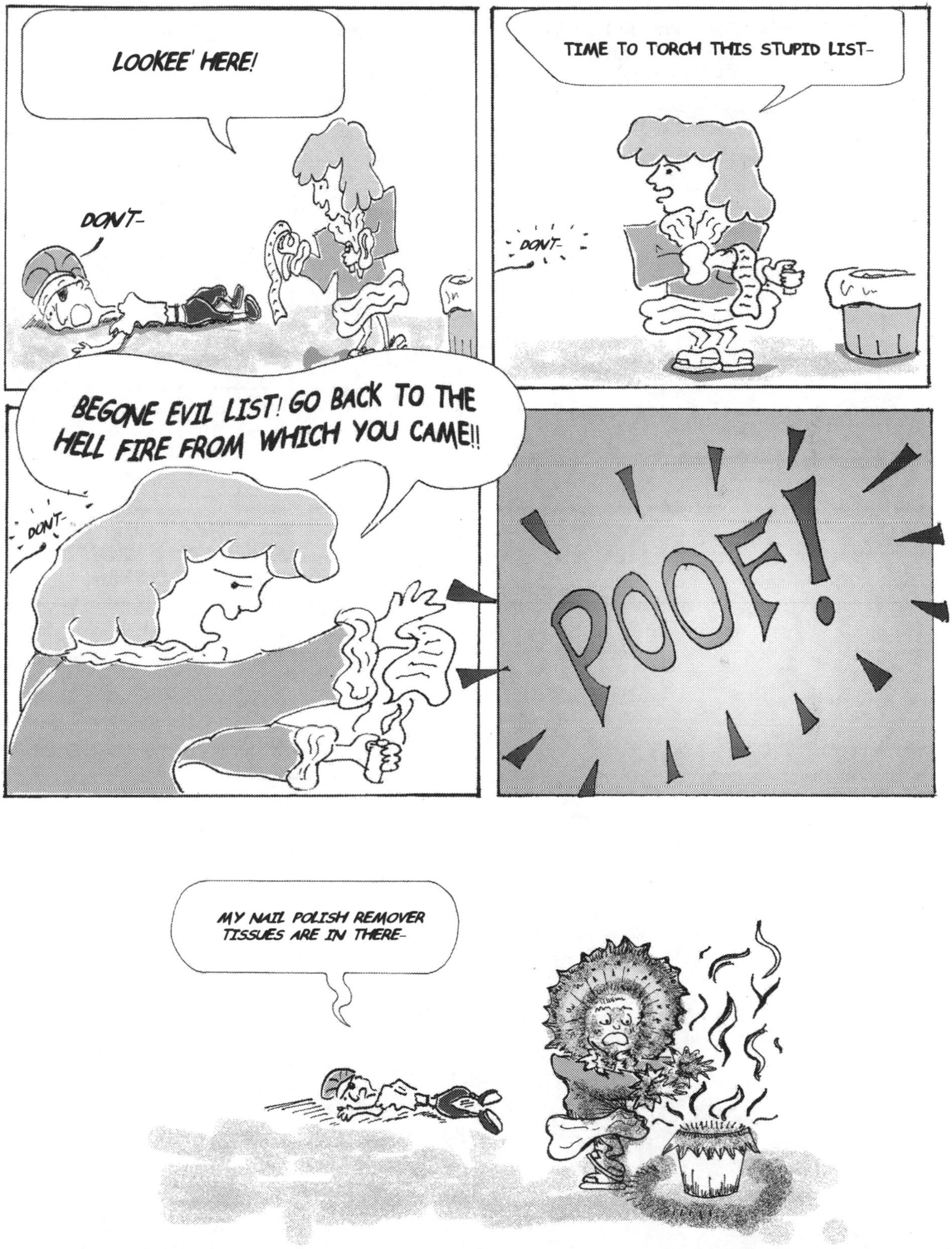
LOOKEE' HERE!
DON'T-
TIME TO TORCH THIS STUPID LIST-
DON'T-
BEGONE EVIL LIST! GO BACK TO THE HELL FIRE FROM WHICH YOU CAME!!
DON'T-
POOF!
MY NAIL POLISH REMOVER TISSUES ARE IN THERE-

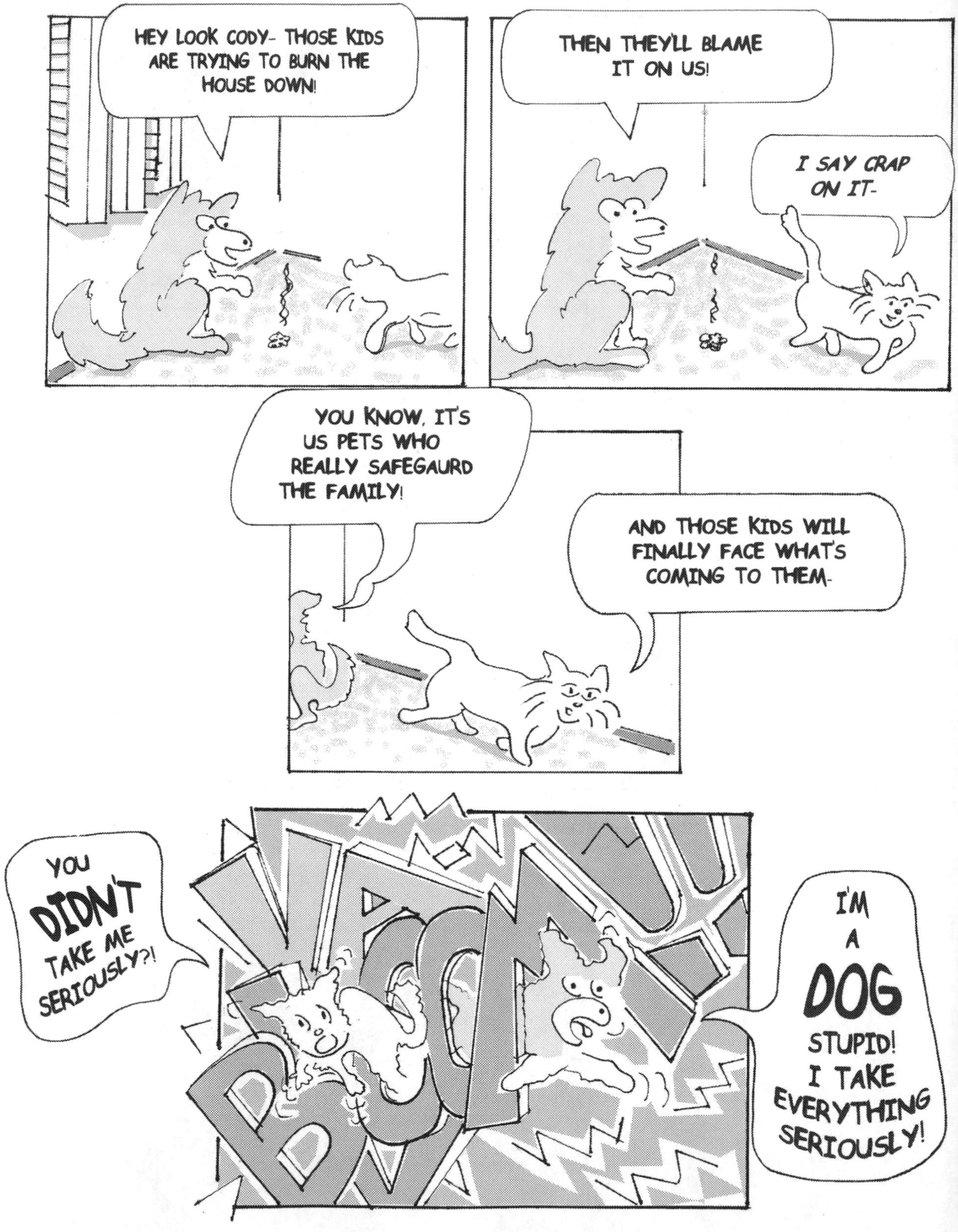
HEY LOOK CODY- THOSE KIDS ARE TRYING TO BURN THE HOUSE DOWN!
THEN THEY'LL BLAME IT ON US!
I SAY CRAP ON IT-
YOU KNOW, IT'S US PETS WHO REALLY SAFEGAURD THE FAMILY!
AND THOSE KIDS WILL FINALLY FACE WHAT'S COMING TO THEM-
YOU DIDN'T TAKE ME SERIOUSLY?!
I'M A DOG STUPID! I TAKE EVERYTHING SERIOUSLY!

CHAPTER
FIVE

JAMAICAN
HOSPITALITY

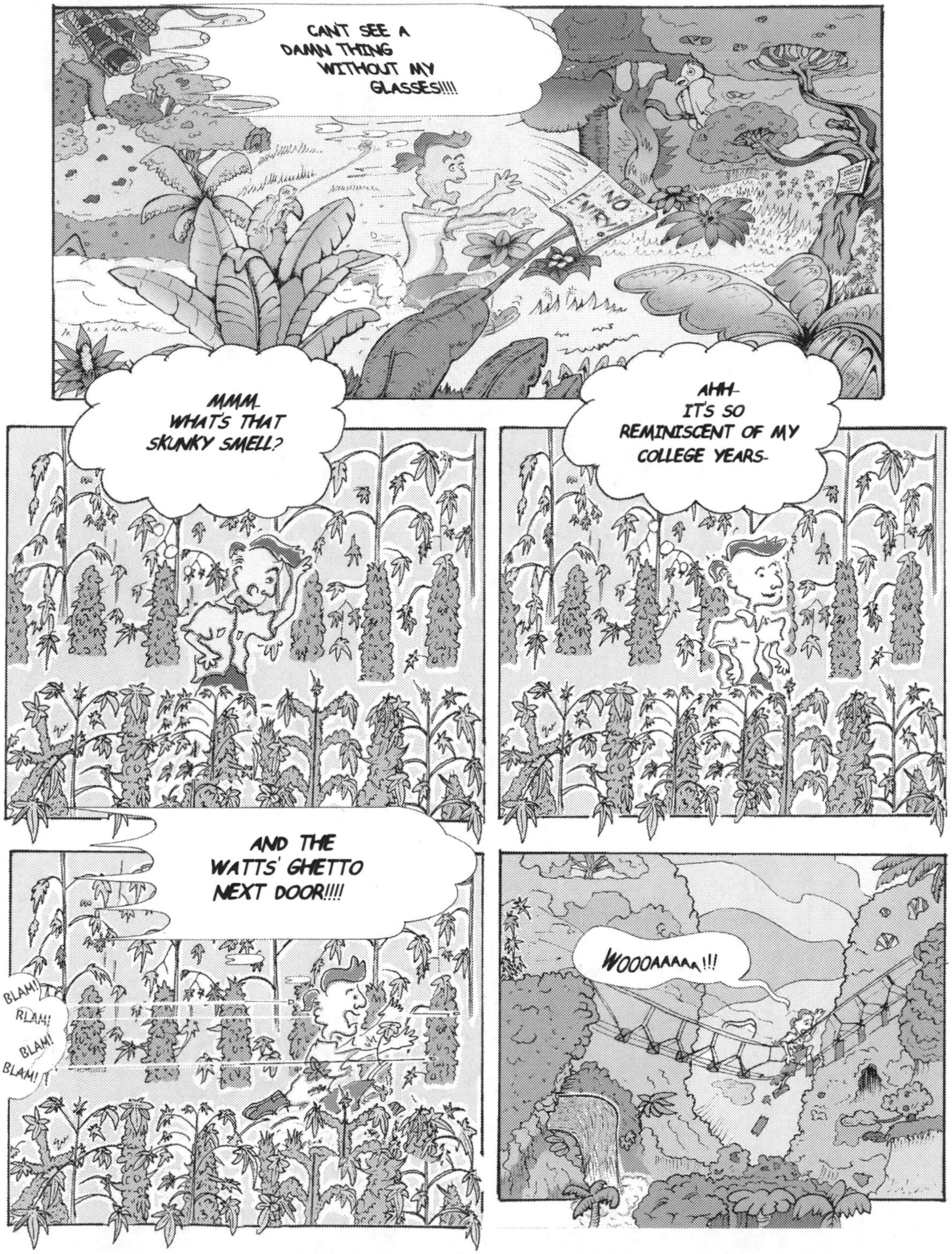
CAN'T SEE A DAMN THING WITHOUT MY GLASSES!!!!
NO ENTR
MMM- WHAT'S THAT SKUNKY SMELL?
AHH- IT'S SO REMINISCENT OF MY COLLEGE YEARS-
AND THE WATTS' GHETTO NEXT DOOR!!!!
BLAM!
BLAM!
BLAM!
BLAM!
WOOOAAAAA!!!

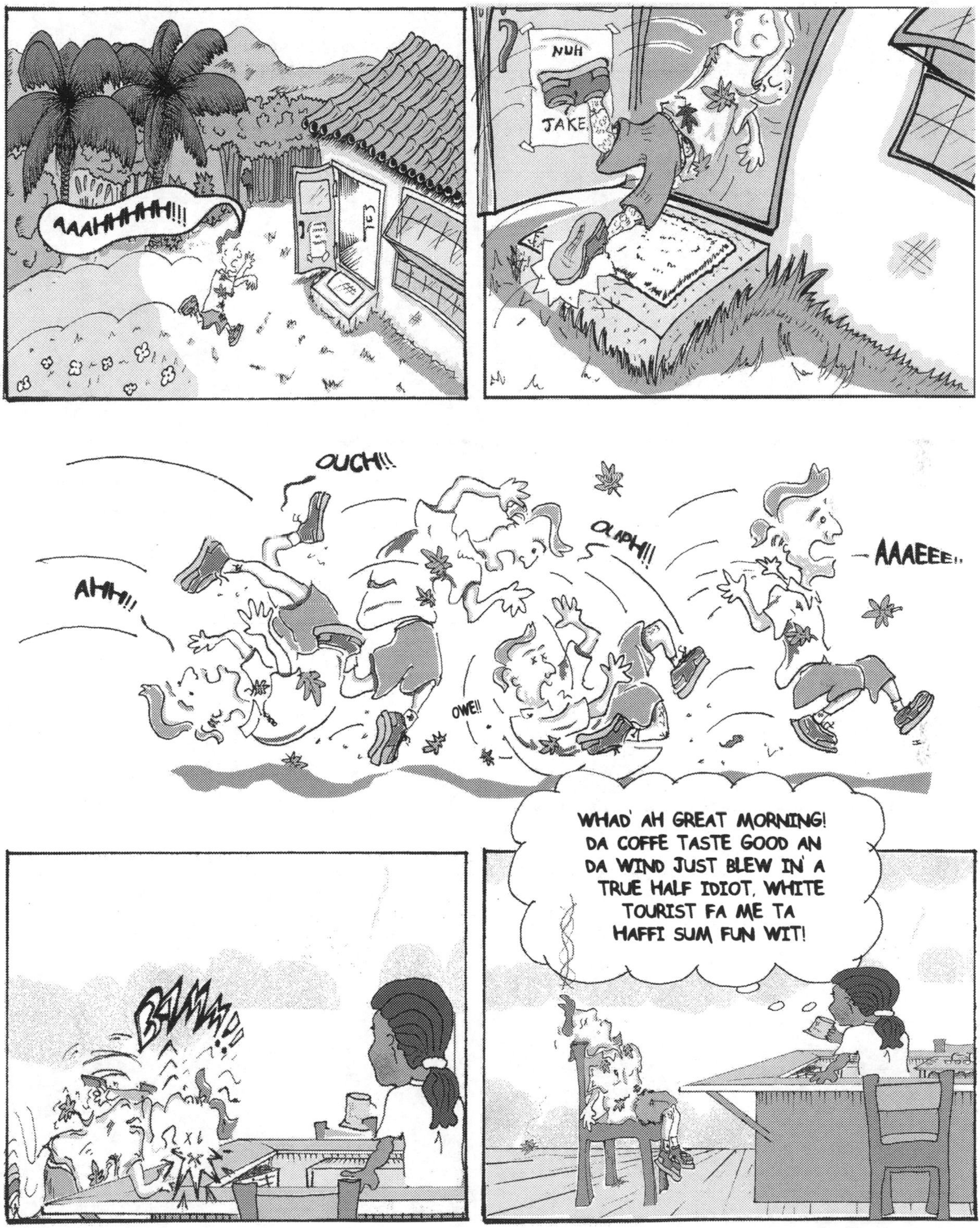
AAAHHHHHH!!!
NUH
JAKE
OUCH!!
AHH!!
OUAPH!!
AAAEEE!!
OWE!!
WHAD' AH GREAT MORNING! DA COFFE TASTE GOOD AN DA WIND JUST BLEW IN' A TRUE HALF IDIOT, WHITE TOURIST FA ME TA HAFFI SUM FUN WIT!

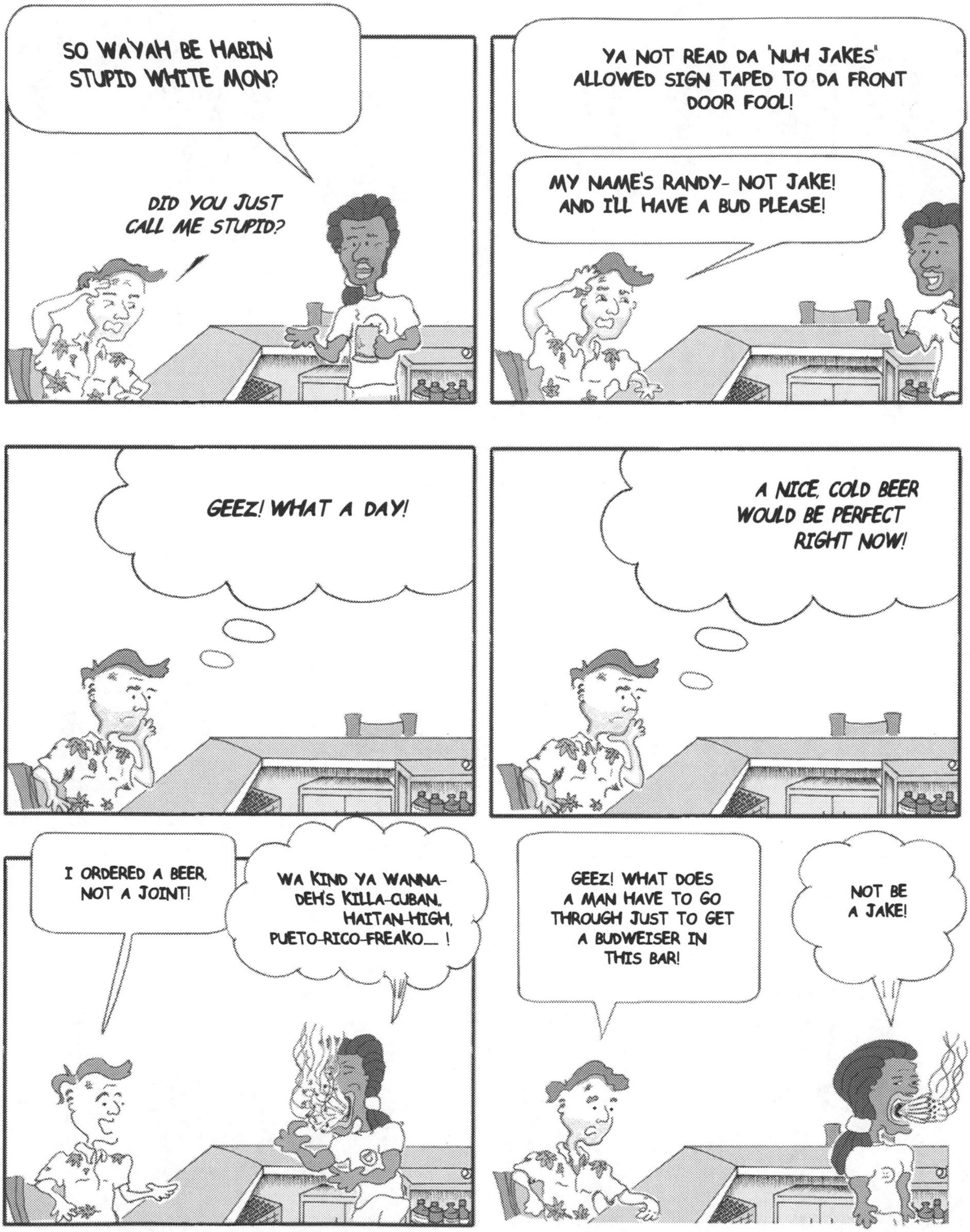
SO WA'YAH BE HABIN' STUPID WHITE MON?
DID YOU JUST CALL ME STUPID?
YA NOT READ DA 'NUH JAKES' ALLOWED SIGN TAPED TO DA FRONT DOOR FOOL!
MY NAME'S RANDY- NOT JAKE! AND I'LL HAVE A BUD PLEASE!
GEEZ! WHAT A DAY!
A NICE, COLD BEER WOULD BE PERFECT RIGHT NOW!
I ORDERED A BEER, NOT A JOINT!
WA KIND YA WANNA- DEH'S KILLA-CUBAN, HAITAN-HIGH, PUETO-RICO-FREAKO.... !
GEEZ! WHAT DOES A MAN HAVE TO GO THROUGH JUST TO GET A BUDWEISER IN THIS BAR!
NOT BE A JAKE!

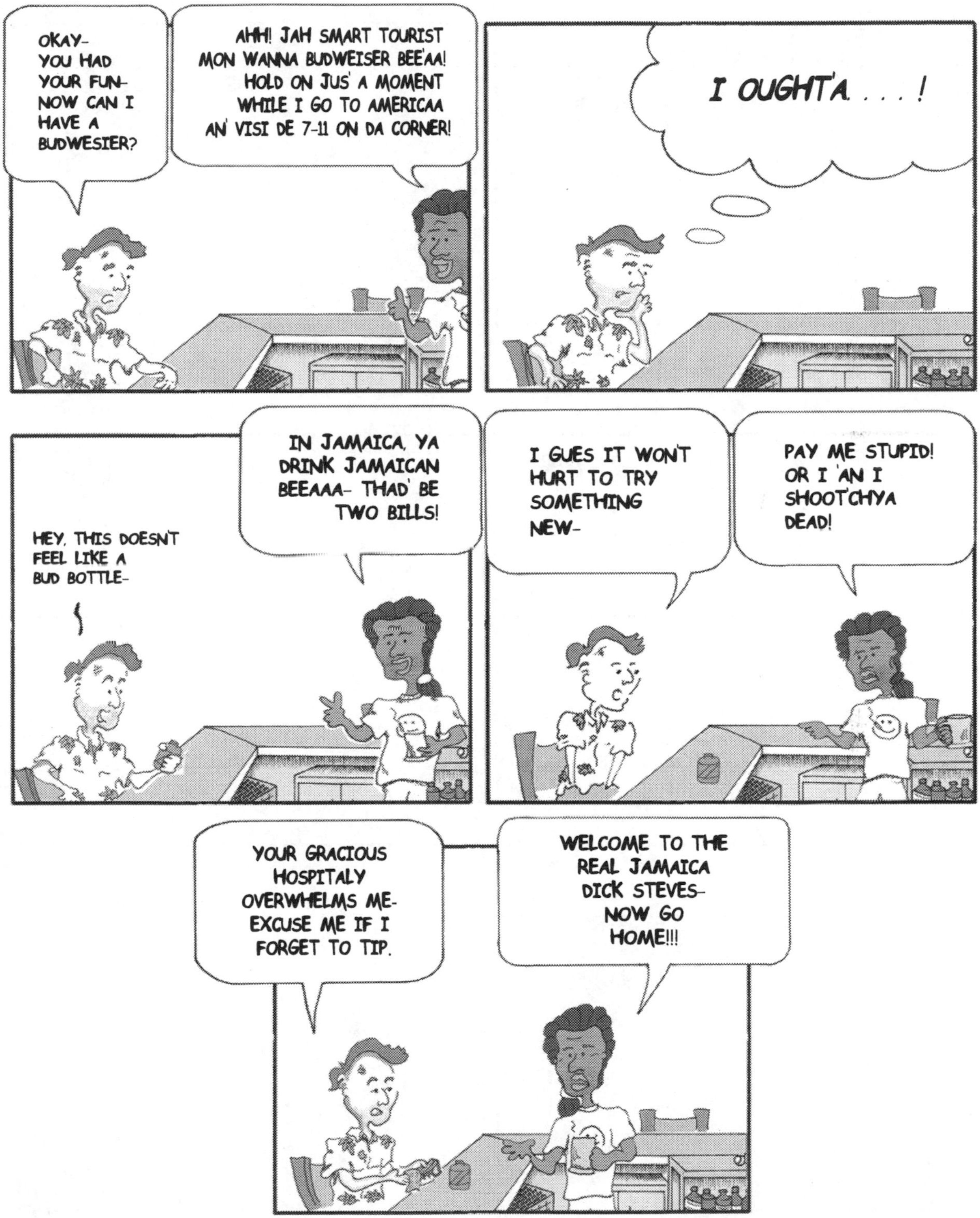
OKAY- YOU HAD YOUR FUN- NOW CAN I HAVE A BUDWESIER?
AHH! JAH SMART TOURIST MON WANNA BUDWEISER BEE'AA! HOLD ON JUS' A MOMENT WHILE I GO TO AMERICAA AN' VISI DE 7-11 ON DA CORNER!
I OUGHT'A . . . !
HEY, THIS DOESN'T FEEL LIKE A BUD BOTTLE-
IN JAMAICA, YA DRINK JAMAICAN BEEAAA- THAD' BE TWO BILLS!
I GUES IT WON'T HURT TO TRY SOMETHING NEW-
PAY ME STUPID! OR I 'AN I SHOOT'CHYA DEAD!
YOUR GRACIOUS HOSPITALY OVERWHELMS ME- EXCUSE ME IF I FORGET TO TIP.
WELCOME TO THE REAL JAMAICA DICK STEVES- NOW GO HOME!!!

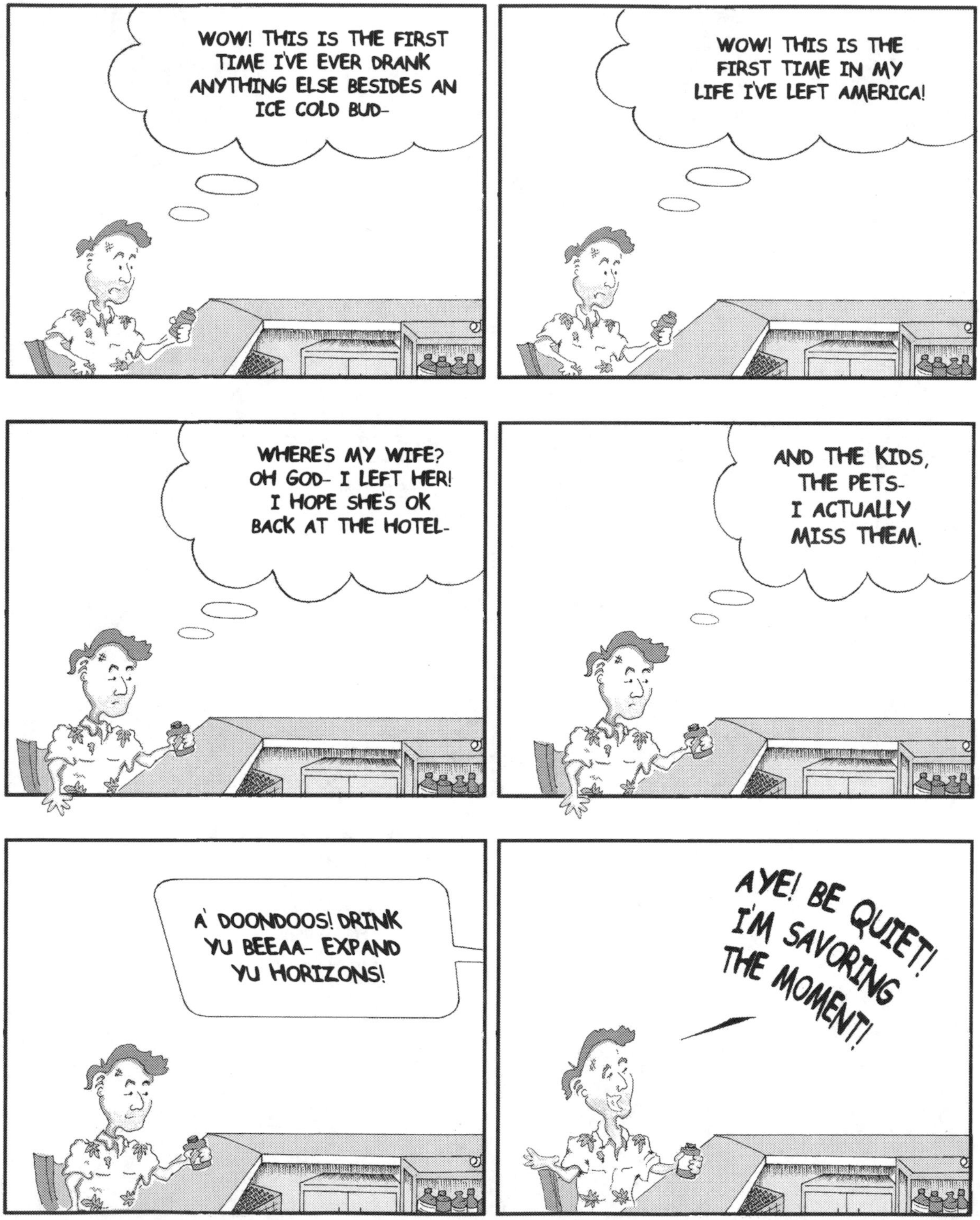
WOW! THIS IS THE FIRST TIME I'VE EVER DRANK ANYTHING ELSE BESIDES AN ICE COLD BUD-
WOW! THIS IS THE FIRST TIME IN MY LIFE I'VE LEFT AMERICA!
WHERE'S MY WIFE? OH GOD- I LEFT HER! I HOPE SHE'S OK BACK AT THE HOTEL-
AND THE KIDS, THE PETS- I ACTUALLY MISS THEM.
A' DOONDOOS! DRINK YU BEEAA- EXPAND YU HORIZONS!
AYE! BE QUIET! I'M SAVORING THE MOMENT!

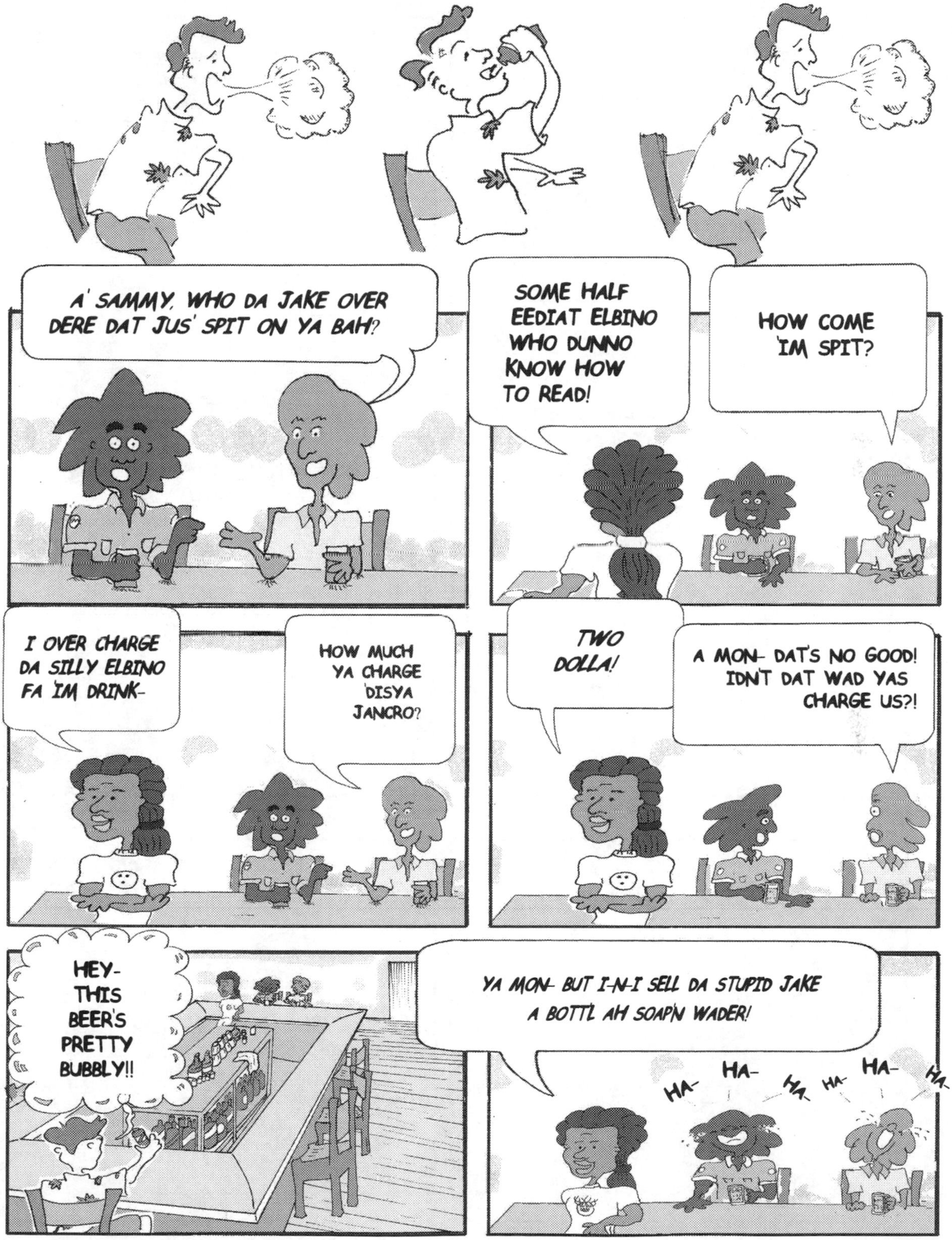
A' SAMMY, WHO DA JAKE OVER DERE DAT JUS' SPIT ON YA BAH?
SOME HALF EEDIAT ELBINO WHO DUNNO KNOW HOW TO READ!
HOW COME 'IM SPIT?
I OVER CHARGE DA SILLY ELBINO FA 'IM DRINK-
HOW MUCH YA CHARGE 'DISYA JANCRO?
TWO DOLLA!
A MON- DAT'S NO GOOD! IDN'T DAT WAD YAS CHARGE US?!
HEY- THIS BEER'S PRETTY BUBBLY!!
YA MON- BUT I-N-I SELL DA STUPID JAKE A BOTTL AH SOAP'N WADER!
HA- HA- HA- HA- HA- HA-

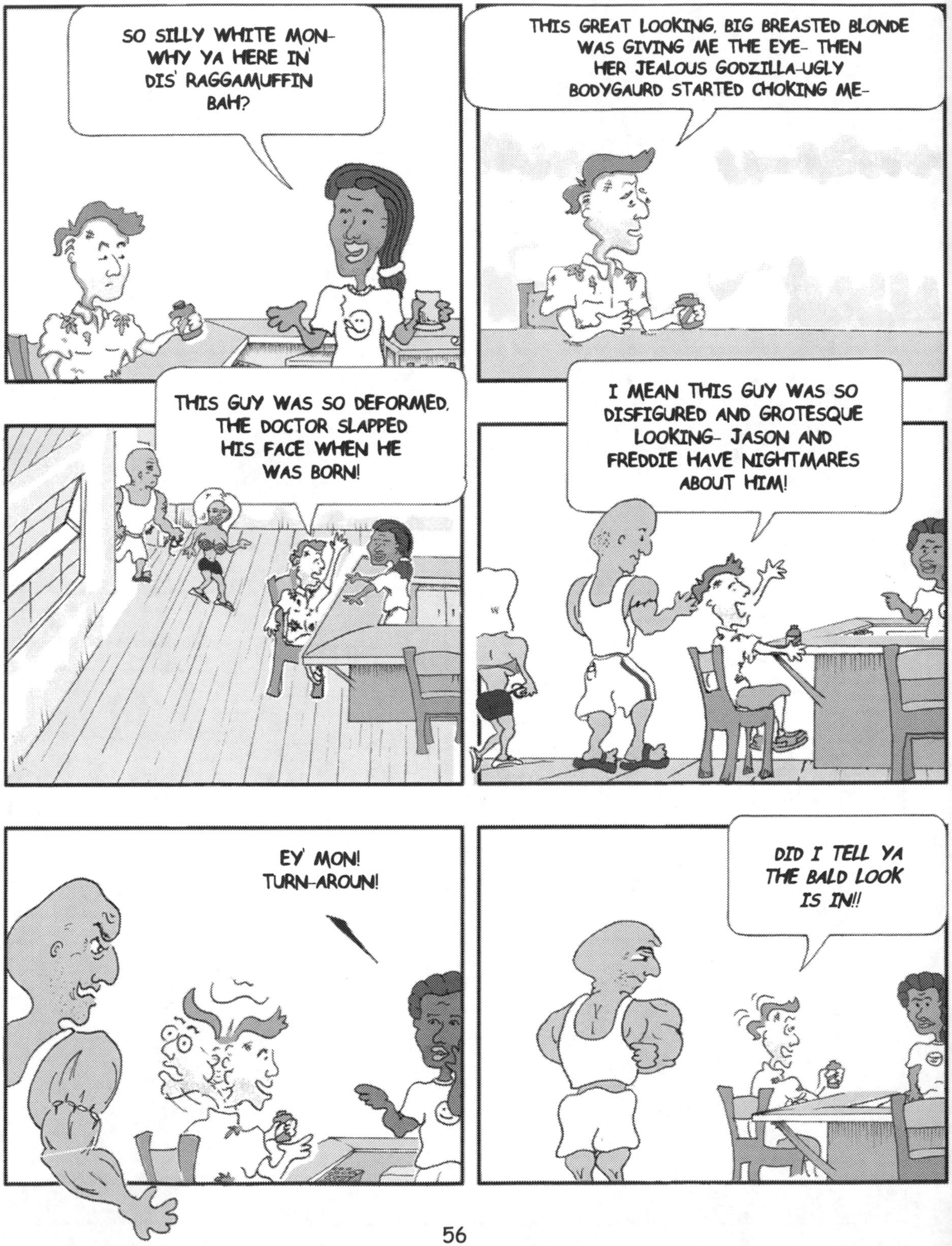
SO SILLY WHITE MON- WHY YA HERE IN' DIS' RAGGAMUFFIN BAH?
THIS GREAT LOOKING, BIG BREASTED BLONDE WAS GIVING ME THE EYE- THEN HER JEALOUS GODZILLA-UGLY BODYGAURD STARTED CHOKING ME-
THIS GUY WAS SO DEFORMED, THE DOCTOR SLAPPED HIS FACE WHEN HE WAS BORN!
I MEAN THIS GUY WAS SO DISFIGURED AND GROTESQUE LOOKING- JASON AND FREDDIE HAVE NIGHTMARES ABOUT HIM!
EY' MON! TURN-AROUN!
DID I TELL YA THE BALD LOOK IS IN!!

CHAPTER SIX

IRIE DESPERATION

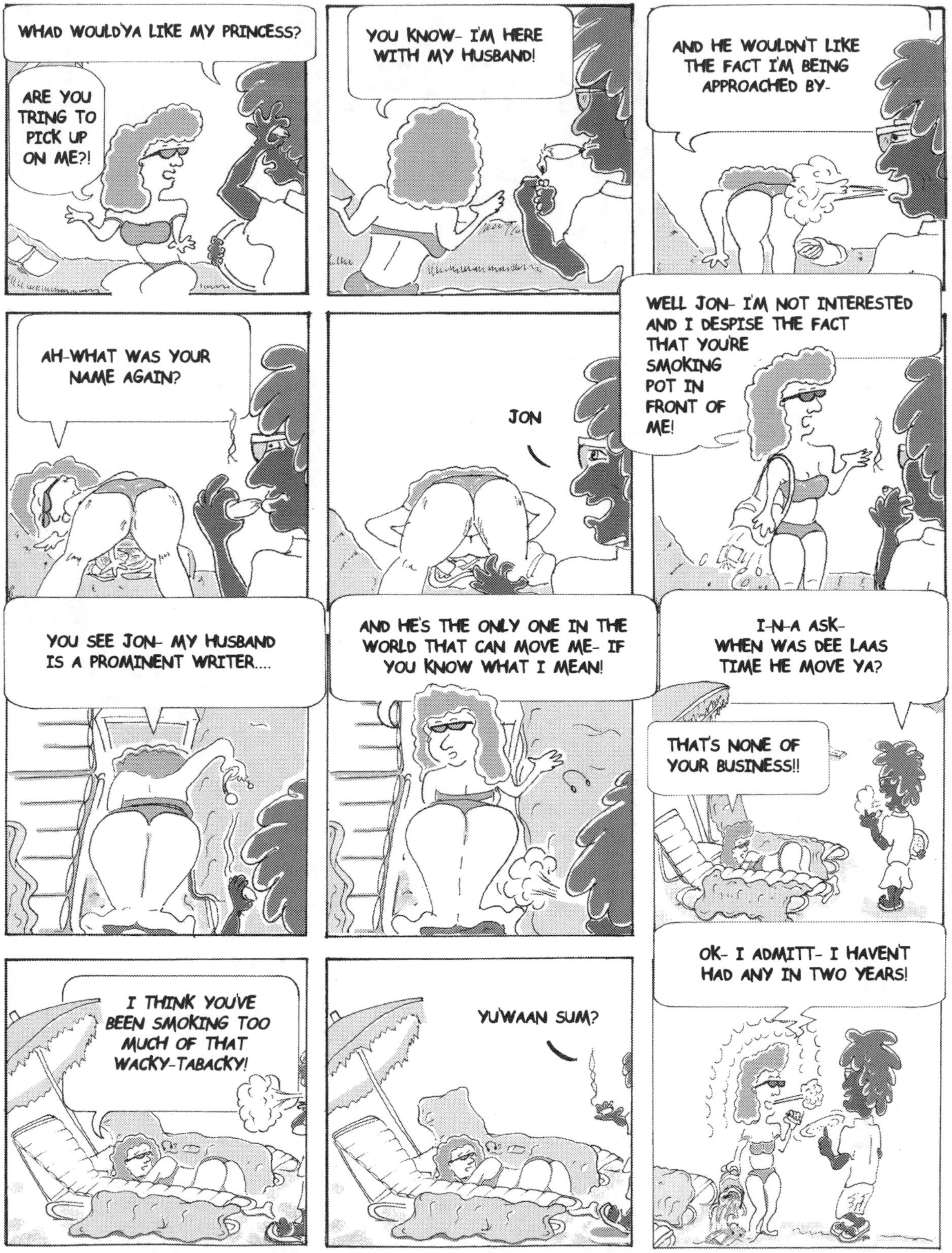
WHAD WOULDYA LIKE MY PRINCESS?
ARE YOU TRING TO PICK UP ON ME?!
YOU KNOW- I'M HERE WITH MY HUSBAND!
AND HE WOULDN'T LIKE THE FACT I'M BEING APPROACHED BY-
AH-WHAT WAS YOUR NAME AGAIN?
JON
WELL JON- I'M NOT INTERESTED AND I DESPISE THE FACT THAT YOU'RE SMOKING POT IN FRONT OF ME!
YOU SEE JON- MY HUSBAND IS A PROMINENT WRITER....
AND HE'S THE ONLY ONE IN THE WORLD THAT CAN MOVE ME- IF YOU KNOW WHAT I MEAN!
I-N-A ASK- WHEN WAS DEE LAAS TIME HE MOVE YA?
THAT'S NONE OF YOUR BUSINESS!!
I THINK YOU'VE BEEN SMOKING TOO MUCH OF THAT WACKY-TABACKY!
YU'WAAN SUM?
OK- I ADMITT- I HAVEN'T HAD ANY IN TWO YEARS!

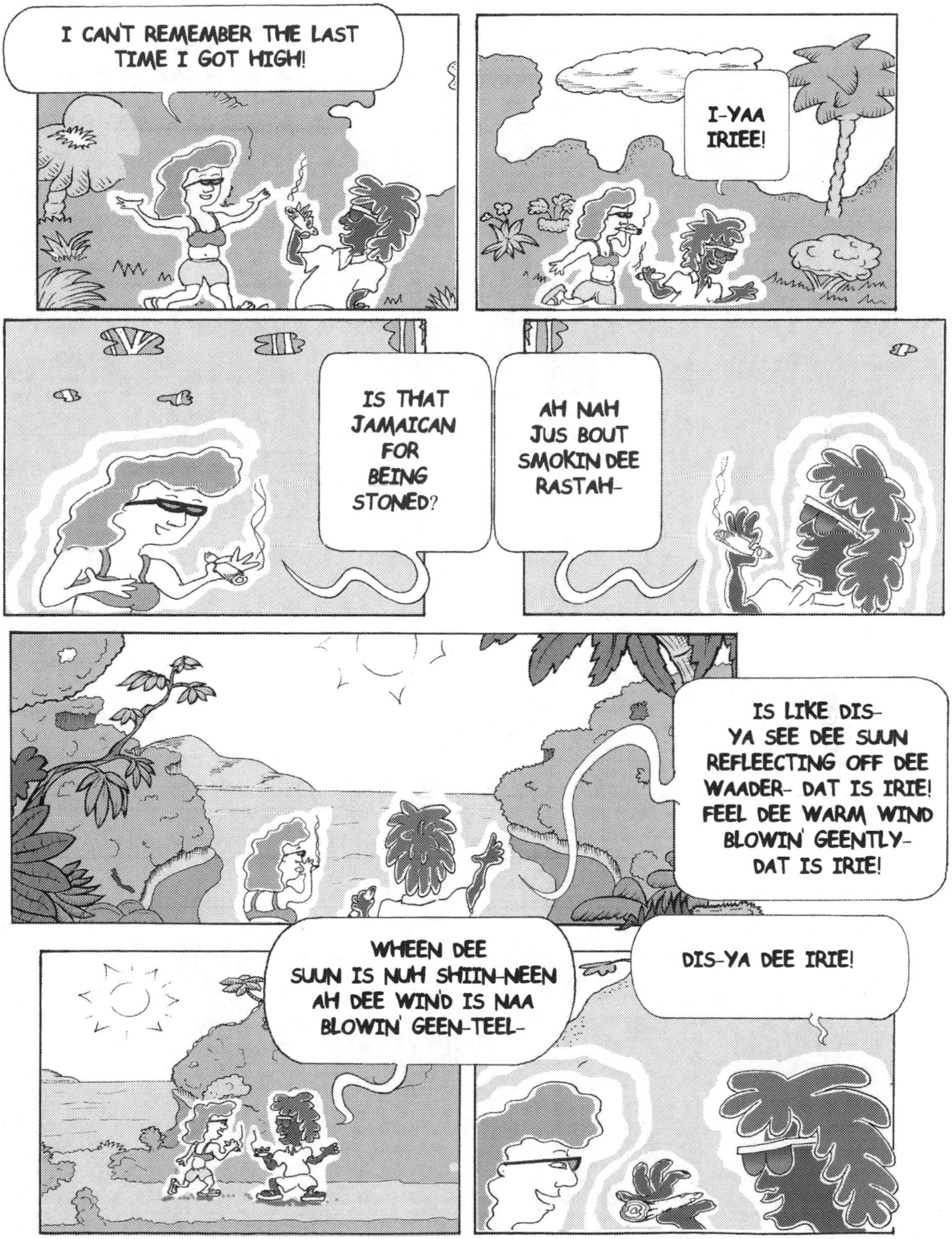
I CAN'T REMEMBER THE LAST TIME I GOT HIGH!
I-YAA IRIEE!
IS THAT JAMAICAN FOR BEING STONED?
AH NAH JUS BOUT SMOKIN DEE RASTAH-
IS LIKE DIS- YA SEE DEE SUUN REFLEECTING OFF DEE WAADER- DAT IS IRIE! FEEL DEE WARM WIND BLOWIN' GEENTLY- DAT IS IRIE!
WHEEN DEE SUUN IS NUH SHIIN-NEEN AH DEE WIND IS NAA BLOWIN' GEEN-TEEL-
DIS-YA DEE IRIE!

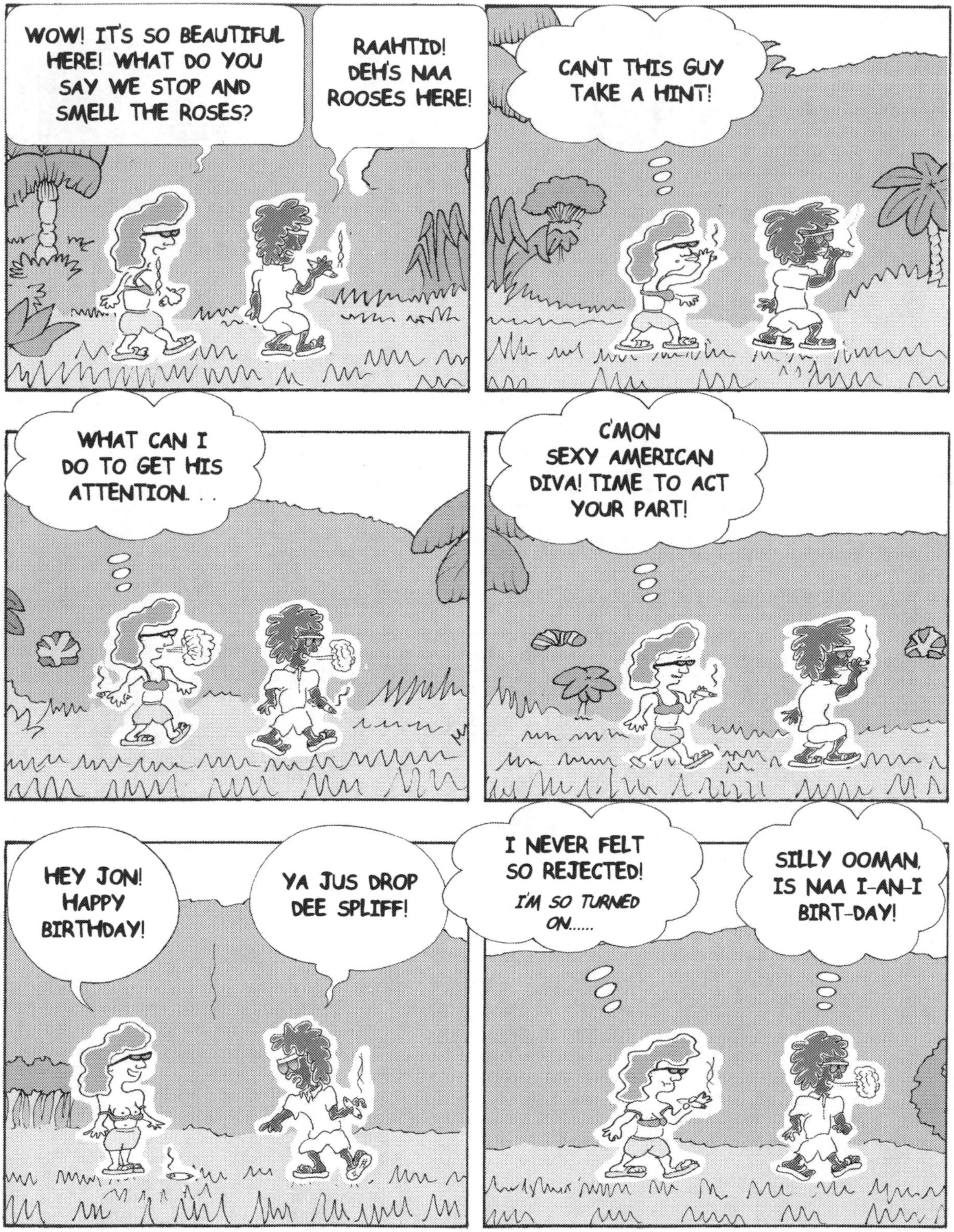
WOW! IT'S SO BEAUTIFUL HERE! WHAT DO YOU SAY WE STOP AND SMELL THE ROSES?
RAAHTID! DEH'S NAA ROOSES HERE!
CAN'T THIS GUY TAKE A HINT!
WHAT CAN I DO TO GET HIS ATTENTION. . .
C'MON SEXY AMERICAN DIVA! TIME TO ACT YOUR PART!
HEY JON! HAPPY BIRTHDAY!
YA JUS DROP DEE SPLIFF!
I NEVER FELT SO REJECTED!
I'M SO TURNED ON.....
SILLY OOMAN, IS NAA I-AN-I BIRT-DAY!

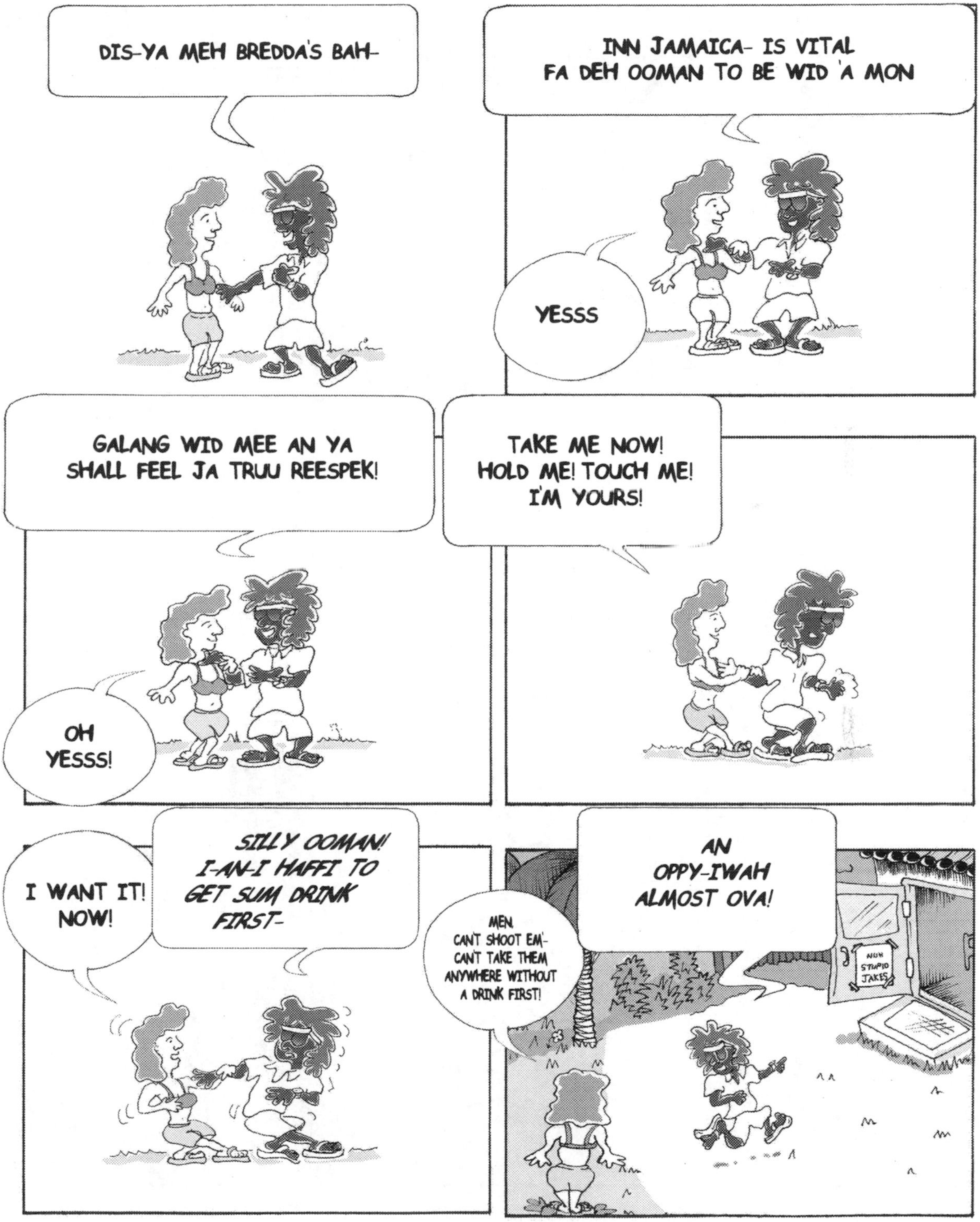
DIS-YA MEH BREDDA'S BAH-
INN JAMAICA- IS VITAL FA DEH OOMAN TO BE WID 'A MON
YESSS
GALANG WID MEE AN YA SHALL FEEL JA TRUU REESPEK!
OH YESSS!
TAKE ME NOW! HOLD ME! TOUCH ME! I'M YOURS!
I WANT IT! NOW!
SILLY OOMAN! I-AN-I HAFFI TO GET SUM DRINK FIRST-
MEN. CAN'T SHOOT EM'- CAN'T TAKE THEM ANYWHERE WITHOUT A DRINK FIRST!
AN OPPY-IWAH ALMOST OVA!
NUH STUPID JAKES

CHAPTER SEVEN

'OPPY IWAH'

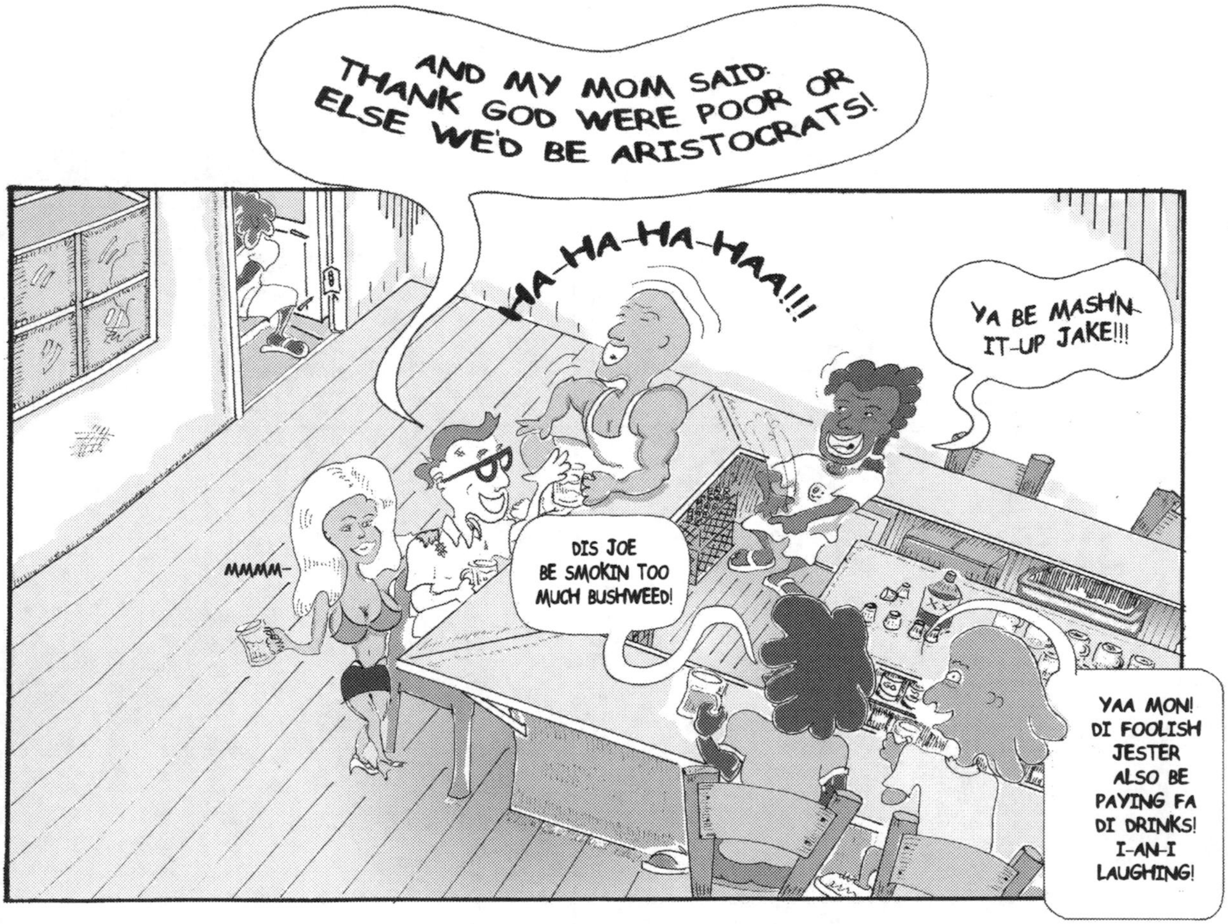
AND MY MOM SAID: THANK GOD WERE POOR OR ELSE WE'D BE ARISTOCRATS!
HA-HA-HA-HAA!!!
YA BE MASH'N-IT-UP JAKE!!!
MMMM-
DIS JOE BE SMOKIN TOO MUCH BUSHWEED!
YAA MON! DI FOOLISH JESTER ALSO BE PAYING FA DI DRINKS! I-AN-I LAUGHING!

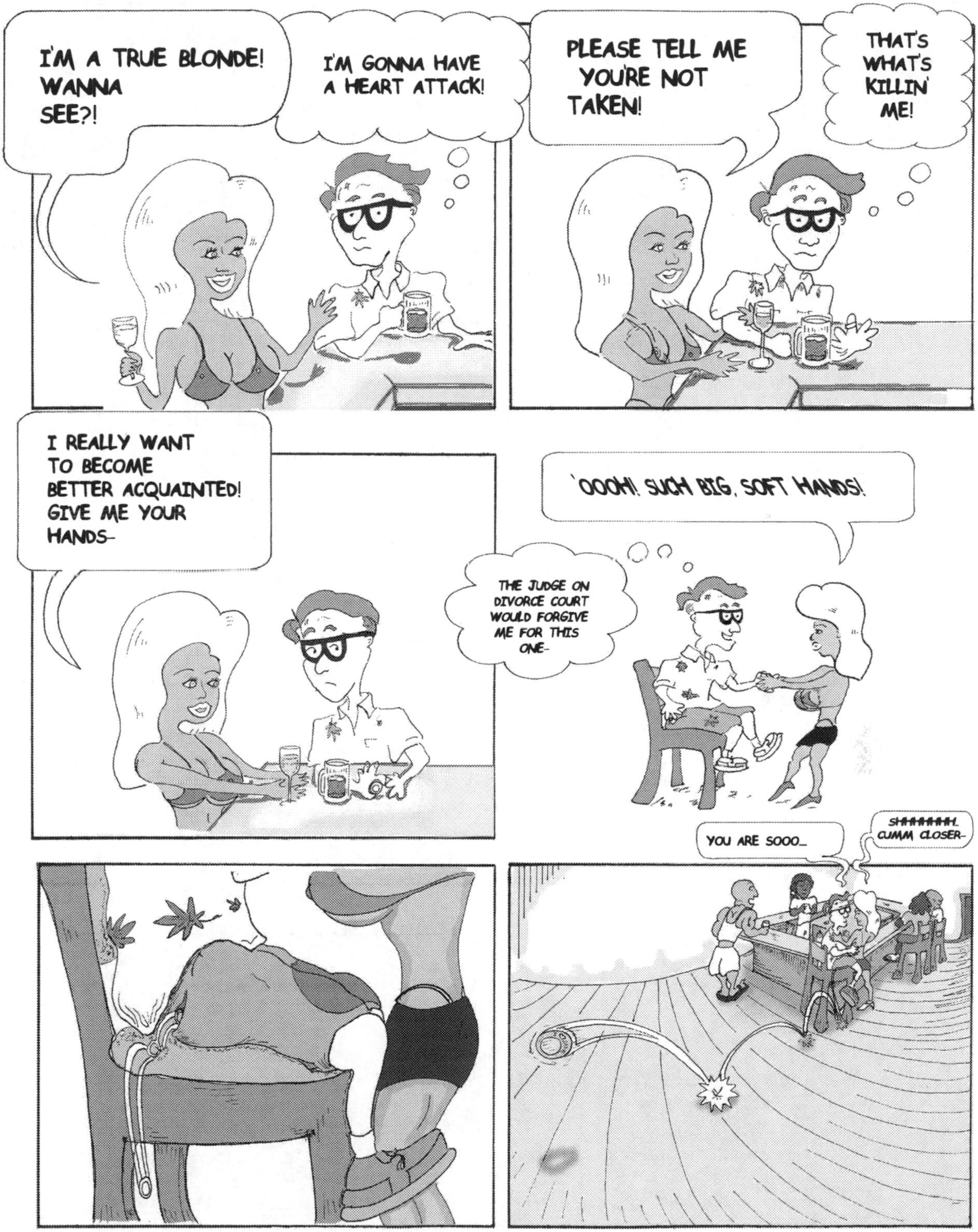
I'M A TRUE BLONDE! WANNA SEE?!
I'M GONNA HAVE A HEART ATTACK!
PLEASE TELL ME YOU'RE NOT TAKEN!
THAT'S WHAT'S KILLIN' ME!
I REALLY WANT TO BECOME BETTER ACQUAINTED! GIVE ME YOUR HANDS-
`OOOH! SUCH BIG, SOFT HANDS!
THE JUDGE ON DIVORCE COURT WOULD FORGIVE ME FOR THIS ONE-
YOU ARE SOOO...
SHHHHHHHH. CUMM CLOSER-

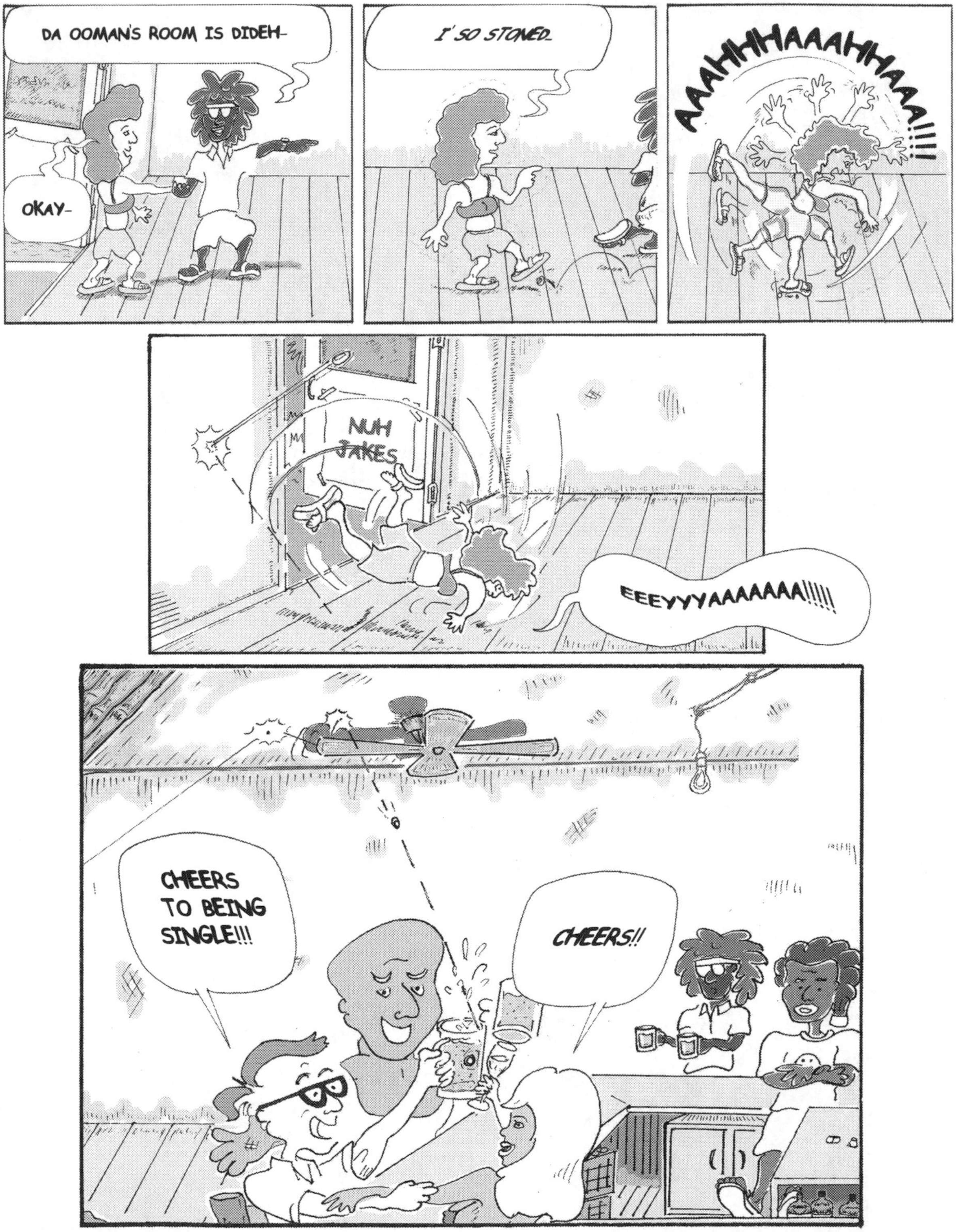
DA OOMAN'S ROOM IS DIDEH-
OKAY-
I' SO STONED-
AAAHHHAAAHHAAA!!!!!
NUH JAKES
EEEYYYAAAAAAA!!!!!
CHEERS TO BEING SINGLE!!!
CHEERS!!

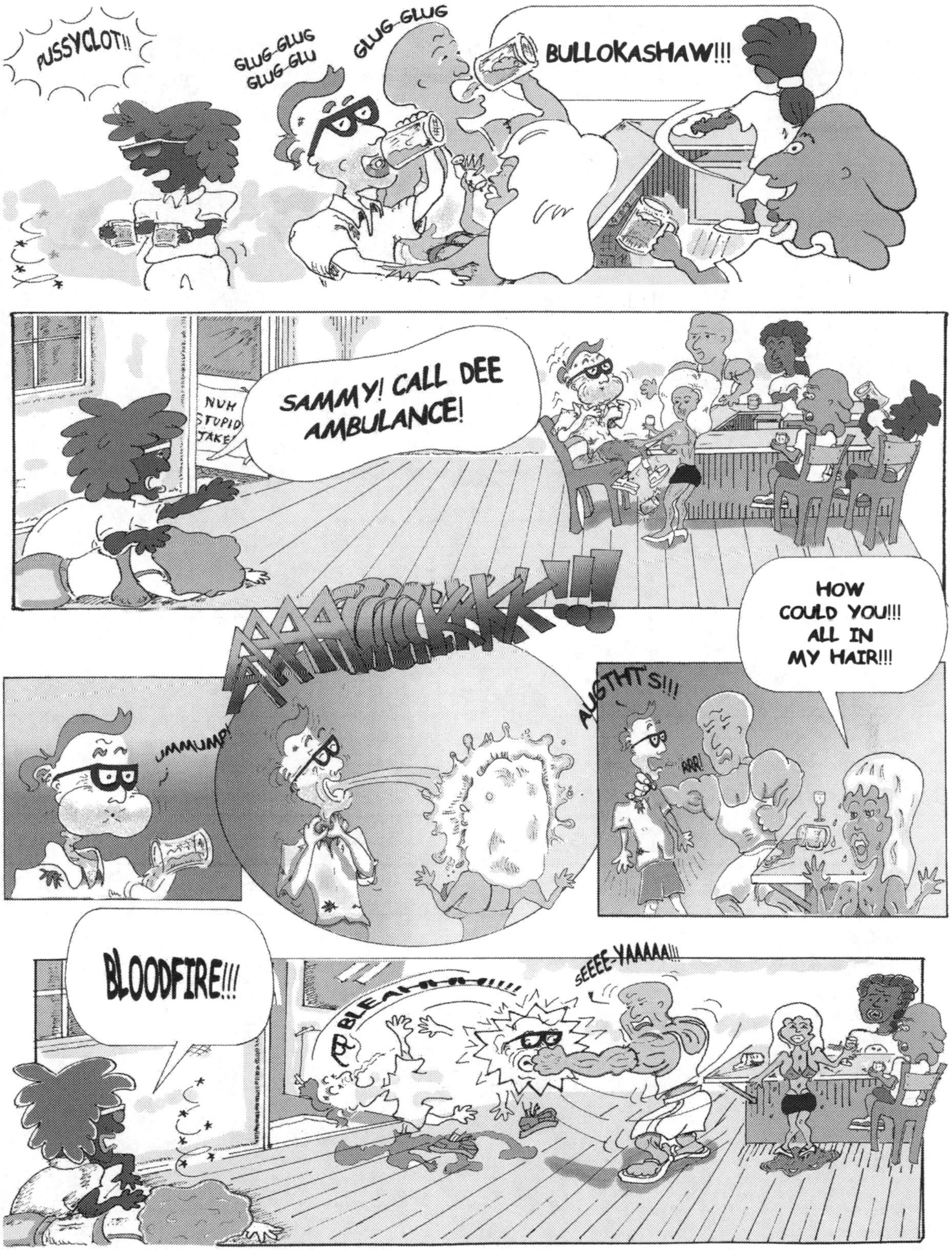
PUSSYCLOT!!
GLUG-GLUG
GLUG-GLU
GLUG-GLUG
BULLOKASHAW!!!
SAMMY! CALL DEE AMBULANCE!
NUH STUPID JAKE
AAAAACCCKKKK!!!
UMMUMP!
AUGHT'S!!!
HOW COULD YOU!!! ALL IN MY HAIR!!!
BLOODFIRE!!!
SEEEE-YAAAAA!!!

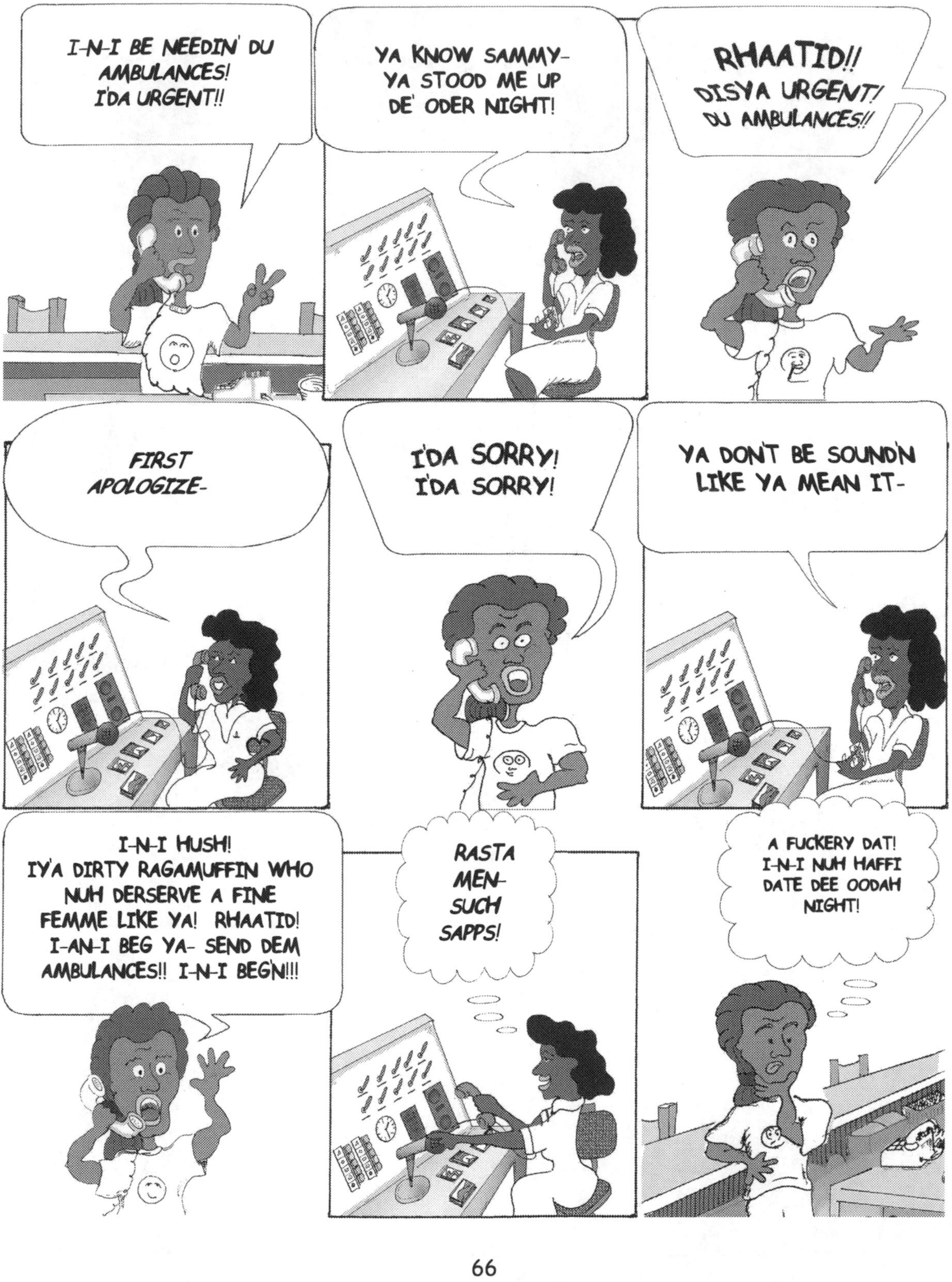
I-N-I BE NEEDIN' DU AMBULANCES! I'DA URGENT!!
YA KNOW SAMMY- YA STOOD ME UP DE' ODER NIGHT!
RHAATID!! DISYA URGENT! DU AMBULANCES!!
FIRST APOLOGIZE-
I'DA SORRY! I'DA SORRY!
YA DON'T BE SOUND'N LIKE YA MEAN IT-
I-N-I HUSH! IY'A DIRTY RAGAMUFFIN WHO NUH DERSERVE A FINE FEMME LIKE YA! RHAATID! I-AN-I BEG YA- SEND DEM AMBULANCES!! I-N-I BEG'N!!!
RASTA MEN- SUCH SAPPS!
A FUCKERY DAT! I-N-I NUH HAFFI DATE DEE OODAH NIGHT!

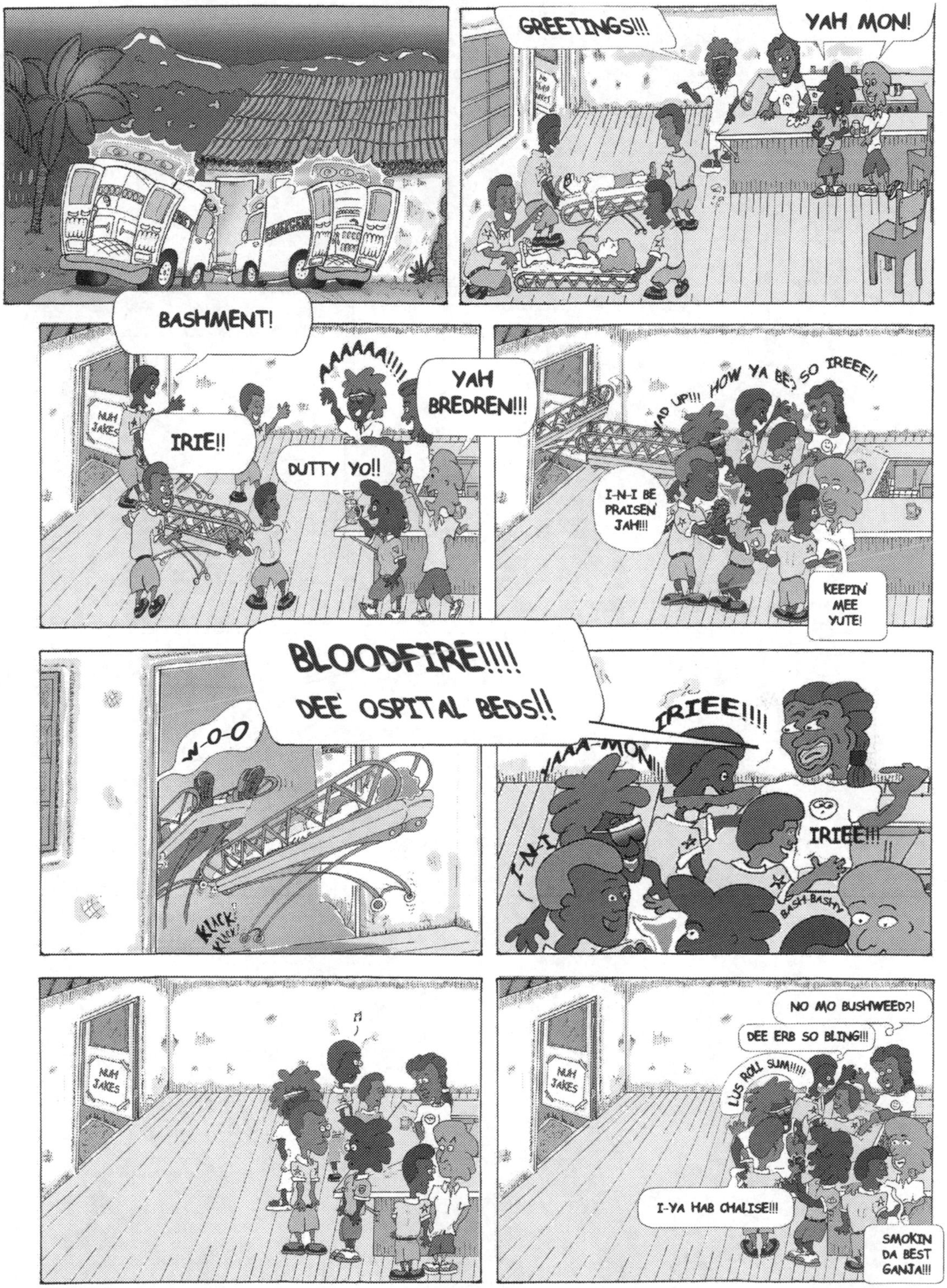
GREETINGS!!!
YAH MON!
BASHMENT!
AAAAAA!!!!
YAH BREDREN!!!
NUH JAKES
IRIE!!
DUTTY YO!!
WAD UP!!! HOW YA BE] SO IREEE!!
I-N-I BE PRAISEN' JAH!!!
KEEPIN' MEE YUTE!
BLOODFIRE!!!!
DEE' OSPITAL BEDS!!
W-O-O
KLICK
IRIEE!!!!
YAAA-MON!!
I-N-I
IRIEE!!!
BASH BASHY
NUH JAKES
NUH JAKES
NO MO BUSHWEED?!
DEE ERB SO BLING!!!
LUS ROLL SUM!!!!!
I-YA HAB CHALISE!!!
SMOKIN DA BEST GANJA!!!

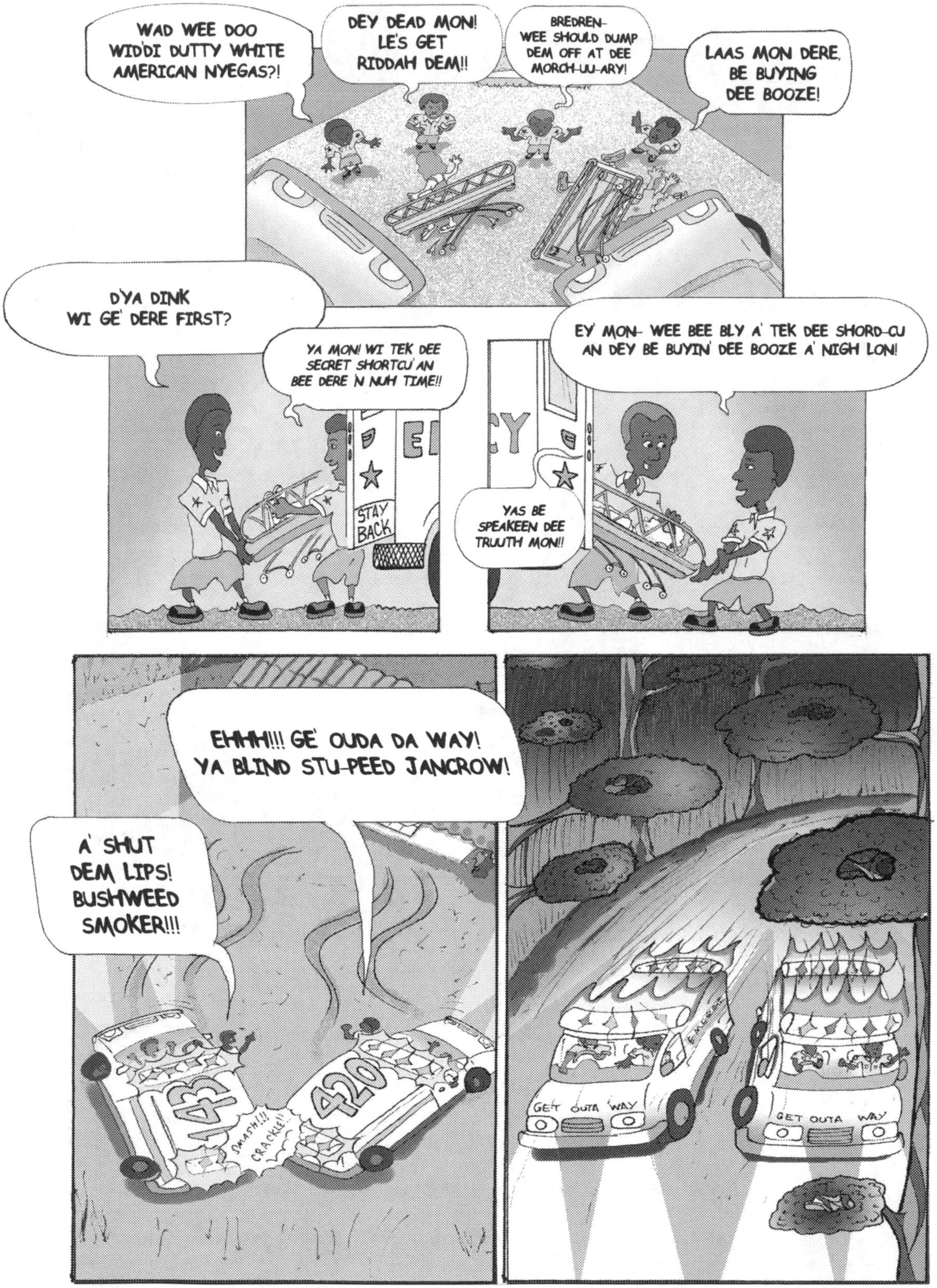
WAD WEE DOO WID'DI DUTTY WHITE AMERICAN NYEGAS?!
DEY DEAD MON! LE'S GET RIDDAH DEM!!
BREDREN- WEE SHOULD DUMP DEM OFF AT DEE MORCH-UU-ARY!
LAAS MON DERE, BE BUYING DEE BOOZE!
D'YA DINK WI GE' DERE FIRST?
YA MON! WI TEK DEE SECRET SHORTCU' AN BEE DERE 'N NUH TIME!!
STAY BACK
EY' MON- WEE BEE BLY A' TEK DEE SHORD-CU AN DEY BE BUYIN' DEE BOOZE A' NIGH LON!
YAS BE SPEAKEEN DEE TRUUTH MON!!
EHHHH!!! GE' OUDA DA WAY! YA BLIND STU-PEED JANCROW!
A' SHUT DEM LIPS! BUSHWEED SMOKER!!!
43
420
SMASH!!!
CRACKLE!!
GET OUTA WAY
GET OUTA WAY

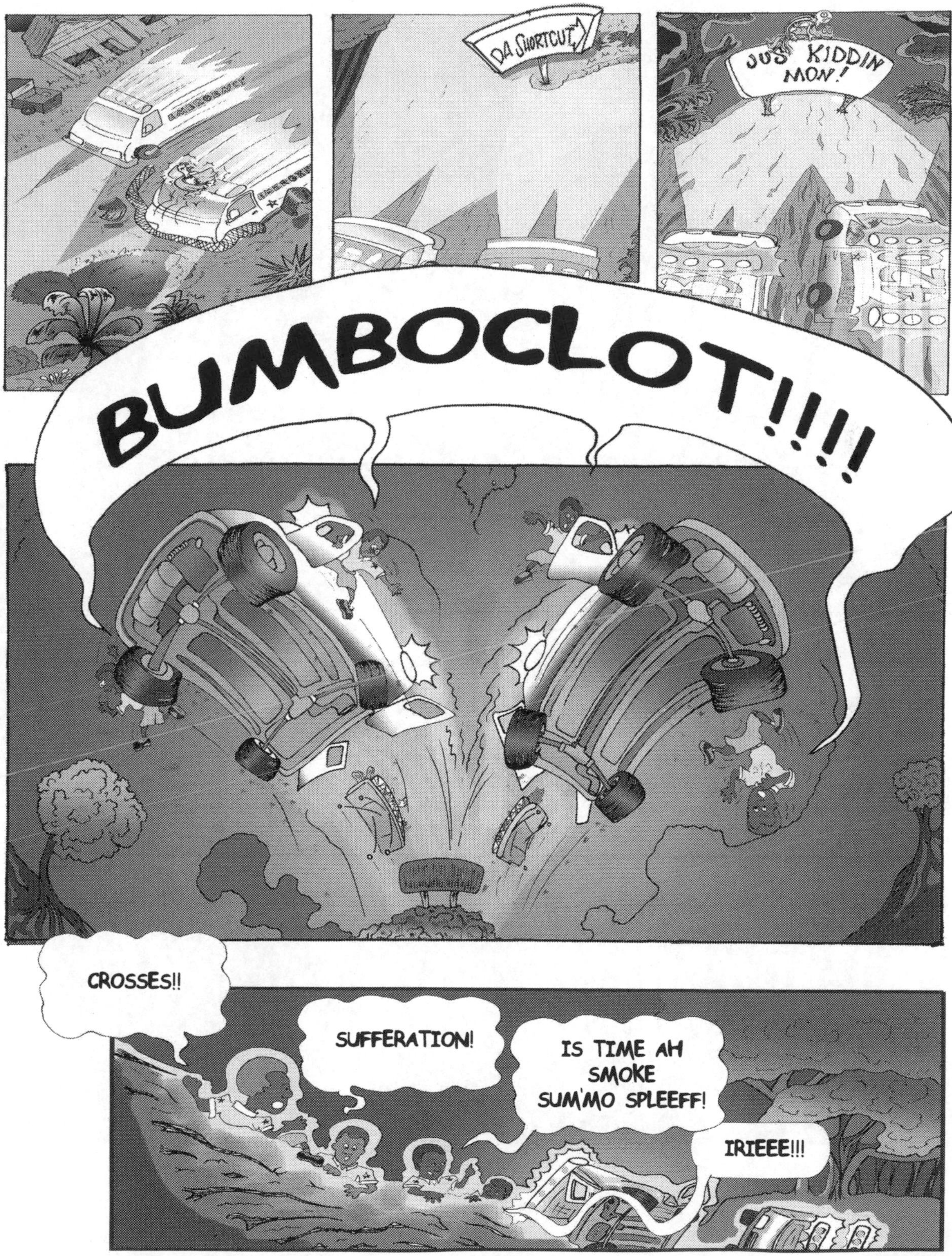
DA SHORTCUT
JUS' KIDDIN MON!
BUMBOCLOT!!!!
CROSSES!!
SUFFERATION!
IS TIME AH SMOKE SUM'MO SPLEEFF!
IRIEEE!!!

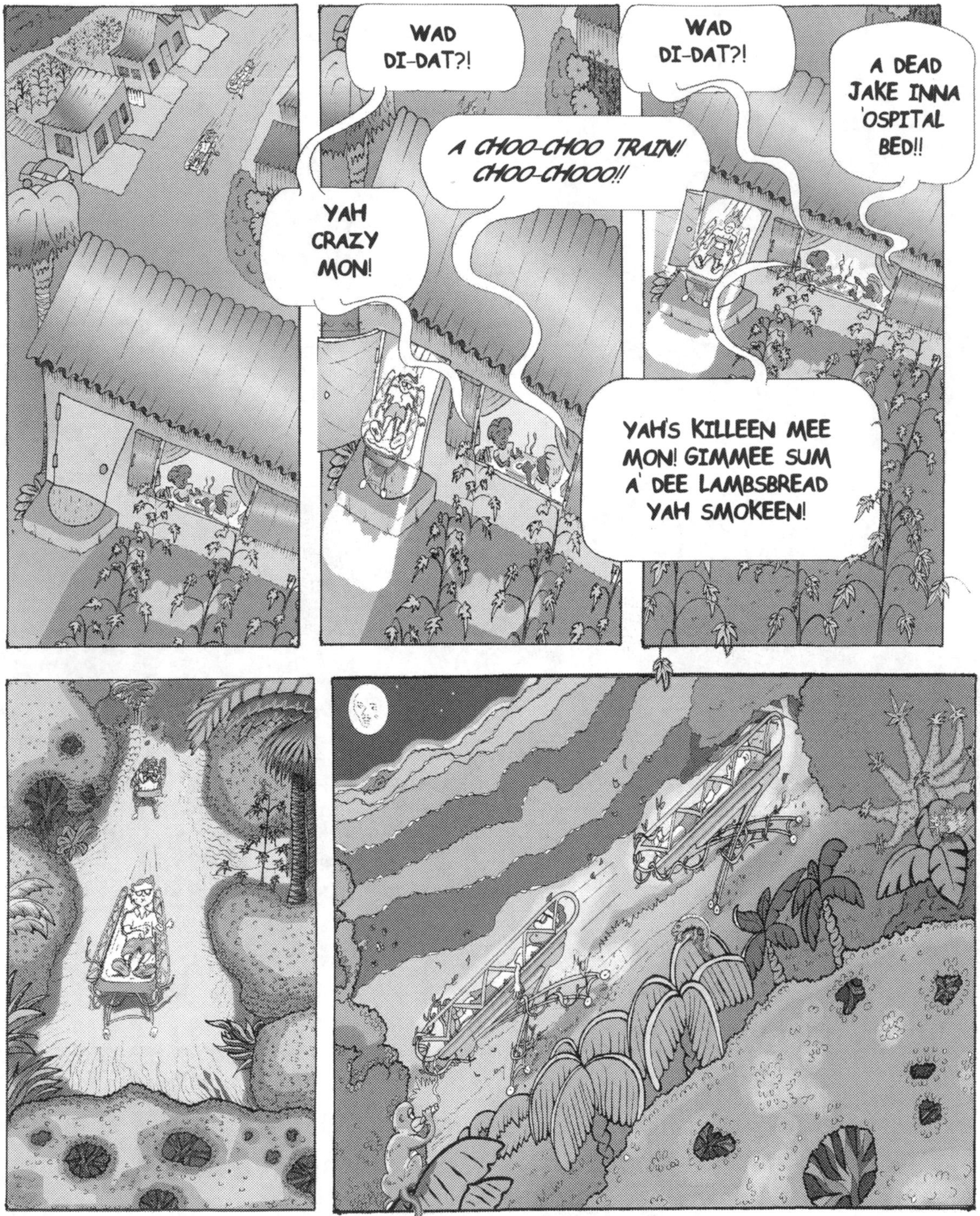
WAD DI-DAT?!
YAH CRAZY MON!
A CHOO-CHOO TRAIN! CHOO-CHOOO!!
WAD DI-DAT?!
A DEAD JAKE INNA 'OSPITAL BED!!
YAH'S KILLEEN MEE MON! GIMMEE SUM A' DEE LAMBSBREAD YAH SMOKEEN!

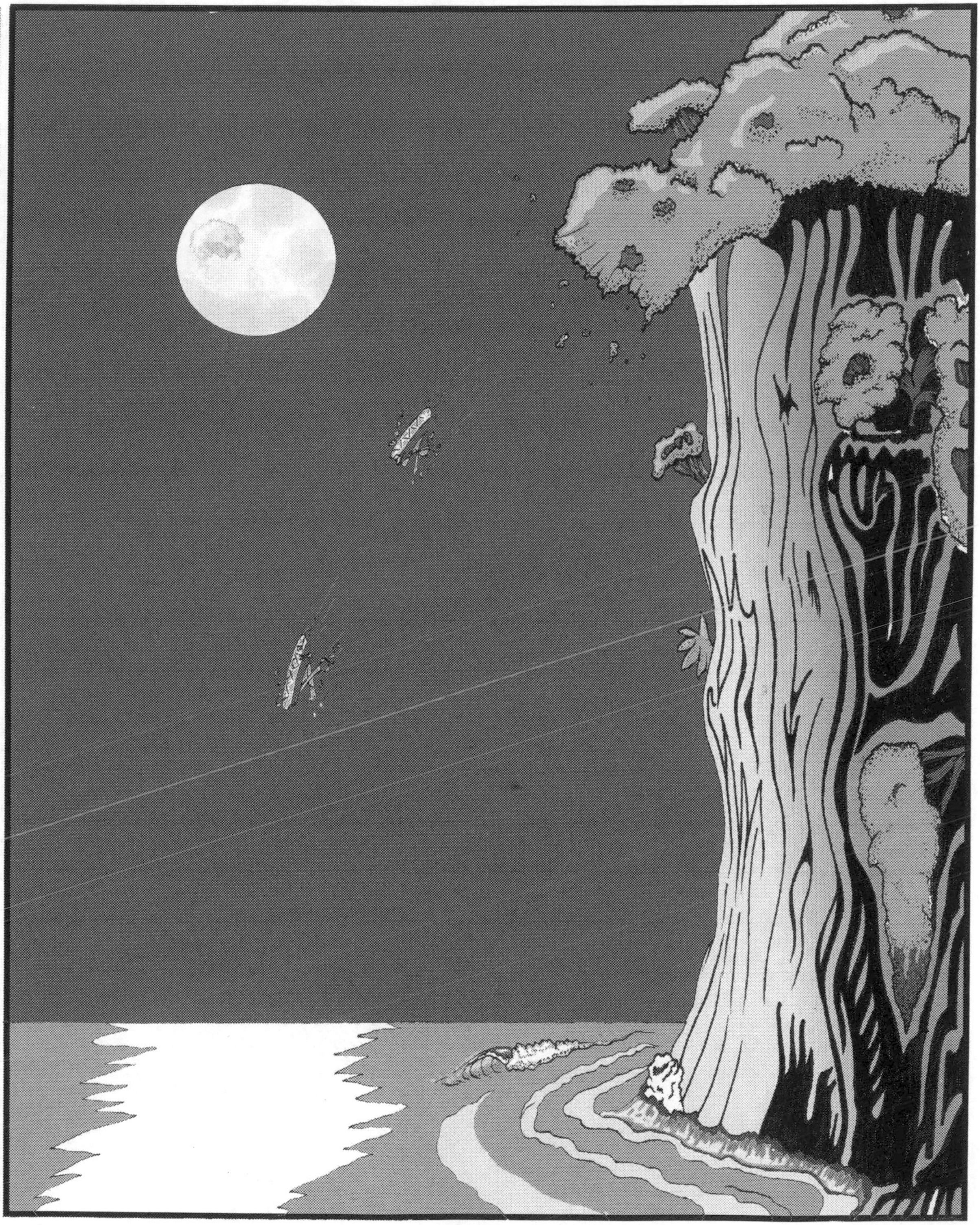

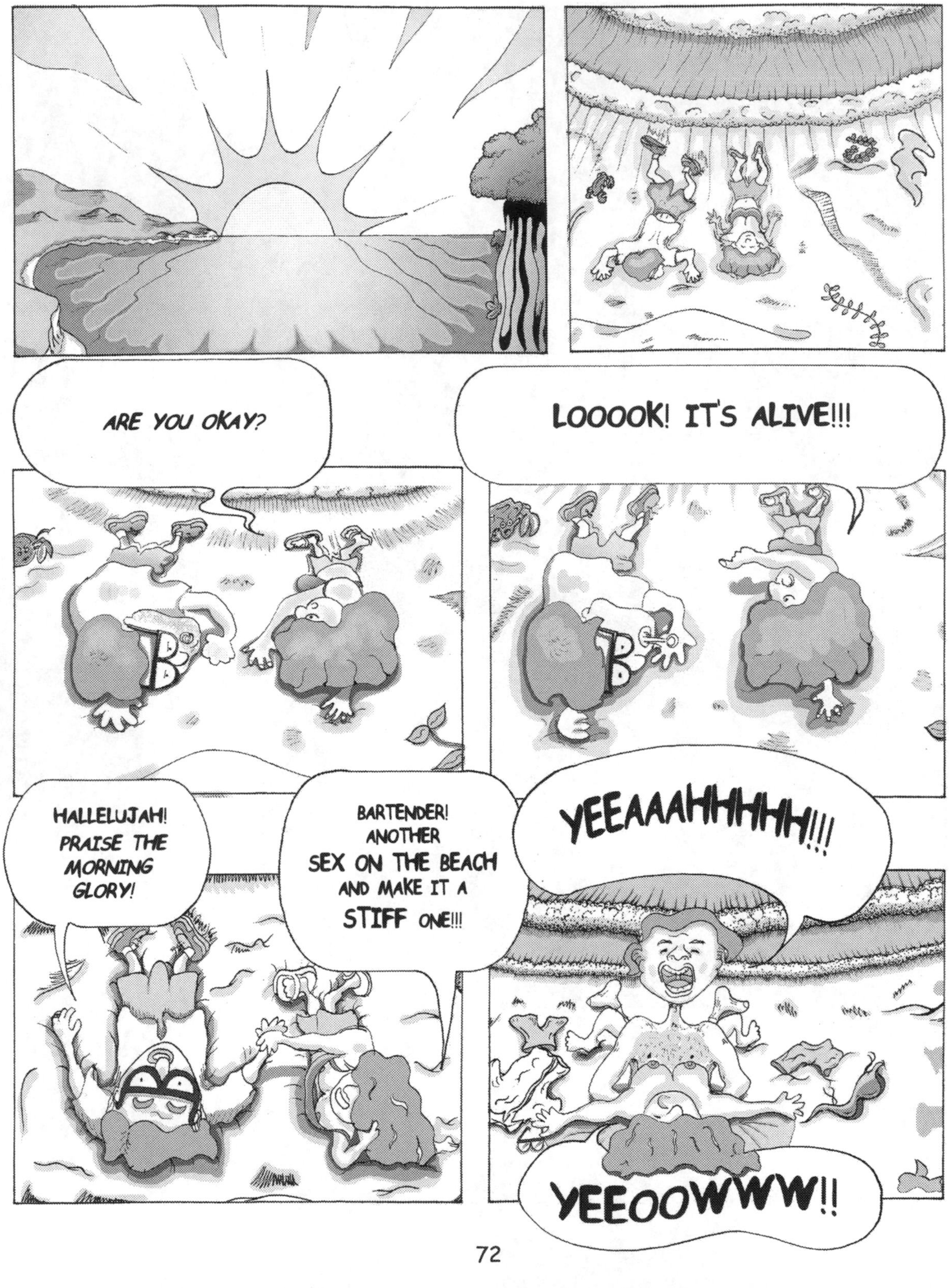
ARE YOU OKAY?
LOOOOK! IT'S ALIVE!!!
HALLELUJAH! PRAISE THE MORNING GLORY!
BARTENDER! ANOTHER SEX ON THE BEACH AND MAKE IT A STIFF ONE!!!
YEEAAAHHHHH!!!
YEEOOWWW!!

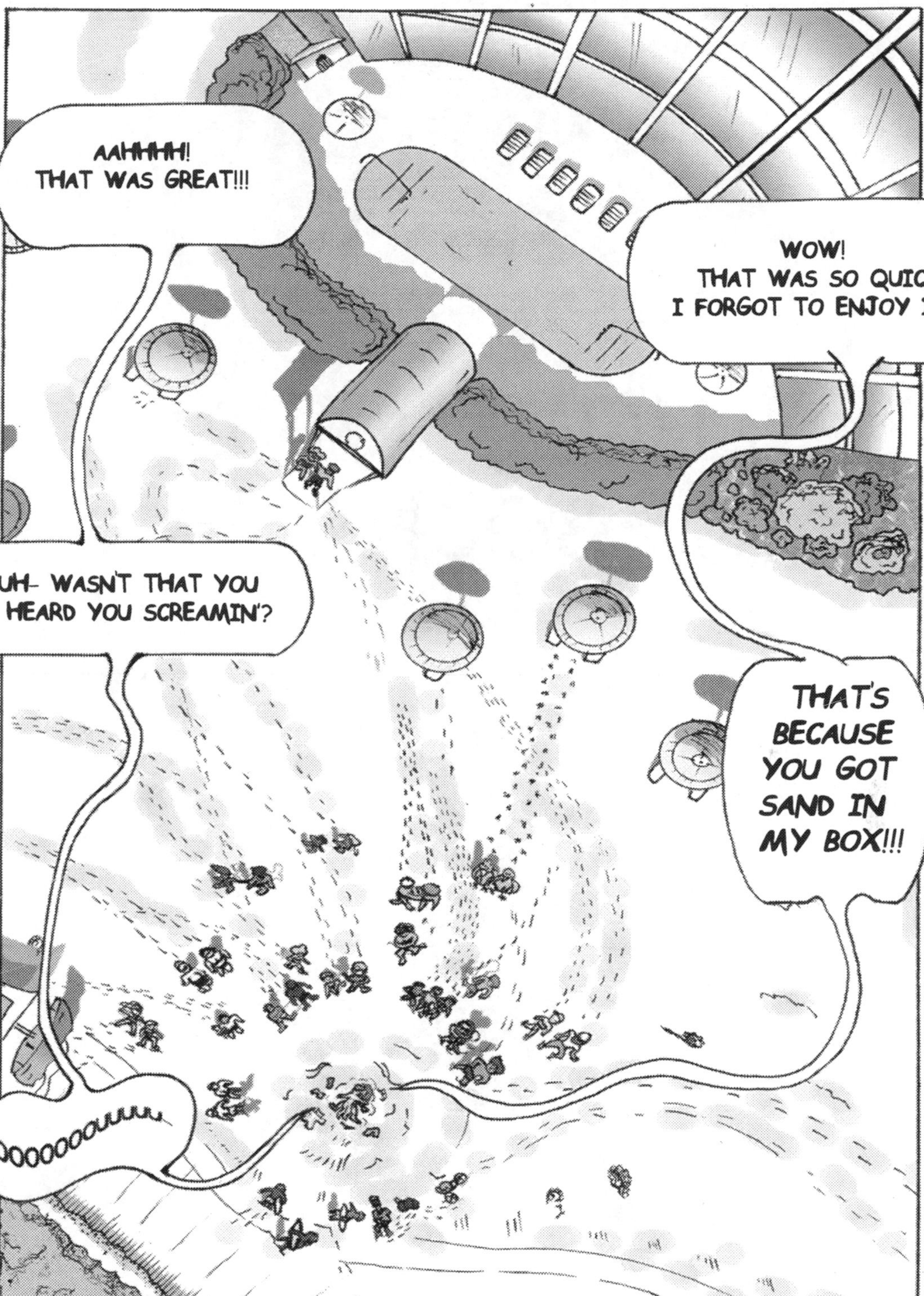
AAHHHHH! THAT WAS GREAT!!!
WOW! THAT WAS SO QUICK I FORGOT TO ENJOY IT!
UH- WASN'T THAT YOU I HEARD YOU SCREAMIN'?
THAT'S BECAUSE YOU GOT SAND IN MY BOX!!!
OOOOOOOUUUUU

CHAPTER EIGHT

HOMEWARD BOUND

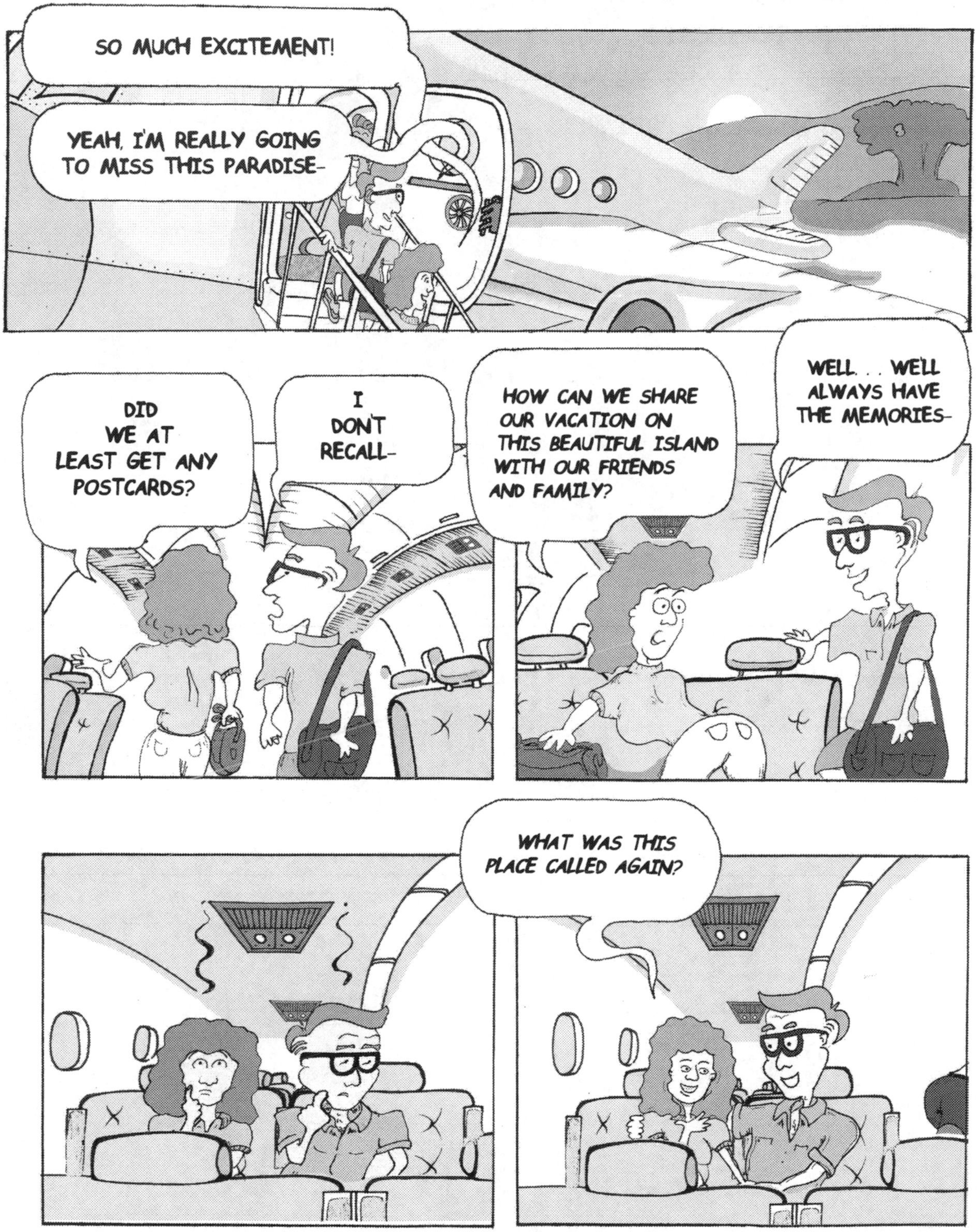
SO MUCH EXCITEMENT!
YEAH, I'M REALLY GOING TO MISS THIS PARADISE—
DID WE AT LEAST GET ANY POSTCARDS?
I DON'T RECALL—
HOW CAN WE SHARE OUR VACATION ON THIS BEAUTIFUL ISLAND WITH OUR FRIENDS AND FAMILY?
WELL . . . WE'LL ALWAYS HAVE THE MEMORIES—
WHAT WAS THIS PLACE CALLED AGAIN?

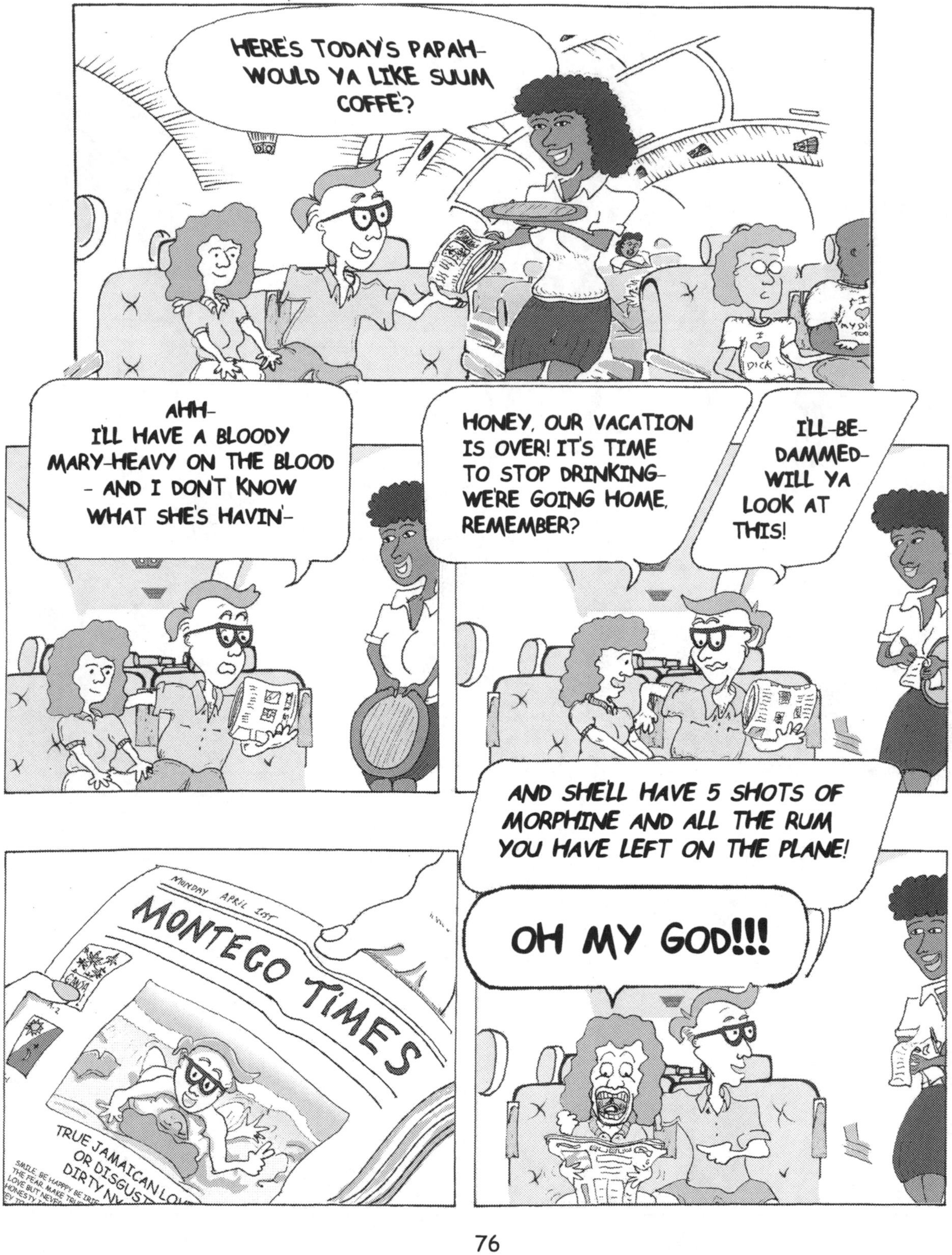
HERE'S TODAY'S PAPAH- WOULD YA LIKE SUUM COFFE'?
AHH- I'LL HAVE A BLOODY MARY-HEAVY ON THE BLOOD - AND I DON'T KNOW WHAT SHE'S HAVIN'-
HONEY, OUR VACATION IS OVER! IT'S TIME TO STOP DRINKING- WE'RE GOING HOME, REMEMBER?
I'LL-BE-DAMMED- WILL YA LOOK AT THIS!
MONTEGO TIMES
AND SHE'LL HAVE 5 SHOTS OF MORPHINE AND ALL THE RUM YOU HAVE LEFT ON THE PLANE!
OH MY GOD!!!

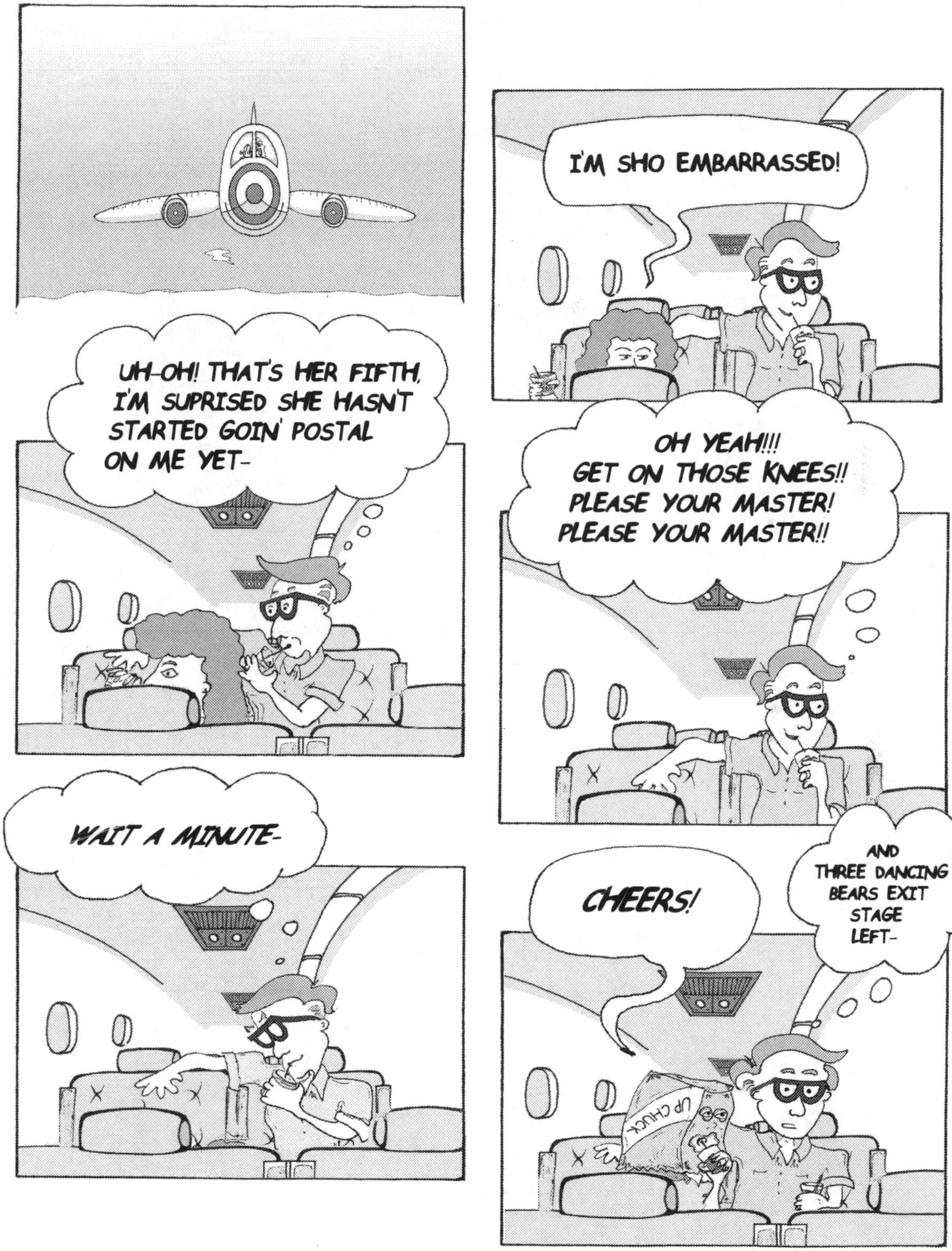
I'M SHO EMBARRASSED!
UH-OH! THAT'S HER FIFTH, I'M SUPRISED SHE HASN'T STARTED GOIN' POSTAL ON ME YET-
OH YEAH!!! GET ON THOSE KNEES!! PLEASE YOUR MASTER! PLEASE YOUR MASTER!!
WAIT A MINUTE-
CHEERS!
AND THREE DANCING BEARS EXIT STAGE LEFT-
UP CHUCK

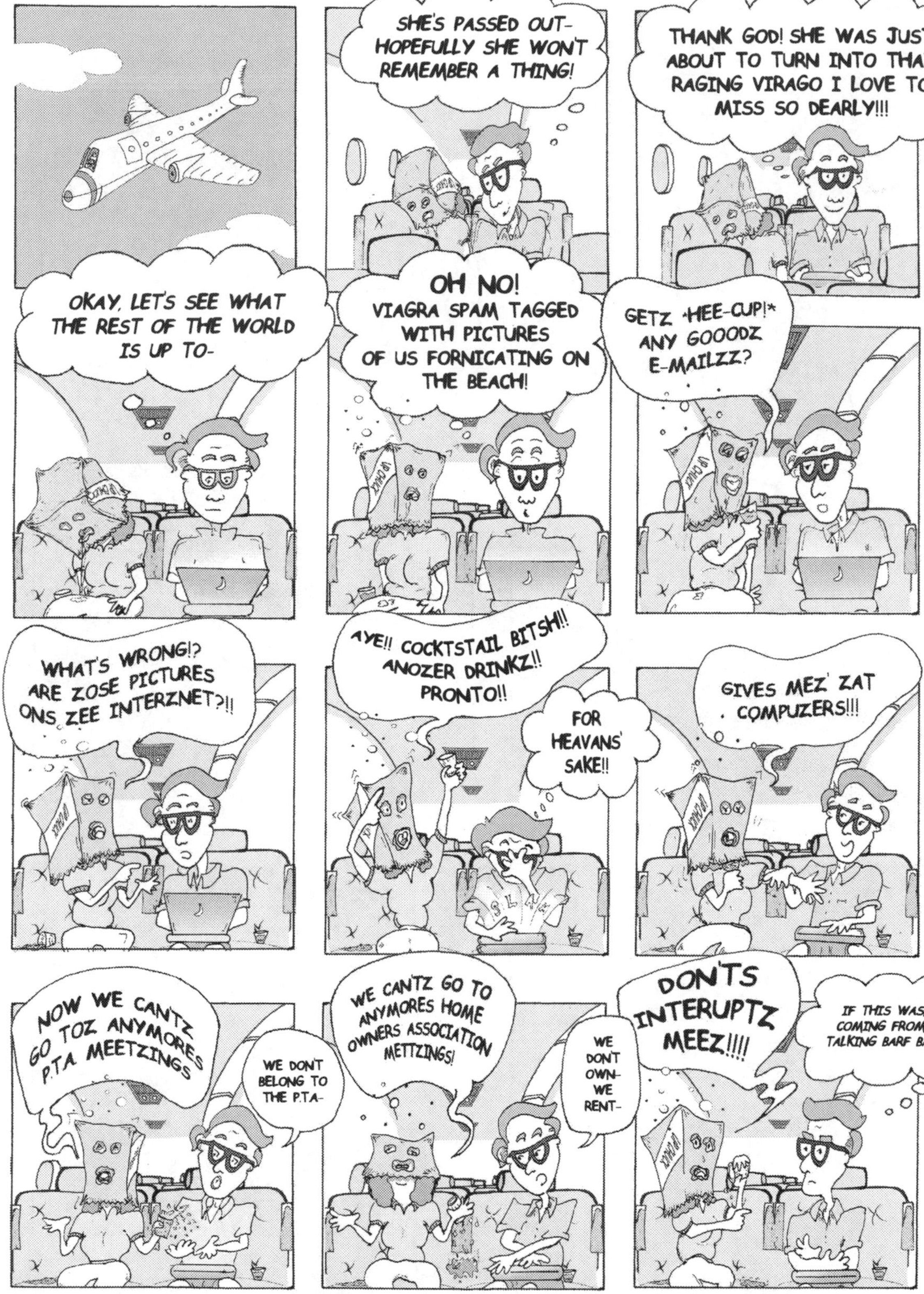
SHE'S PASSED OUT- HOPEFULLY SHE WON'T REMEMBER A THING!
THANK GOD! SHE WAS JUST ABOUT TO TURN INTO THAT RAGING VIRAGO I LOVE TO MISS SO DEARLY!!!
OKAY, LET'S SEE WHAT THE REST OF THE WORLD IS UP TO-
OH NO! VIAGRA SPAM TAGGED WITH PICTURES OF US FORNICATING ON THE BEACH!
GETZ *HEE-CUP!* ANY GOOODZ E-MAILZZ?
WHAT'S WRONG!? ARE ZOSE PICTURES ONS ZEE INTERZNET?!!
AYE!! COCKTSTAIL BITSH!! ANOZER DRINKZ!! PRONTO!!
FOR HEAVANS' SAKE!!
GIVES MEZ' ZAT COMPUZERS!!!
NOW WE CAN'TZ GO TOZ ANYMORES P.T.A MEETZINGS
WE DON'T BELONG TO THE P.T.A-
WE CAN'TZ GO TO ANYMORES HOME OWNERS ASSOCIATION METTZINGS!
WE DON'T OWN- WE RENT-
DON'TS INTERUPTZ MEEZ!!!!
IF THIS WASN'T COMING FROM A TALKING BARF BAG...

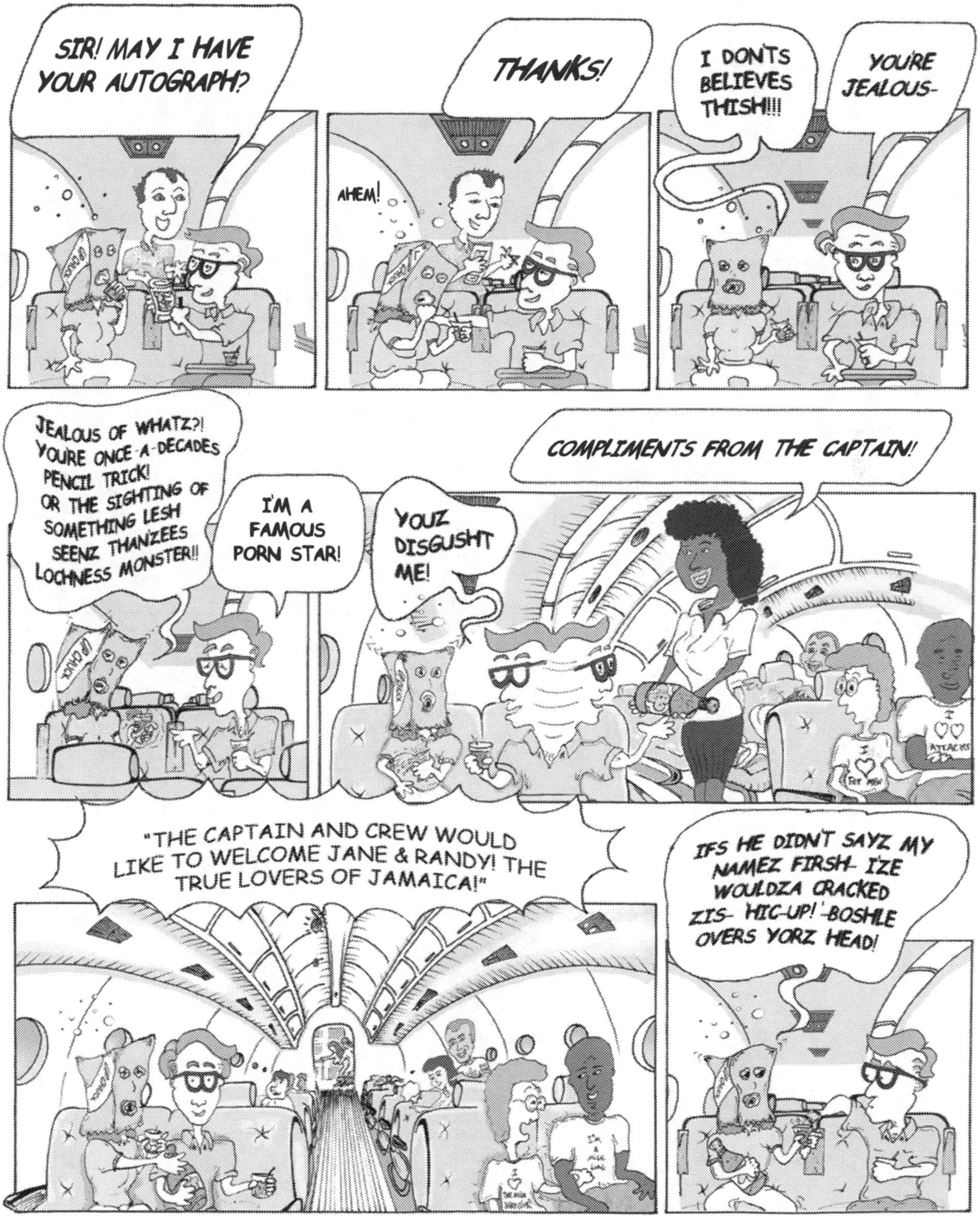
SIR! MAY I HAVE YOUR AUTOGRAPH?
AHEM!
THANKS!
I DON'TS BELIEVES THISH!!!
YOU'RE JEALOUS-
JEALOUS OF WHATZ?! YOU'RE ONCE-A-DECADES PENCIL TRICK! OR THE SIGHTING OF SOMETHING LESH SEENZ THANZEES LOCHNESS MONSTER!!
I'M A FAMOUS PORN STAR!
YOUZ DISGUSHT ME!
COMPLIMENTS FROM THE CAPTAIN!
"THE CAPTAIN AND CREW WOULD LIKE TO WELCOME JANE & RANDY! THE TRUE LOVERS OF JAMAICA!"
IFS HE DIDN'T SAYZ MY NAMEZ FIRSH- IZE WOULDZA CRACKED ZIS- 'HIC-UP!'-BOSHLE OVERS YORZ HEAD!

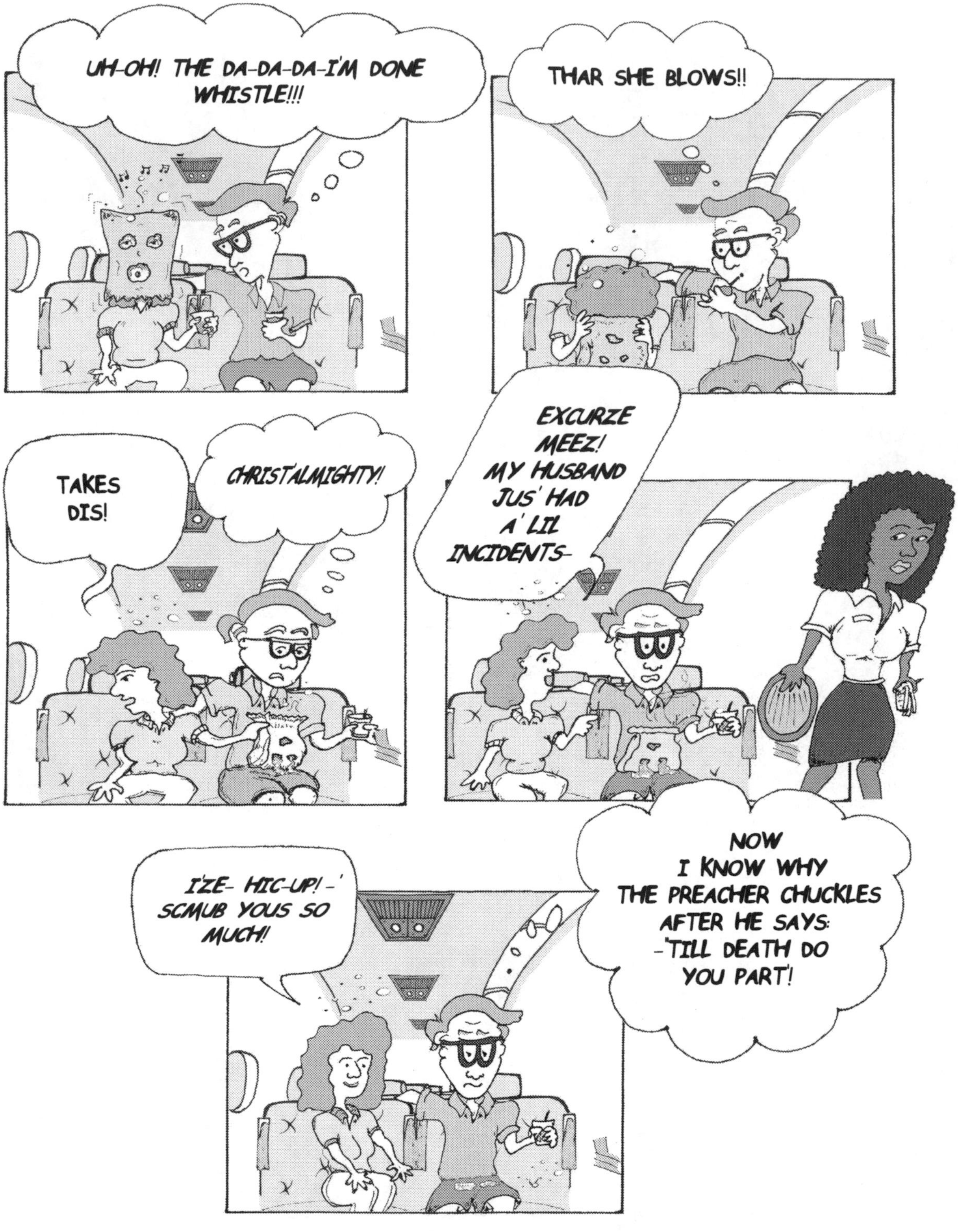
UH-OH! THE DA-DA-DA-I'M DONE WHISTLE!!!
THAR SHE BLOWS!!
TAKES DIS!
CHRIST'ALMIGHTY!
EXCURZE MEEZ! MY HUSBAND JUS' HAD A' LIL INCIDENTS-
I'ZE- HIC-UP! -' SCMUB YOUS SO MUCH!
NOW I KNOW WHY THE PREACHER CHUCKLES AFTER HE SAYS: -'TILL DEATH DO YOU PART'!

CHAPTER NINE

PETS ARE PEOPLE TOO

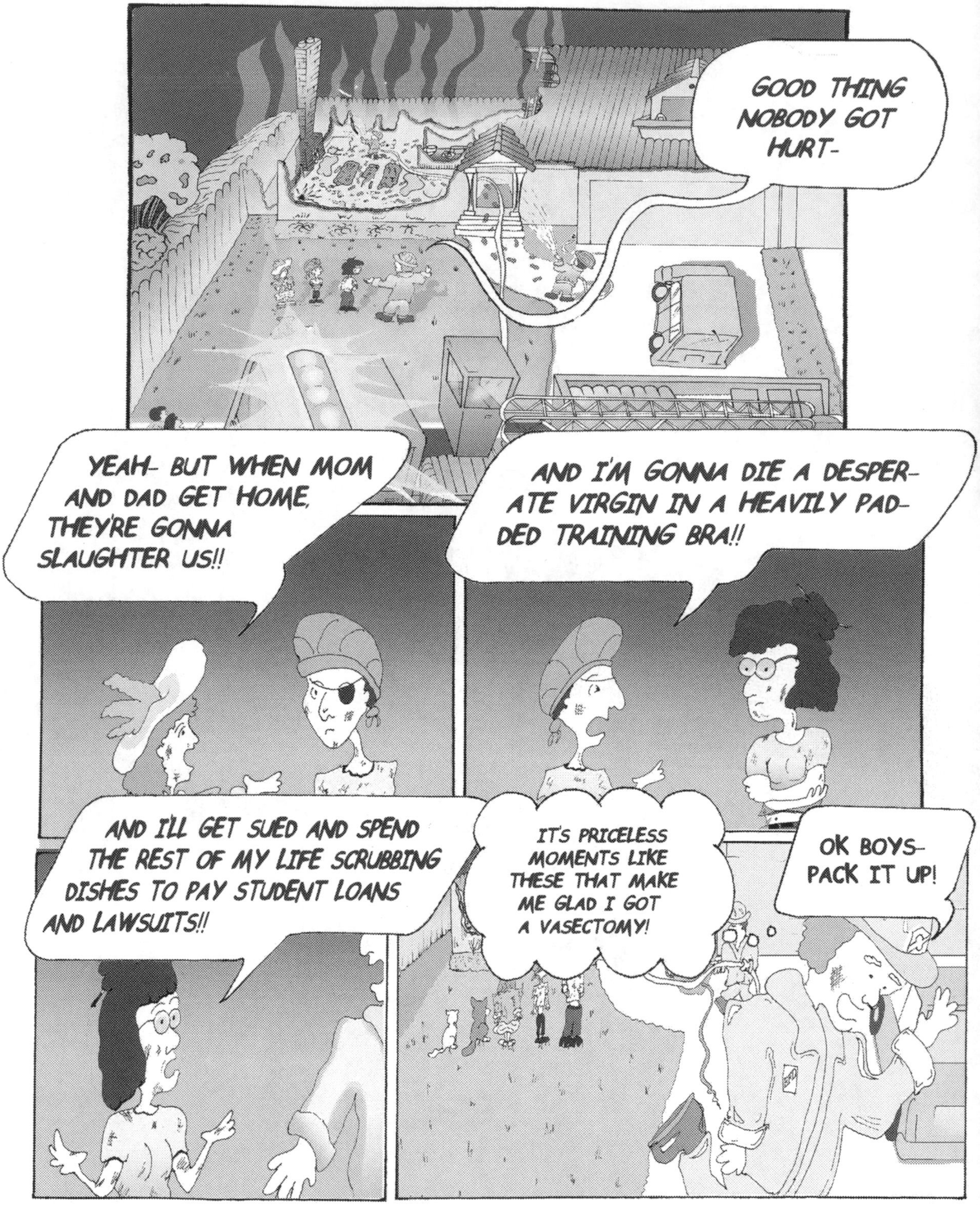
GOOD THING NOBODY GOT HURT-
YEAH- BUT WHEN MOM AND DAD GET HOME, THEY'RE GONNA SLAUGHTER US!!
AND I'M GONNA DIE A DESPER- ATE VIRGIN IN A HEAVILY PAD- DED TRAINING BRA!!
AND I'LL GET SUED AND SPEND THE REST OF MY LIFE SCRUBBING DISHES TO PAY STUDENT LOANS AND LAWSUITS!!
IT'S PRICELESS MOMENTS LIKE THESE THAT MAKE ME GLAD I GOT A VASECTOMY!
OK BOYS- PACK IT UP!

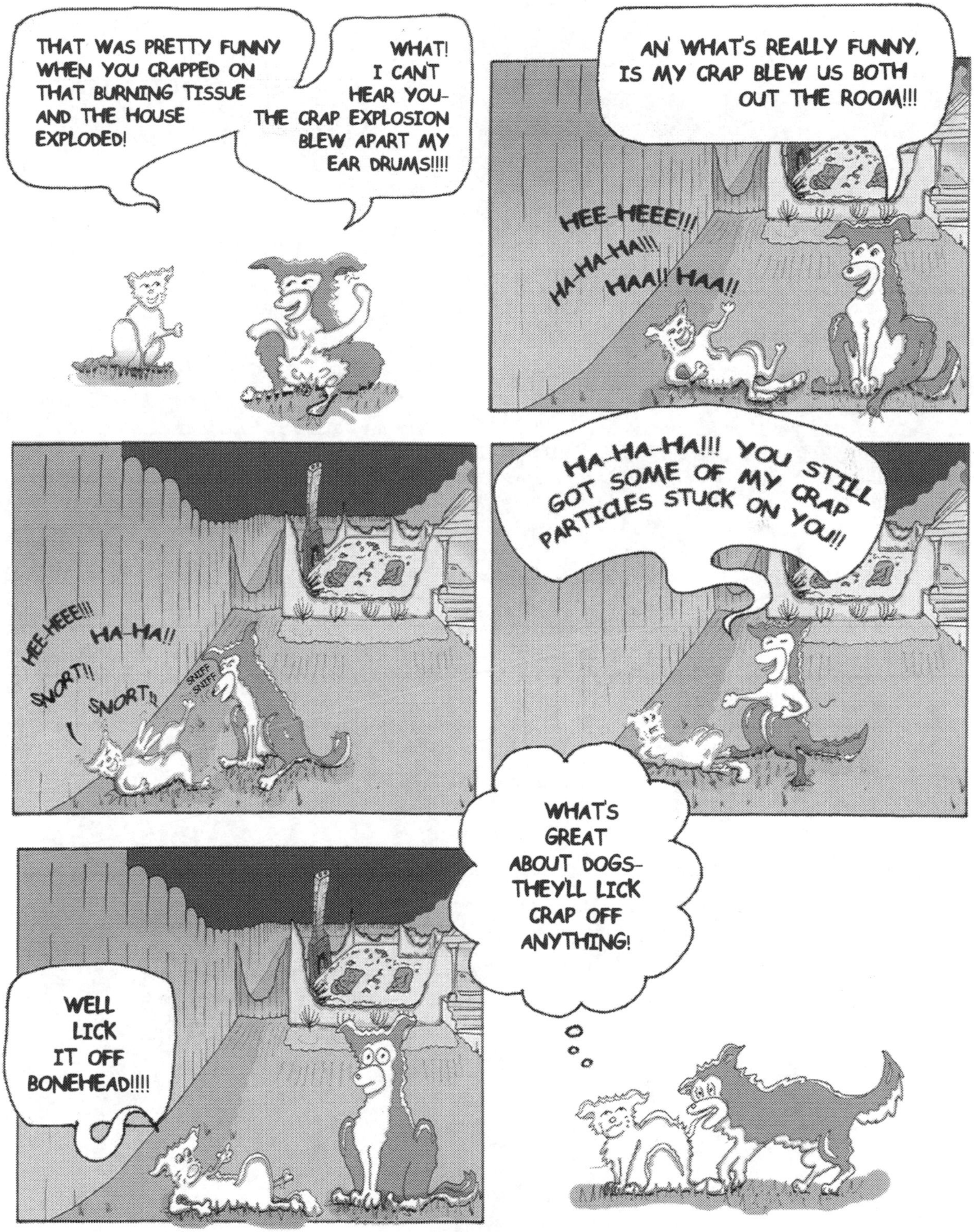
THAT WAS PRETTY FUNNY WHEN YOU CRAPPED ON THAT BURNING TISSUE AND THE HOUSE EXPLODED!
WHAT! I CAN'T HEAR YOU- THE CRAP EXPLOSION BLEW APART MY EAR DRUMS!!!!
AN' WHAT'S REALLY FUNNY, IS MY CRAP BLEW US BOTH OUT THE ROOM!!!
HEE-HEEE!!!
HA-HA-HA!!!
HAA!! HAA!!
HEE-HEEE!!!
HA-HA!!
SNORT!!
SNORT!!
SNIFF SNIFF
HA-HA-HA!!! YOU STILL GOT SOME OF MY CRAP PARTICLES STUCK ON YOU!!
WELL LICK IT OFF BONEHEAD!!!!
WHAT'S GREAT ABOUT DOGS- THEY'LL LICK CRAP OFF ANYTHING!

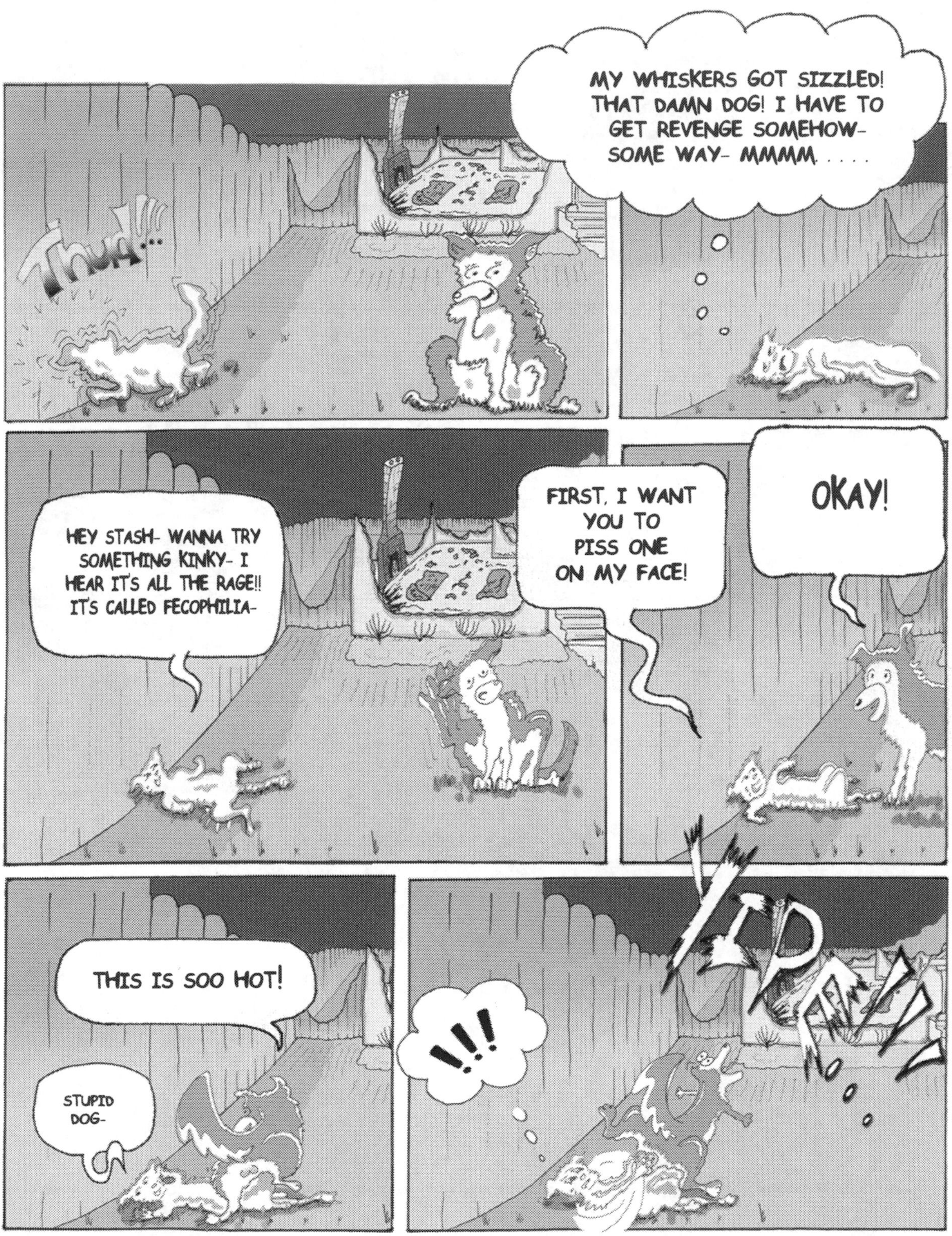

Thud
MY WHISKERS GOT SIZZLED! THAT DAMN DOG! I HAVE TO GET REVENGE SOMEHOW- SOME WAY- MMMM.....
HEY STASH- WANNA TRY SOMETHING KINKY- I HEAR IT'S ALL THE RAGE!! IT'S CALLED FECOPHILIA-
FIRST, I WANT YOU TO PISS ONE ON MY FACE!
OKAY!
THIS IS SOO HOT!
STUPID DOG-
!!!

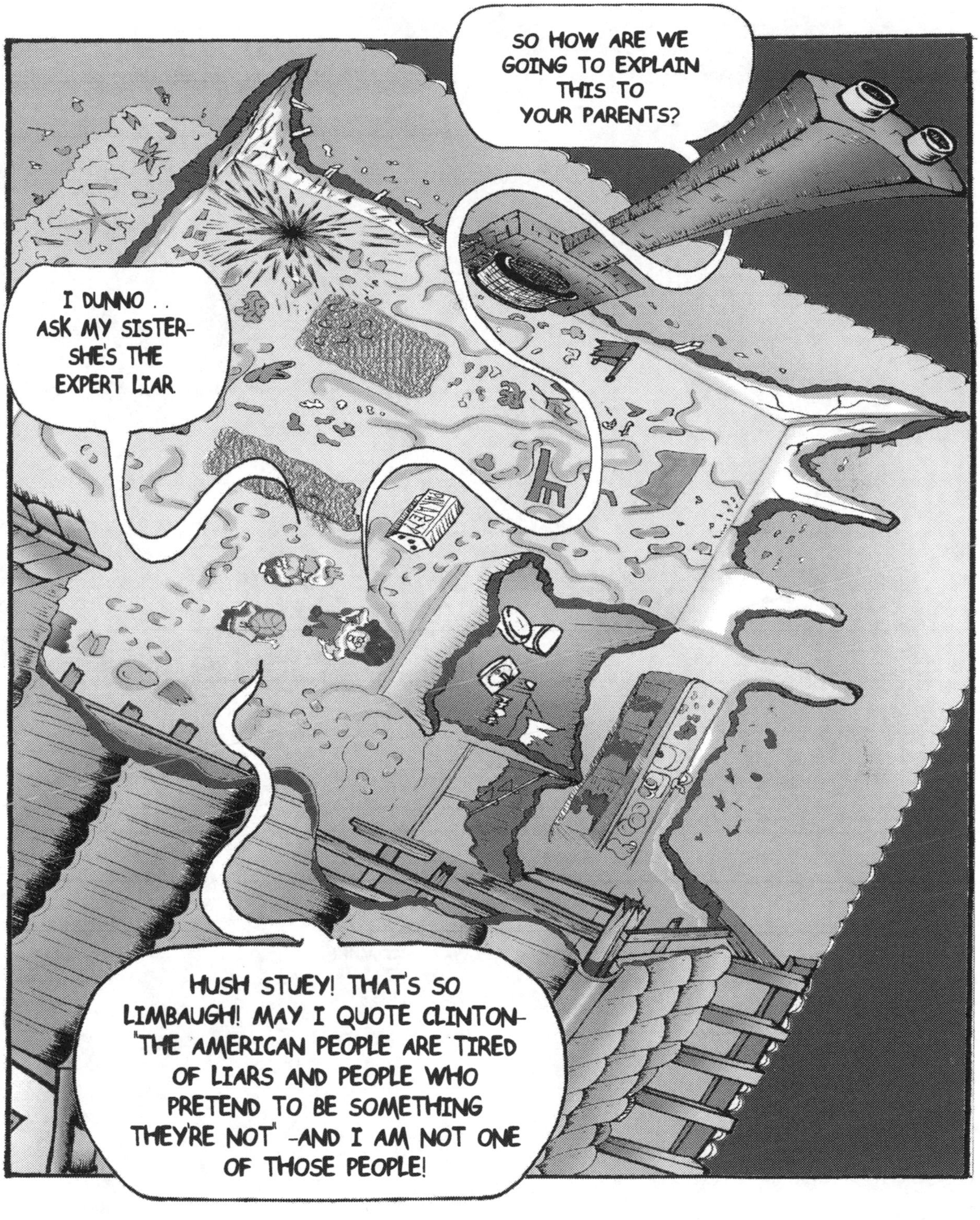
SO HOW ARE WE GOING TO EXPLAIN THIS TO YOUR PARENTS?
I DUNNO . . ASK MY SISTER- SHE'S THE EXPERT LIAR.
HUSH STUEY! THAT'S SO LIMBAUGH! MAY I QUOTE CLINTON- "THE AMERICAN PEOPLE ARE TIRED OF LIARS AND PEOPLE WHO PRETEND TO BE SOMETHING THEY'RE NOT" -AND I AM NOT ONE OF THOSE PEOPLE!

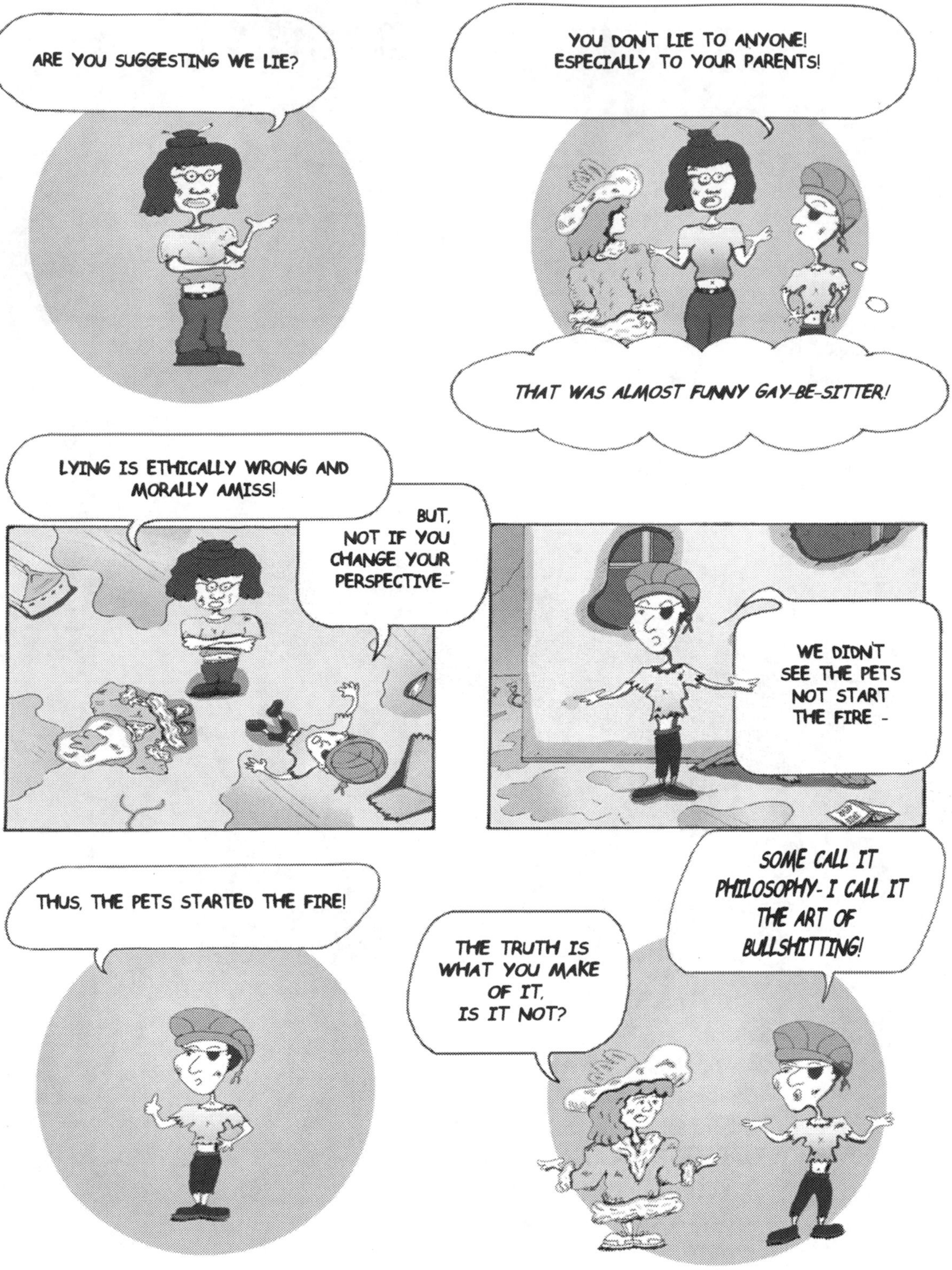
ARE YOU SUGGESTING WE LIE?
YOU DON'T LIE TO ANYONE! ESPECIALLY TO YOUR PARENTS!
THAT WAS ALMOST FUNNY GAY-BE-SITTER!
LYING IS ETHICALLY WRONG AND MORALLY AMISS!
BUT, NOT IF YOU CHANGE YOUR PERSPECTIVE-
WE DIDN'T SEE THE PETS NOT START THE FIRE -
THUS, THE PETS STARTED THE FIRE!
THE TRUTH IS WHAT YOU MAKE OF IT, IS IT NOT?
SOME CALL IT PHILOSOPHY- I CALL IT THE ART OF BULLSHITTING!

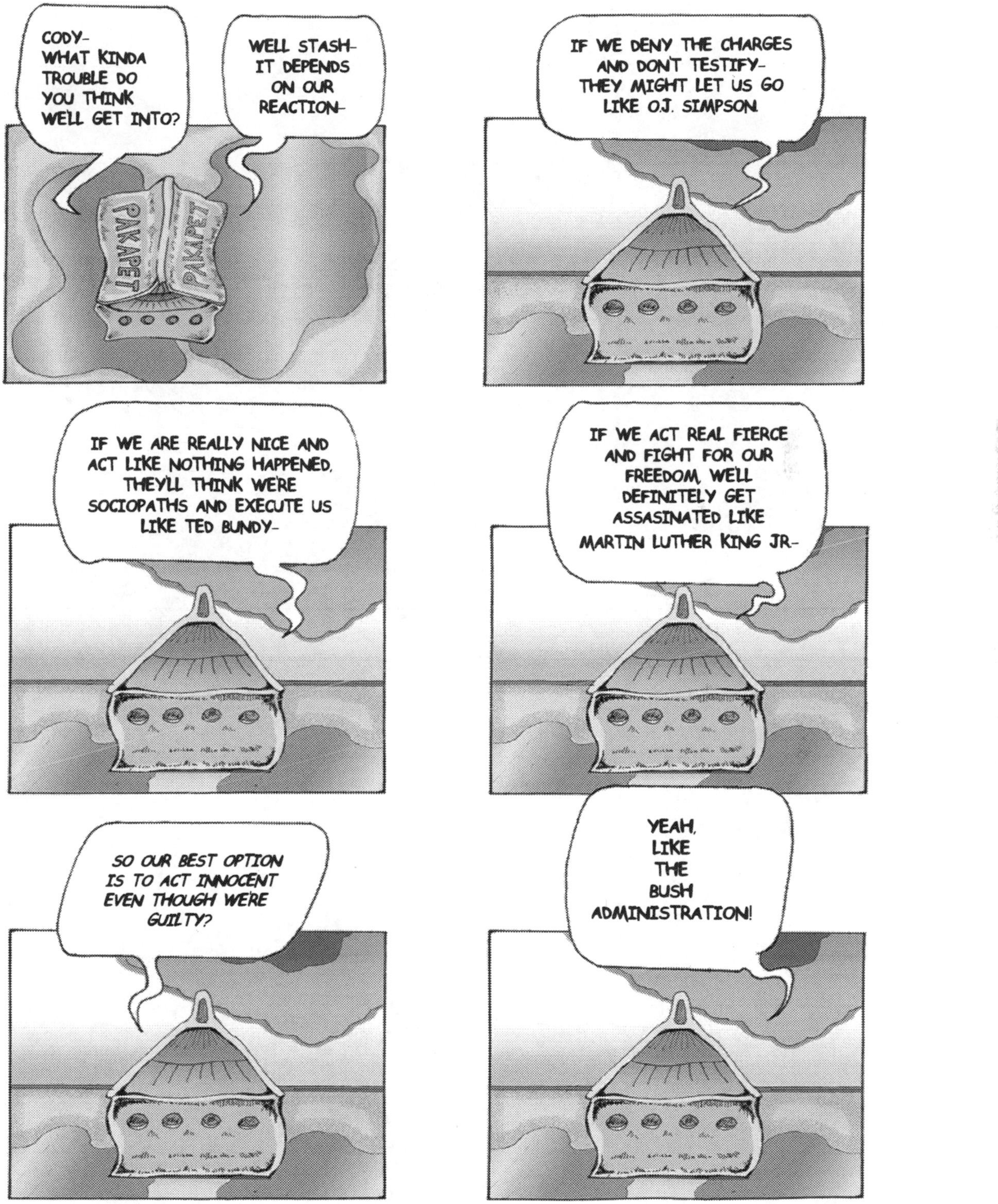
CODY- WHAT KINDA TROUBLE DO YOU THINK WE'LL GET INTO?
WELL STASH- IT DEPENDS ON OUR REACTION-
PAKAPET
PAKAPET
IF WE DENY THE CHARGES AND DON'T TESTIFY- THEY MIGHT LET US GO LIKE O.J. SIMPSON.
IF WE ARE REALLY NICE AND ACT LIKE NOTHING HAPPENED, THEY'LL THINK WE'RE SOCIOPATHS AND EXECUTE US LIKE TED BUNDY-
IF WE ACT REAL FIERCE AND FIGHT FOR OUR FREEDOM, WE'LL DEFINITELY GET ASSASINATED LIKE MARTIN LUTHER KING JR.-
SO OUR BEST OPTION IS TO ACT INNOCENT EVEN THOUGH WE'RE GUILTY?
YEAH, LIKE THE BUSH ADMINISTRATION!

CHAPTER
10

LAST
CALL!!!

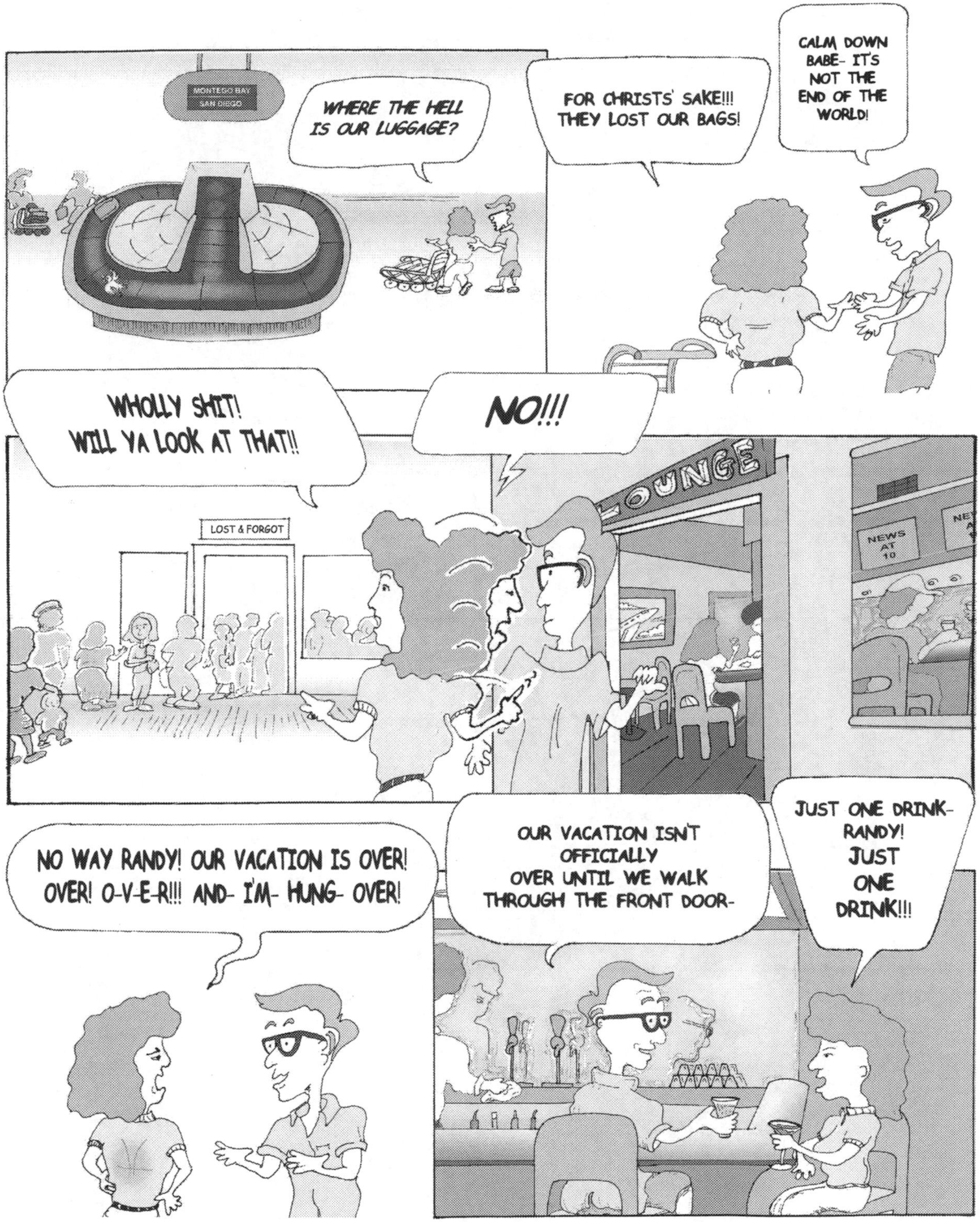
MONTEGO BAY
SAN DIEGO
WHERE THE HELL IS OUR LUGGAGE?
FOR CHRISTS' SAKE!!! THEY LOST OUR BAGS!
CALM DOWN BABE- IT'S NOT THE END OF THE WORLD!
WHOLLY SHIT! WILL YA LOOK AT THAT!!
NO!!!
LOST & FORGOT
LOUNGE
NEWS AT 10
NO WAY RANDY! OUR VACATION IS OVER! OVER! O-V-E-R!!! AND- I'M- HUNG- OVER!
OUR VACATION ISN'T OFFICIALLY OVER UNTIL WE WALK THROUGH THE FRONT DOOR-
JUST ONE DRINK- RANDY! JUST ONE DRINK!!!

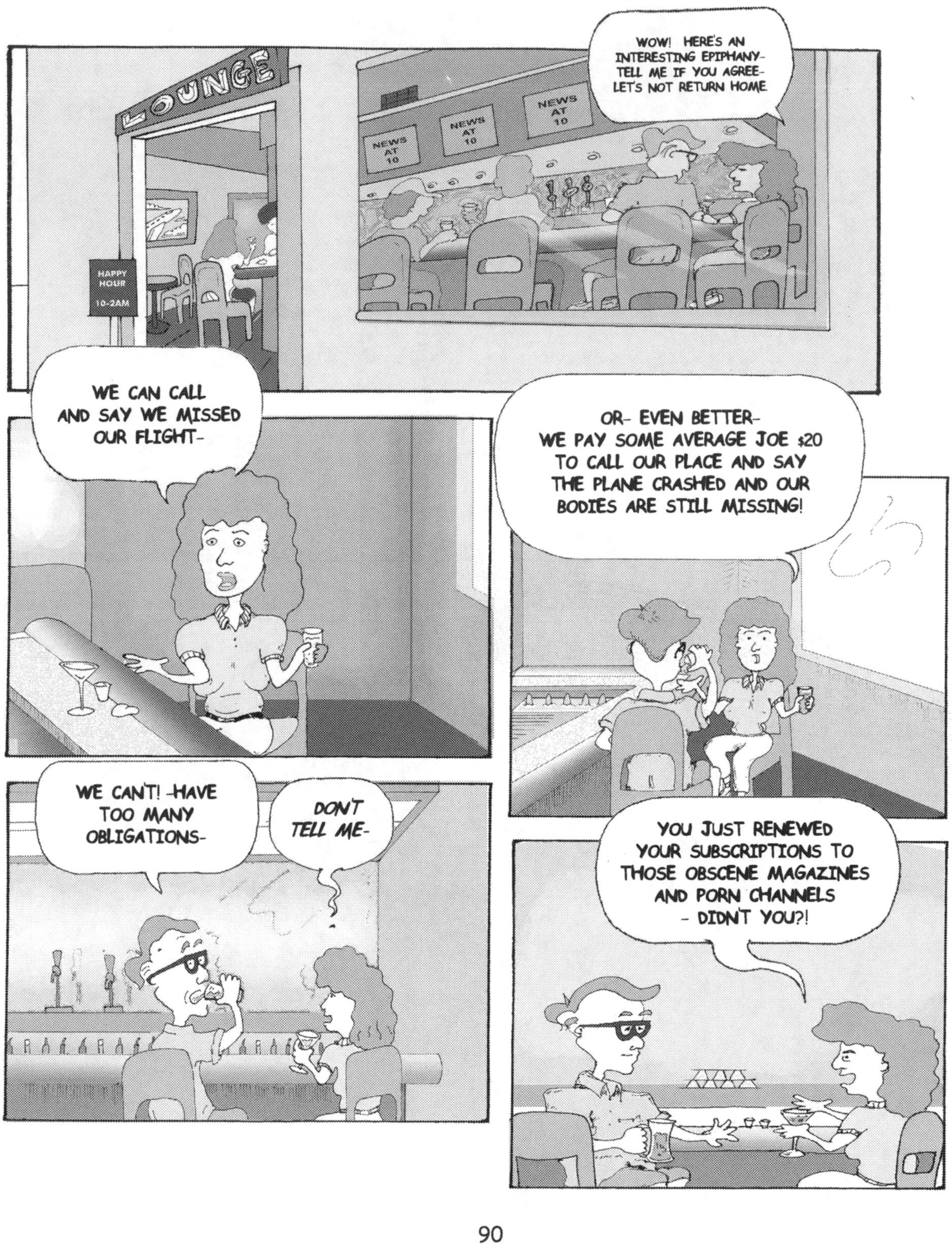
WOW! HERE'S AN INTERESTING EPIPHANY- TELL ME IF YOU AGREE- LET'S NOT RETURN HOME.
LOUNGE
NEWS AT 10
NEWS AT 10
NEWS AT 10
HAPPY HOUR 10-2AM
WE CAN CALL AND SAY WE MISSED OUR FLIGHT-
OR- EVEN BETTER- WE PAY SOME AVERAGE JOE $20 TO CALL OUR PLACE AND SAY THE PLANE CRASHED AND OUR BODIES ARE STILL MISSING!
WE CAN'T! -HAVE TOO MANY OBLIGATIONS-
DON'T TELL ME-
YOU JUST RENEWED YOUR SUBSCRIPTIONS TO THOSE OBSCENE MAGAZINES AND PORN CHANNELS - DIDN'T YOU?!

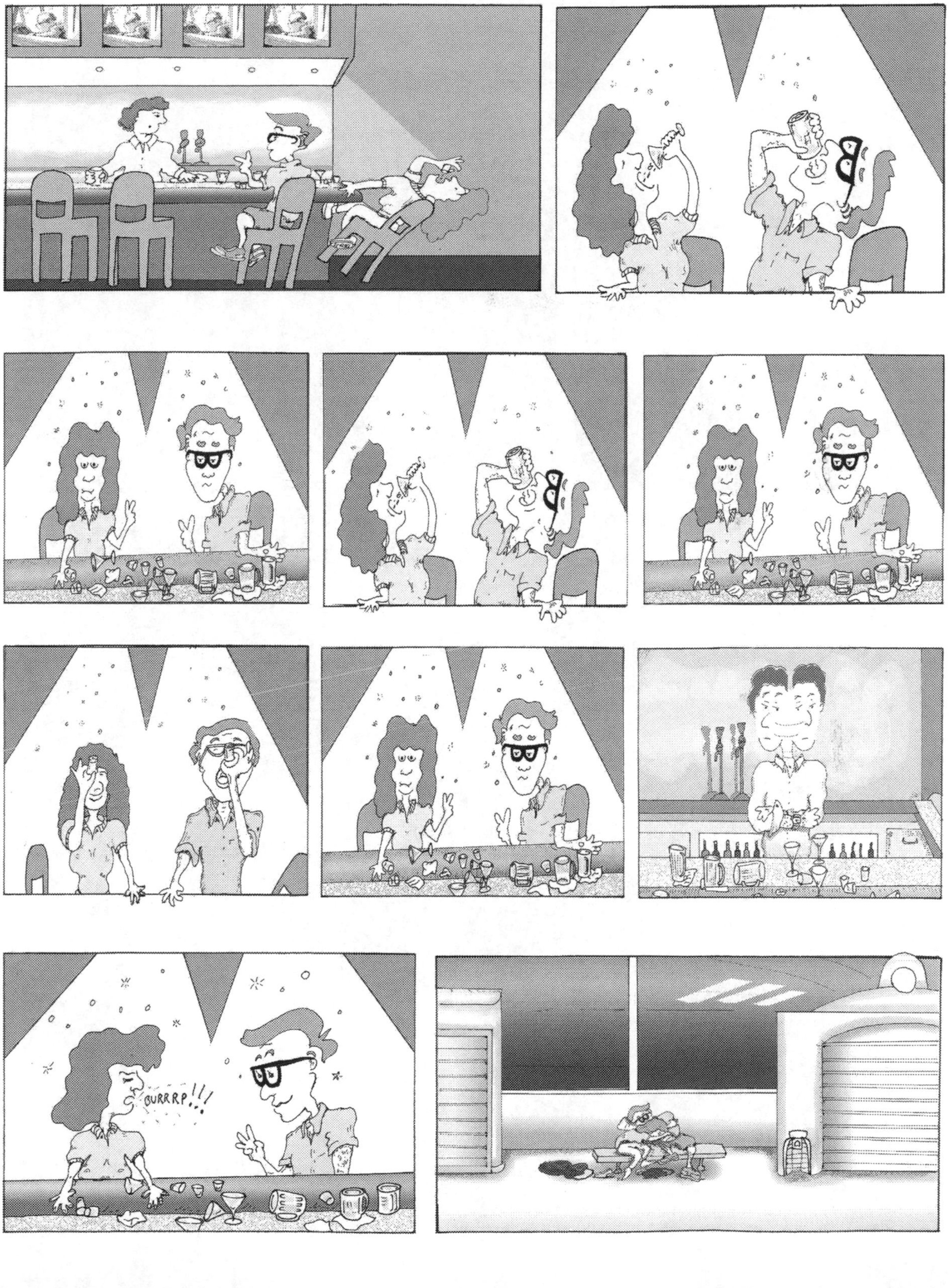
BURRRP!!!

AND 30 SECONDS EARLIER
AT THE NOOD HOMESTEAD-

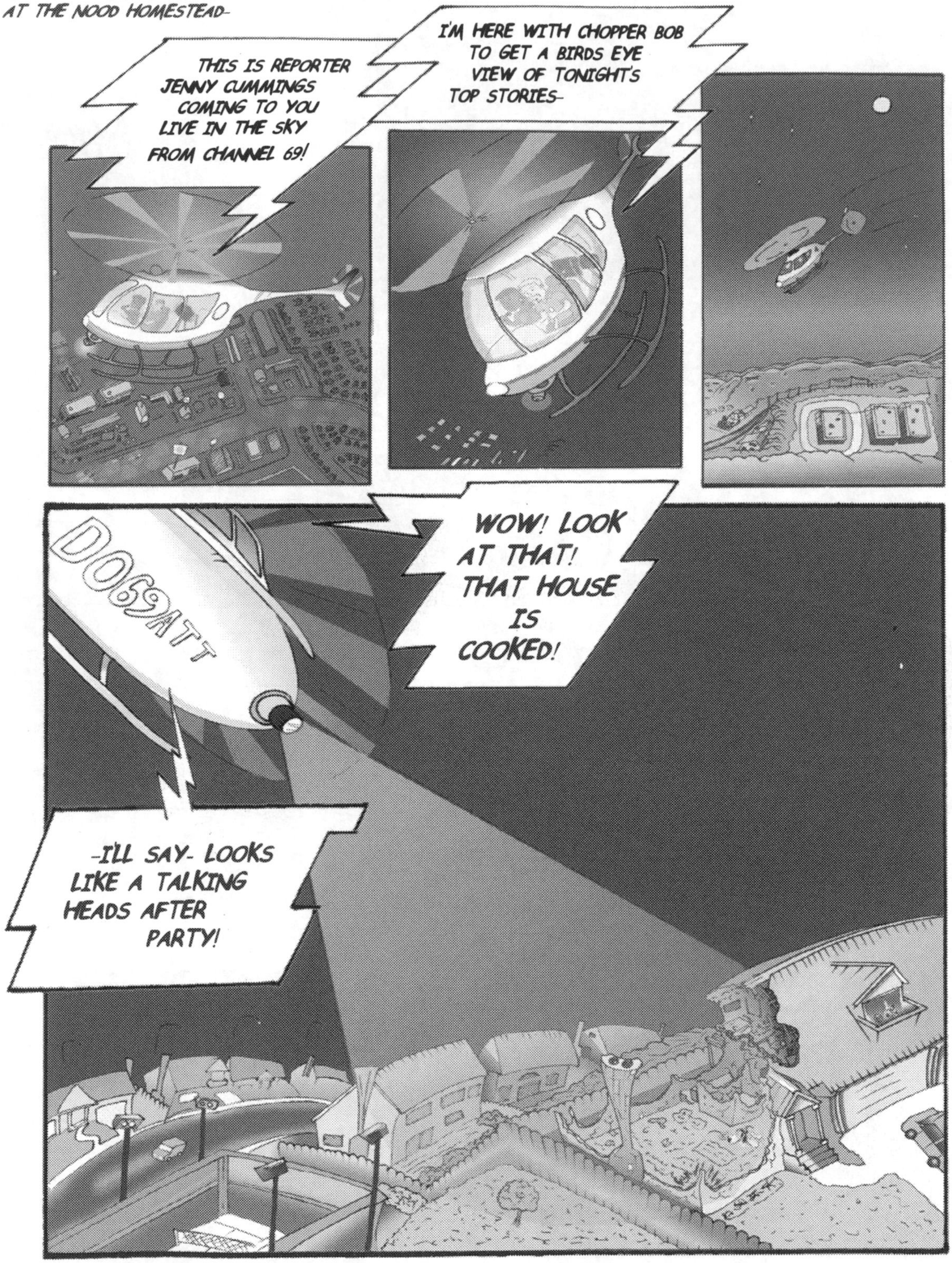
THIS IS REPORTER JENNY CUMMINGS COMING TO YOU LIVE IN THE SKY FROM CHANNEL 69!
I'M HERE WITH CHOPPER BOB TO GET A BIRDS EYE VIEW OF TONIGHT'S TOP STORIES-
DOG9ATT
WOW! LOOK AT THAT! THAT HOUSE IS COOKED!
-I'LL SAY- LOOKS LIKE A TALKING HEADS AFTER PARTY!

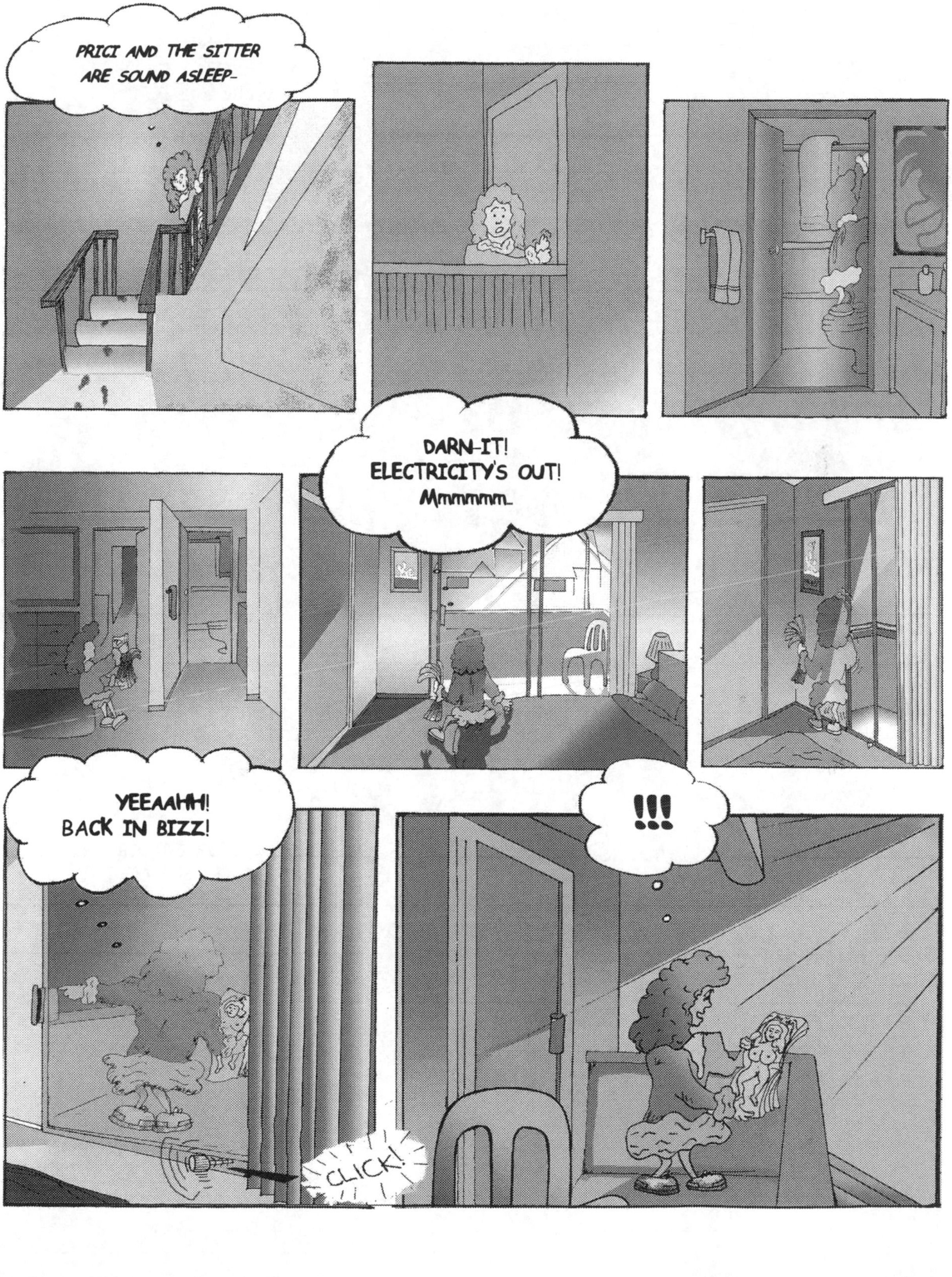
PRICI AND THE SITTER ARE SOUND ASLEEP-
DARN-IT! ELECTRICITY'S OUT! Mmmmmm...
YEEAAHH! BACK IN BIZZ!
CLICK!
!!!

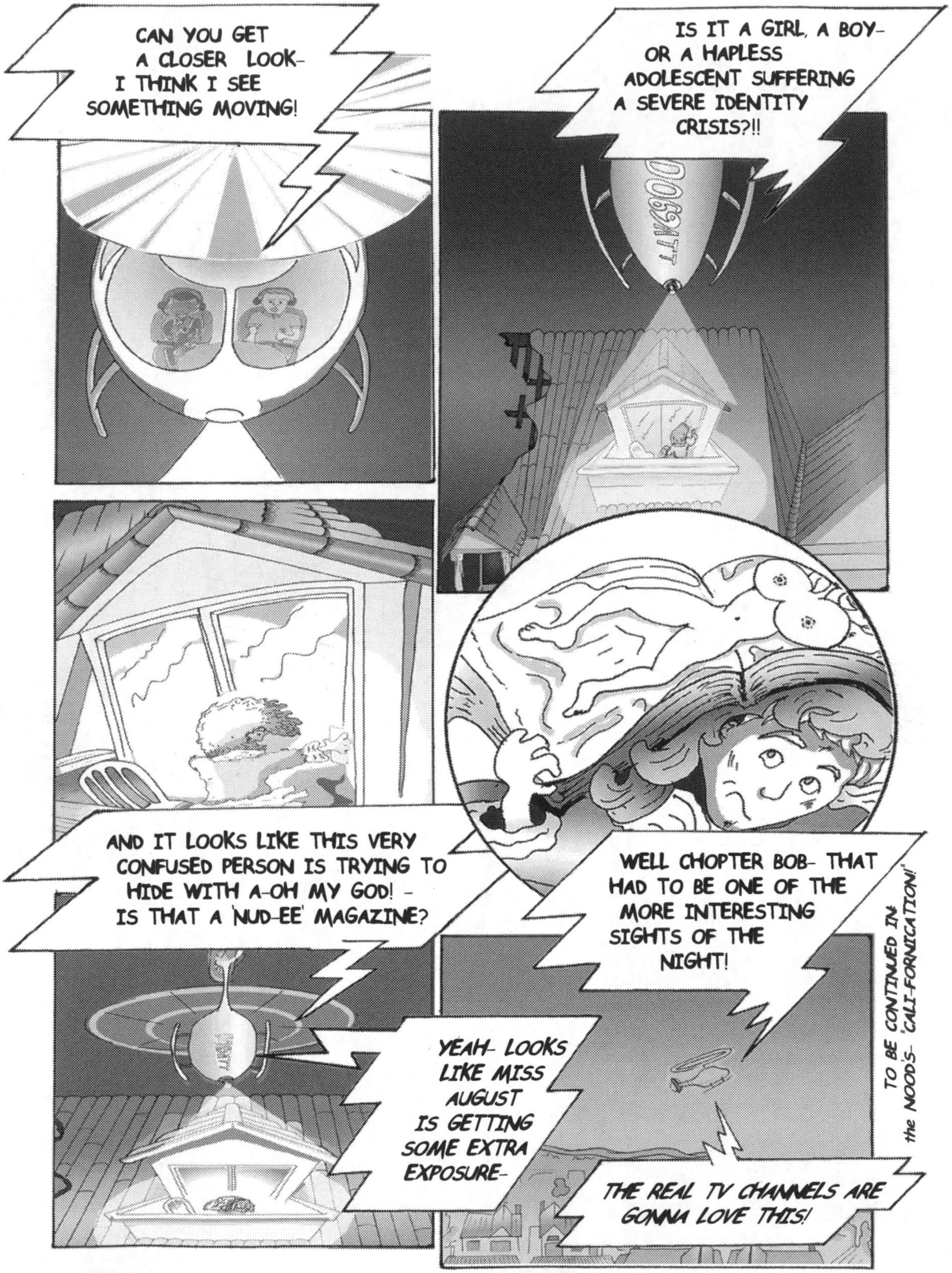
CAN YOU GET A CLOSER LOOK- I THINK I SEE SOMETHING MOVING!
IS IT A GIRL, A BOY- OR A HAPLESS ADOLESCENT SUFFERING A SEVERE IDENTITY CRISIS?!!
AND IT LOOKS LIKE THIS VERY CONFUSED PERSON IS TRYING TO HIDE WITH A-OH MY GOD! - IS THAT A 'NUD-EE' MAGAZINE?
WELL CHOPTER BOB- THAT HAD TO BE ONE OF THE MORE INTERESTING SIGHTS OF THE NIGHT!
YEAH- LOOKS LIKE MISS AUGUST IS GETTING SOME EXTRA EXPOSURE-
THE REAL TV CHANNELS ARE GONNA LOVE THIS!
TO BE CONTINUED IN: the NOOD'S- "CALI-FORNICATION!"

CHAPTER
11

HOME...
SWEET...
HOME...

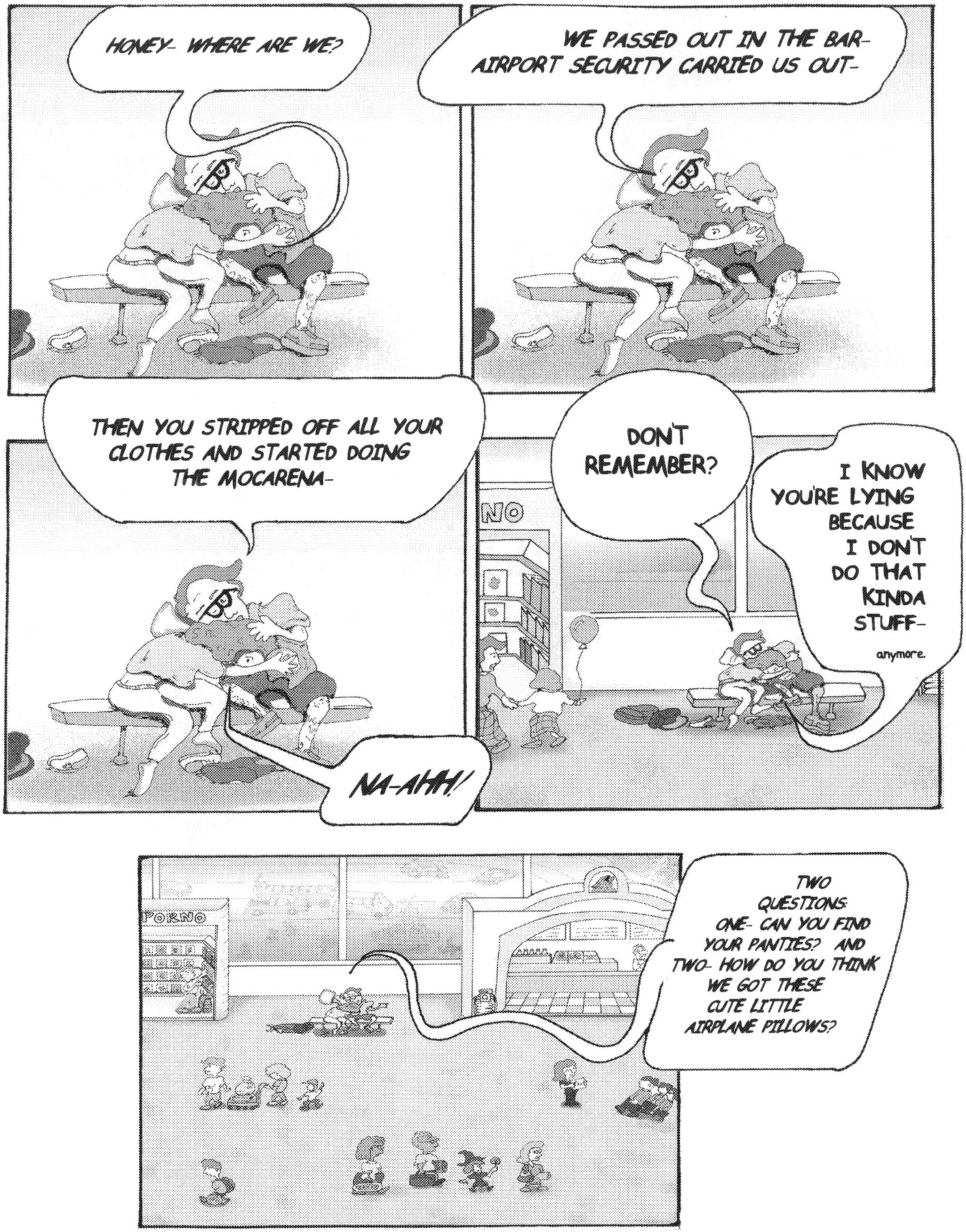
HONEY- WHERE ARE WE?
WE PASSED OUT IN THE BAR- AIRPORT SECURITY CARRIED US OUT-
THEN YOU STRIPPED OFF ALL YOUR CLOTHES AND STARTED DOING THE MOCARENA-
NA-AHH!
DON'T REMEMBER?
I KNOW YOU'RE LYING BECAUSE I DON'T DO THAT KINDA STUFF-
anymore.
PORNO
TWO QUESTIONS: ONE- CAN YOU FIND YOUR PANTIES? AND TWO- HOW DO YOU THINK WE GOT THESE CUTE LITTLE AIRPLANE PILLOWS?

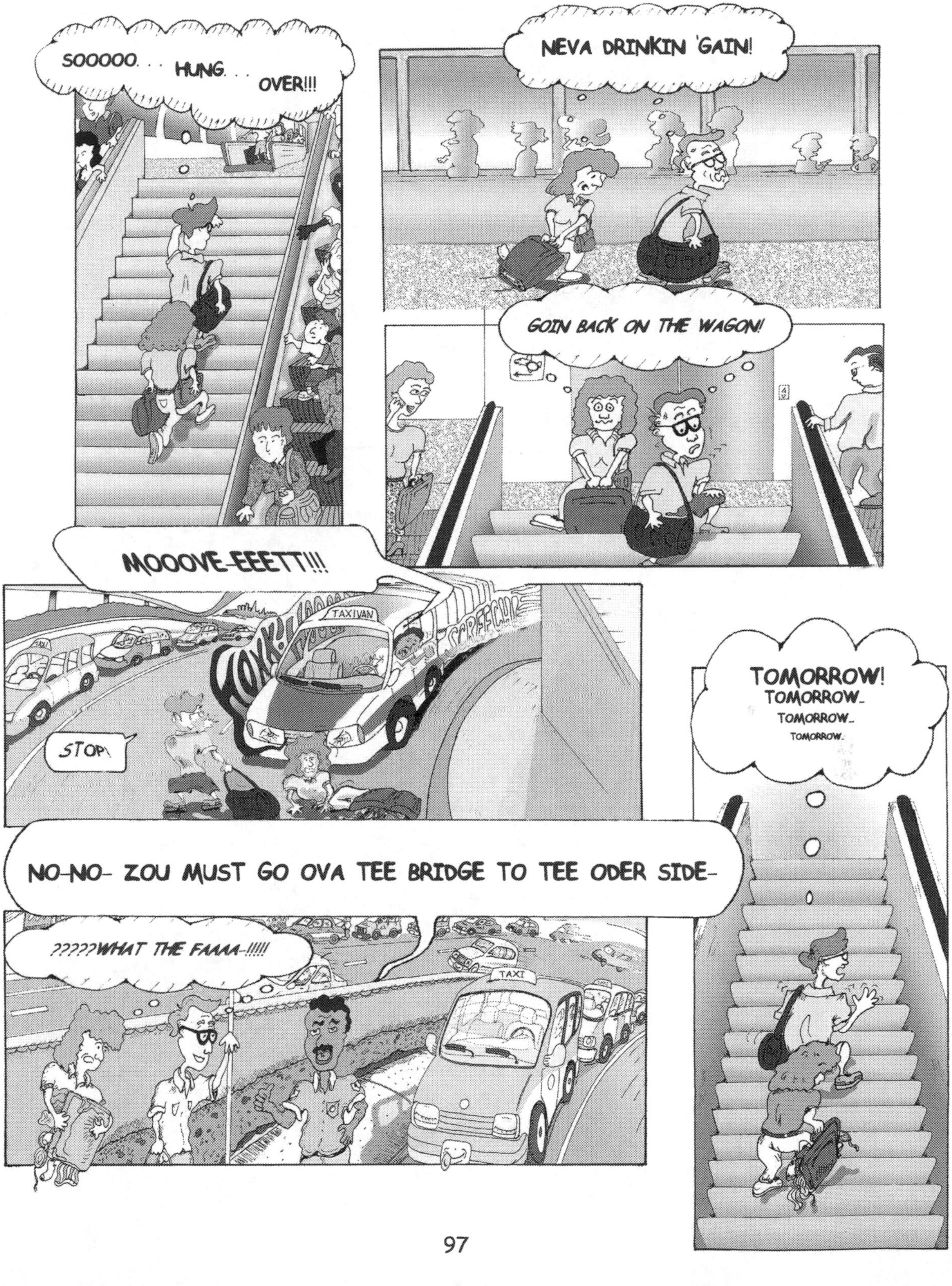
SOOOOO... HUNG... OVER!!!
NEVA DRINKIN 'GAIN!
GOIN BACK ON THE WAGON!
MOOOVE-EEETT!!!
TAXIVAN
STOP!
NO-NO- ZOU MUST GO OVA TEE BRIDGE TO TEE ODER SIDE-
?????WHAT THE FAAAA-!!!!!
TAXI
TOMORROW!
TOMORROW...
TOMORROW...
TOMORROW...

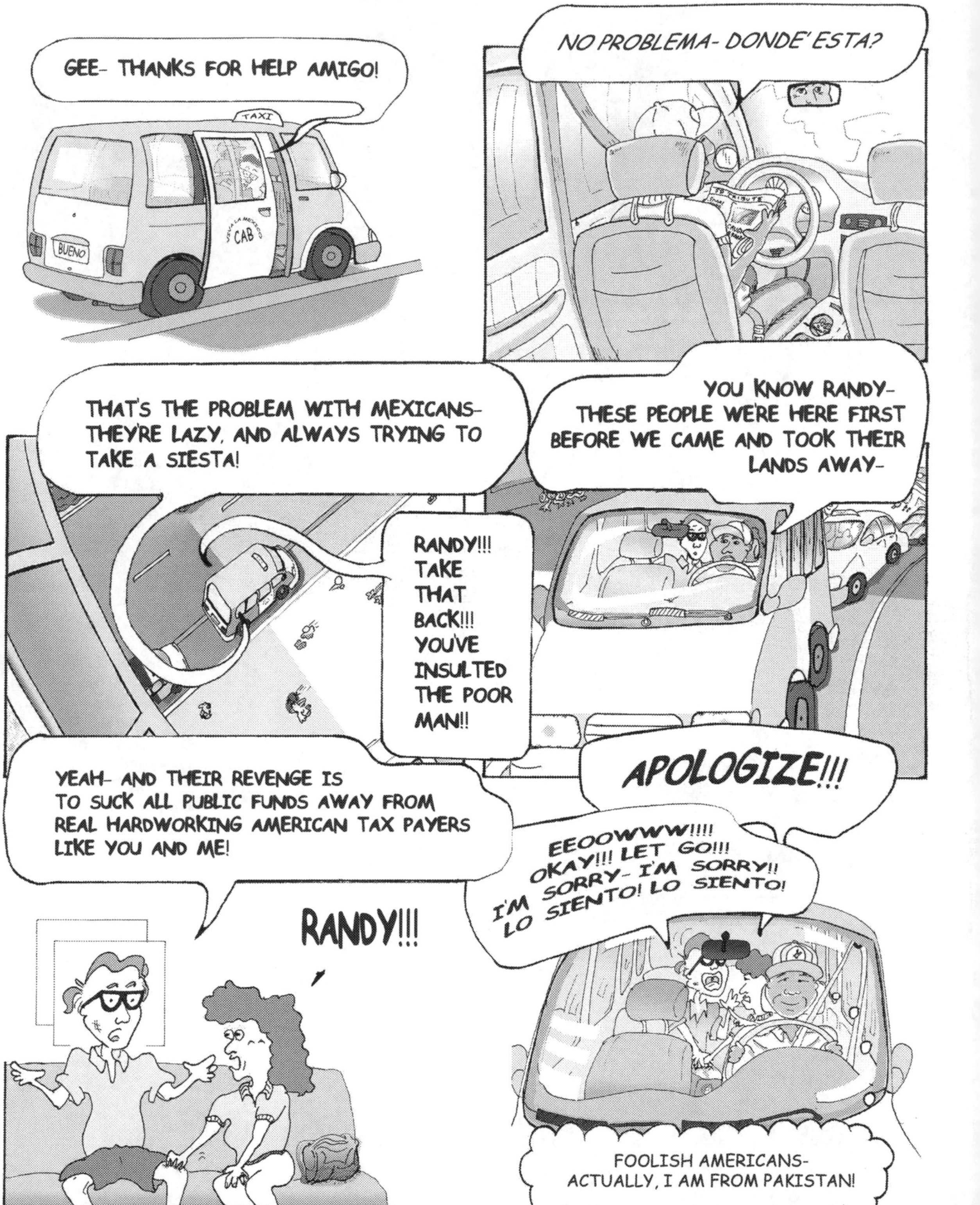

GEE- THANKS FOR HELP AMIGO!
TAXI
BUENO
VIVA LA MEXICO CAB
NO PROBLEMA- DONDE' ESTA?
THAT'S THE PROBLEM WITH MEXICANS- THEY'RE LAZY, AND ALWAYS TRYING TO TAKE A SIESTA!
YOU KNOW RANDY- THESE PEOPLE WE'RE HERE FIRST BEFORE WE CAME AND TOOK THEIR LANDS AWAY-
RANDY!!! TAKE THAT BACK!!! YOU'VE INSULTED THE POOR MAN!!
YEAH- AND THEIR REVENGE IS TO SUCK ALL PUBLIC FUNDS AWAY FROM REAL HARDWORKING AMERICAN TAX PAYERS LIKE YOU AND ME!
APOLOGIZE!!!
RANDY!!!
EEOOWWW!!!! OKAY!!! LET GO!!! I'M SORRY- I'M SORRY!! LO SIENTO! LO SIENTO!
FOOLISH AMERICANS- ACTUALLY, I AM FROM PAKISTAN!

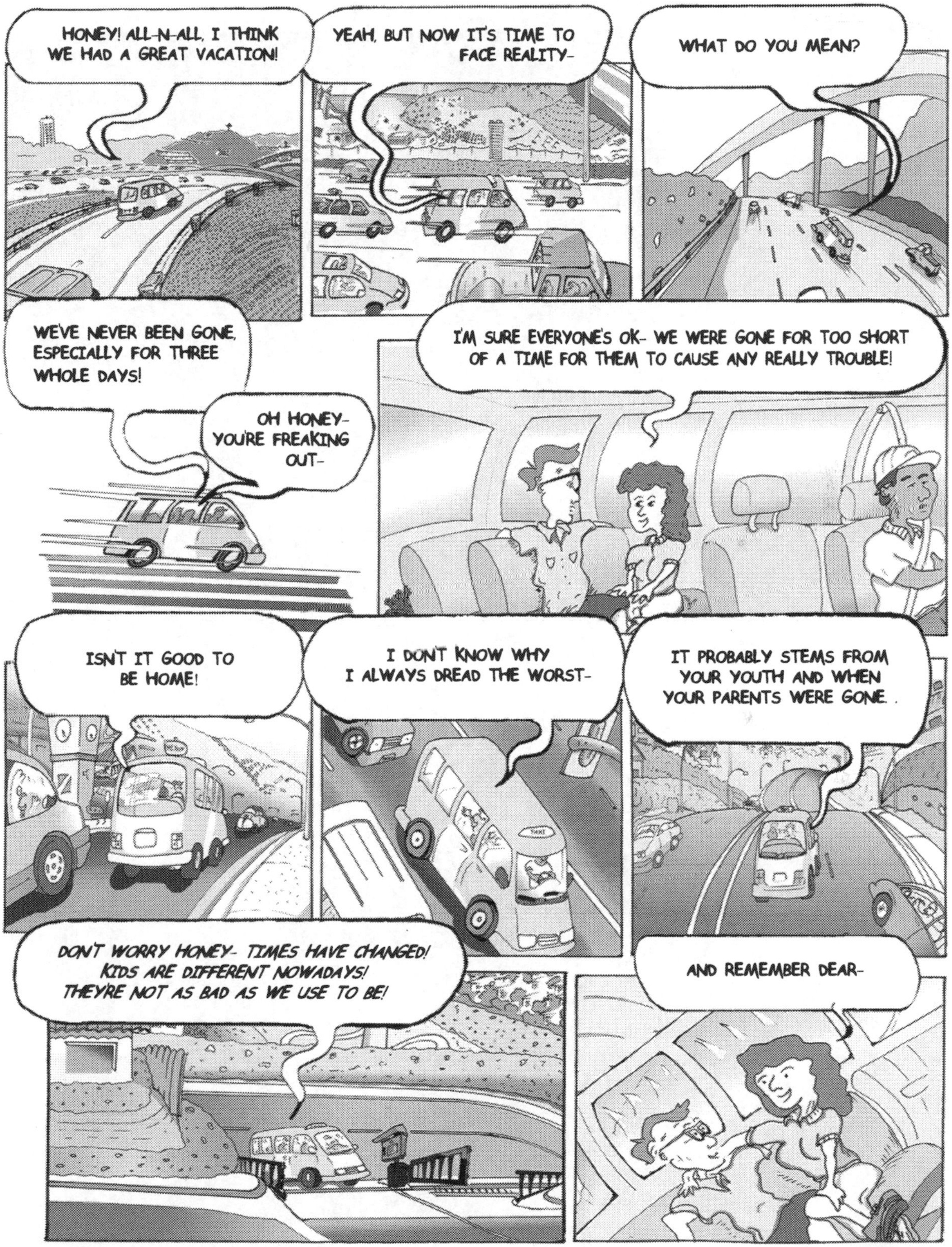
HONEY! ALL-N-ALL, I THINK WE HAD A GREAT VACATION!
YEAH, BUT NOW IT'S TIME TO FACE REALITY-
WHAT DO YOU MEAN?
WE'VE NEVER BEEN GONE, ESPECIALLY FOR THREE WHOLE DAYS!
OH HONEY- YOU'RE FREAKING OUT-
I'M SURE EVERYONE'S OK- WE WERE GONE FOR TOO SHORT OF A TIME FOR THEM TO CAUSE ANY REALLY TROUBLE!
ISN'T IT GOOD TO BE HOME!
I DON'T KNOW WHY I ALWAYS DREAD THE WORST-
IT PROBABLY STEMS FROM YOUR YOUTH AND WHEN YOUR PARENTS WERE GONE.
DON'T WORRY HONEY- TIMES HAVE CHANGED! KIDS ARE DIFFERENT NOWADAYS! THEY'RE NOT AS BAD AS WE USE TO BE!
AND REMEMBER DEAR-

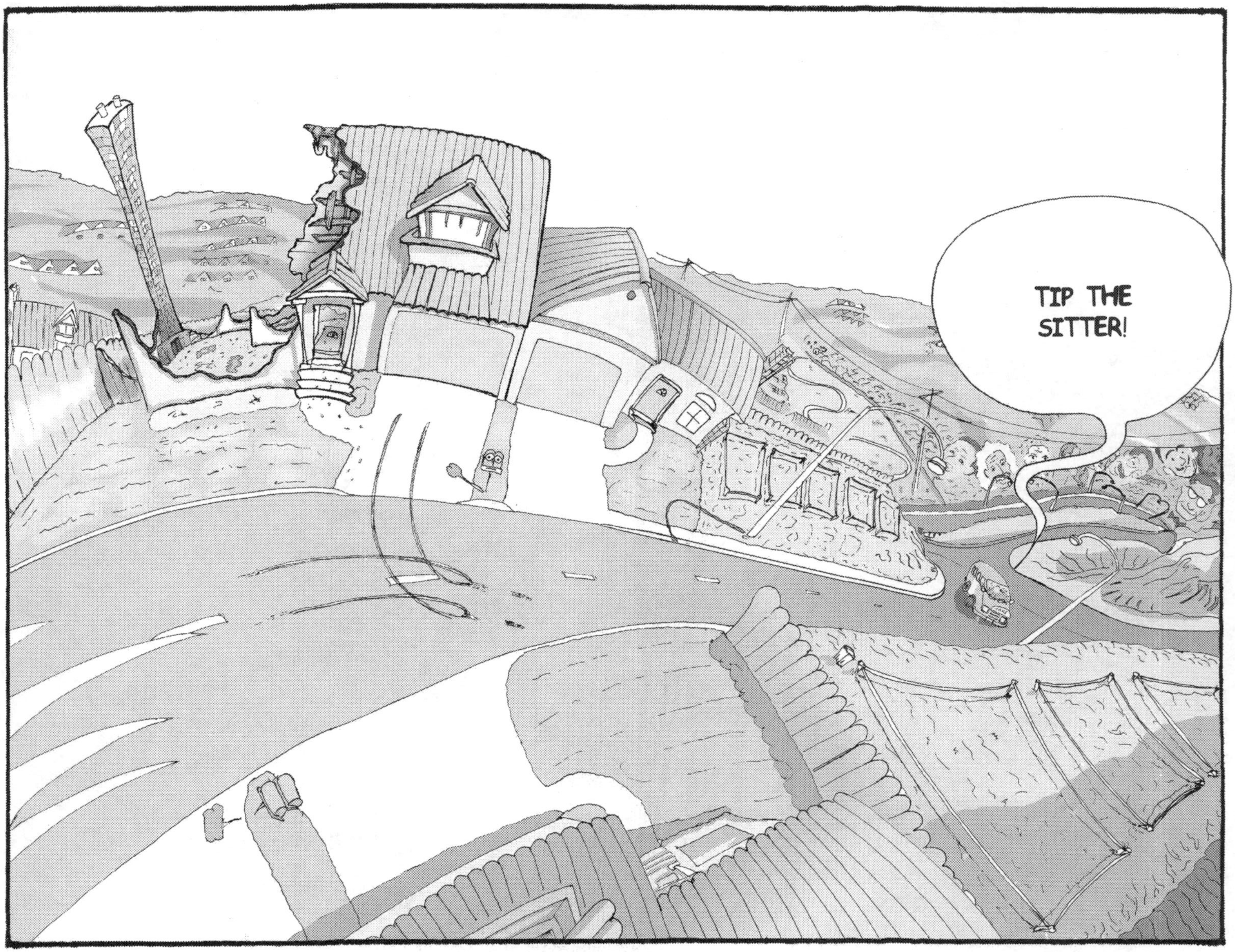
TIP THE SITTER!

EPILOGUE

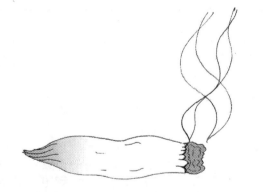

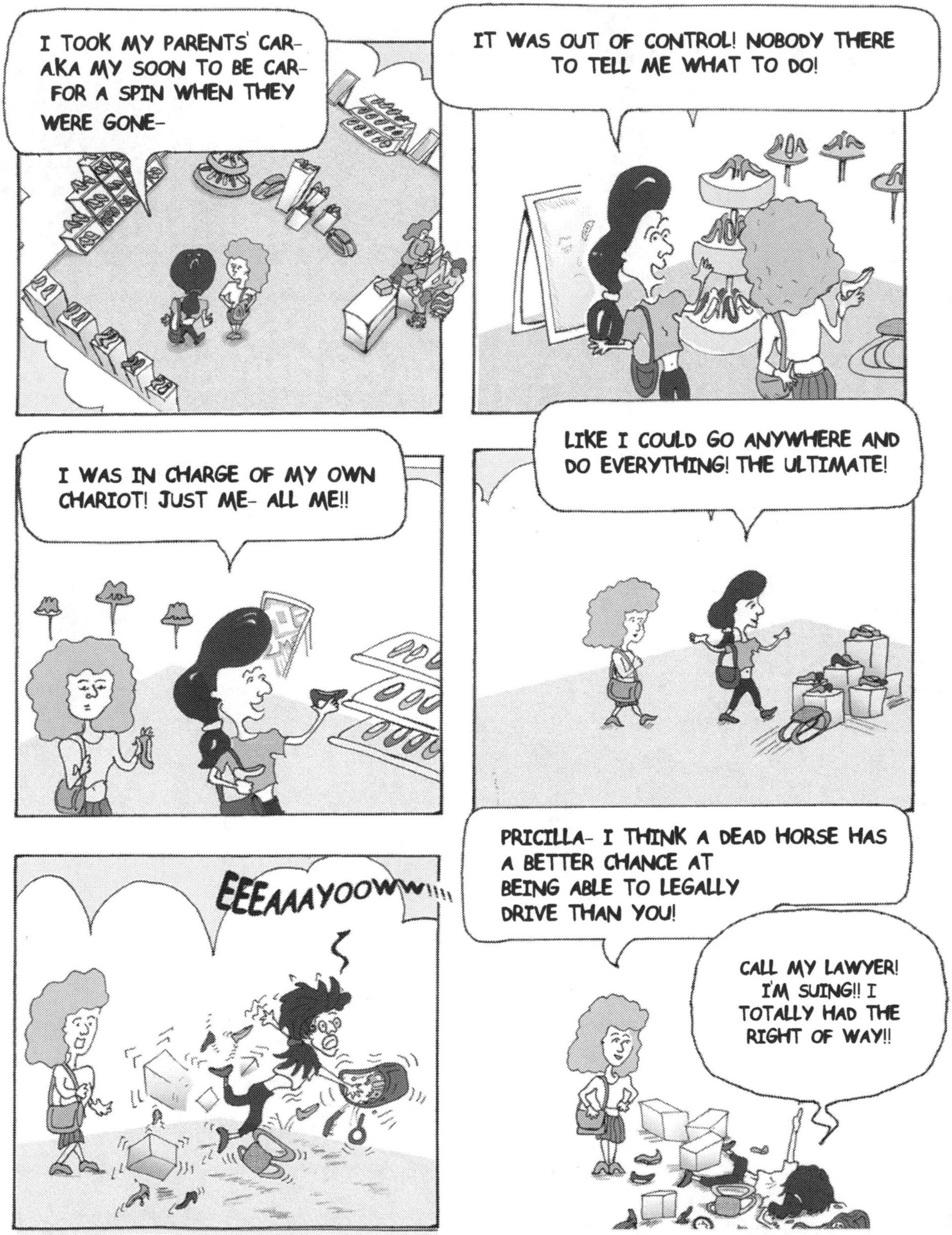
I TOOK MY PARENTS' CAR- A.KA MY SOON TO BE CAR- FOR A SPIN WHEN THEY WERE GONE-
IT WAS OUT OF CONTROL! NOBODY THERE TO TELL ME WHAT TO DO!
I WAS IN CHARGE OF MY OWN CHARIOT! JUST ME- ALL ME!!
LIKE I COULD GO ANYWHERE AND DO EVERYTHING! THE ULTIMATE!
EEEAAAYOOWW!!!!
PRICILLA- I THINK A DEAD HORSE HAS A BETTER CHANCE AT BEING ABLE TO LEGALLY DRIVE THAN YOU!
CALL MY LAWYER! I'M SUING!! I TOTALLY HAD THE RIGHT OF WAY!!

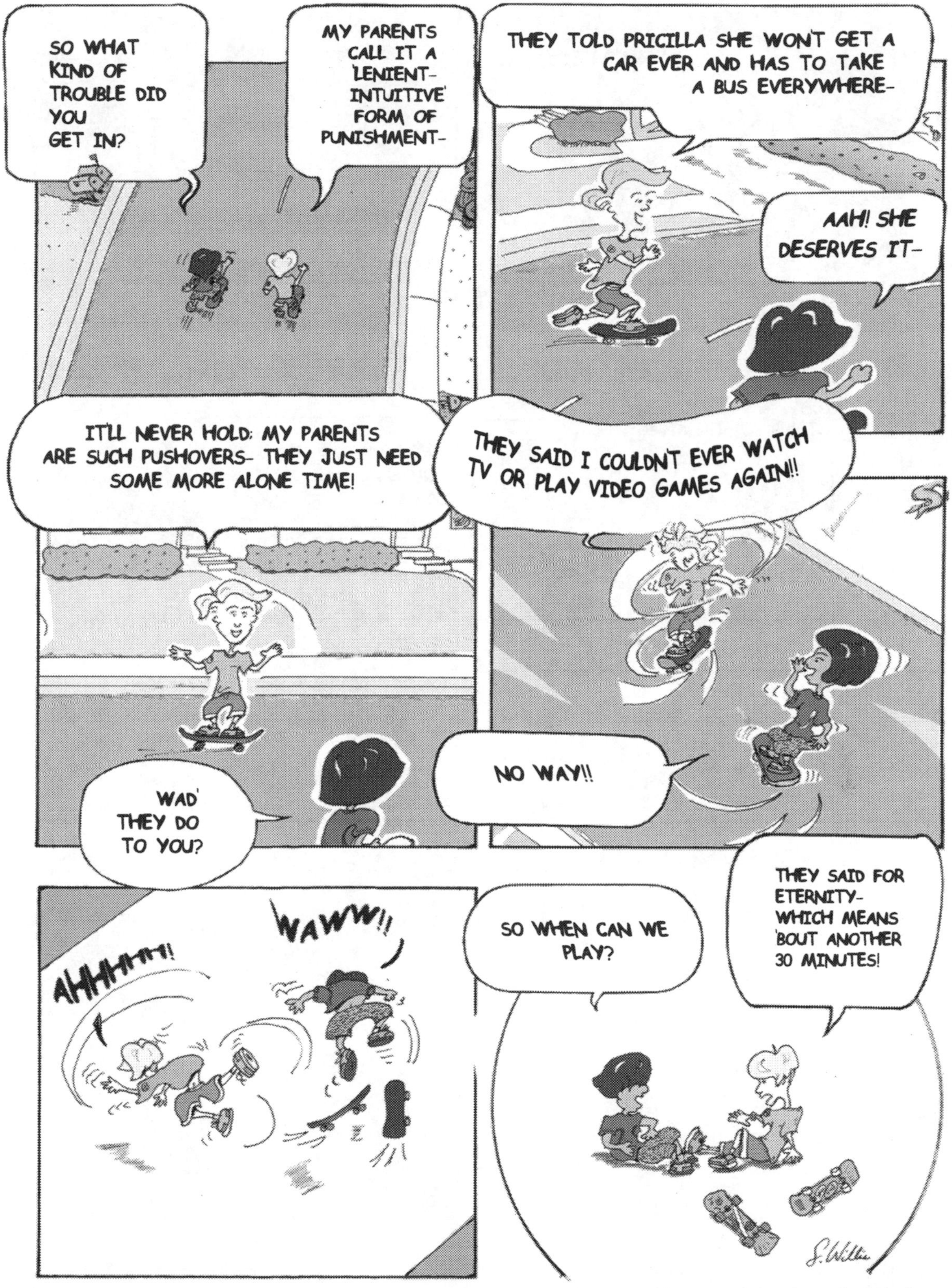
SO WHAT KIND OF TROUBLE DID YOU GET IN?
MY PARENTS CALL IT A 'LENIENT-INTUITIVE' FORM OF PUNISHMENT-
THEY TOLD PRICILLA SHE WON'T GET A CAR EVER AND HAS TO TAKE A BUS EVERYWHERE-
AAH! SHE DESERVES IT-
IT'LL NEVER HOLD; MY PARENTS ARE SUCH PUSHOVERS- THEY JUST NEED SOME MORE ALONE TIME!
THEY SAID I COULDN'T EVER WATCH TV OR PLAY VIDEO GAMES AGAIN!!
WAD' THEY DO TO YOU?
NO WAY!!
AHHHHH!
WAWW!!
SO WHEN CAN WE PLAY?
THEY SAID FOR ETERNITY- WHICH MEANS 'BOUT ANOTHER 30 MINUTES!
S. Willis

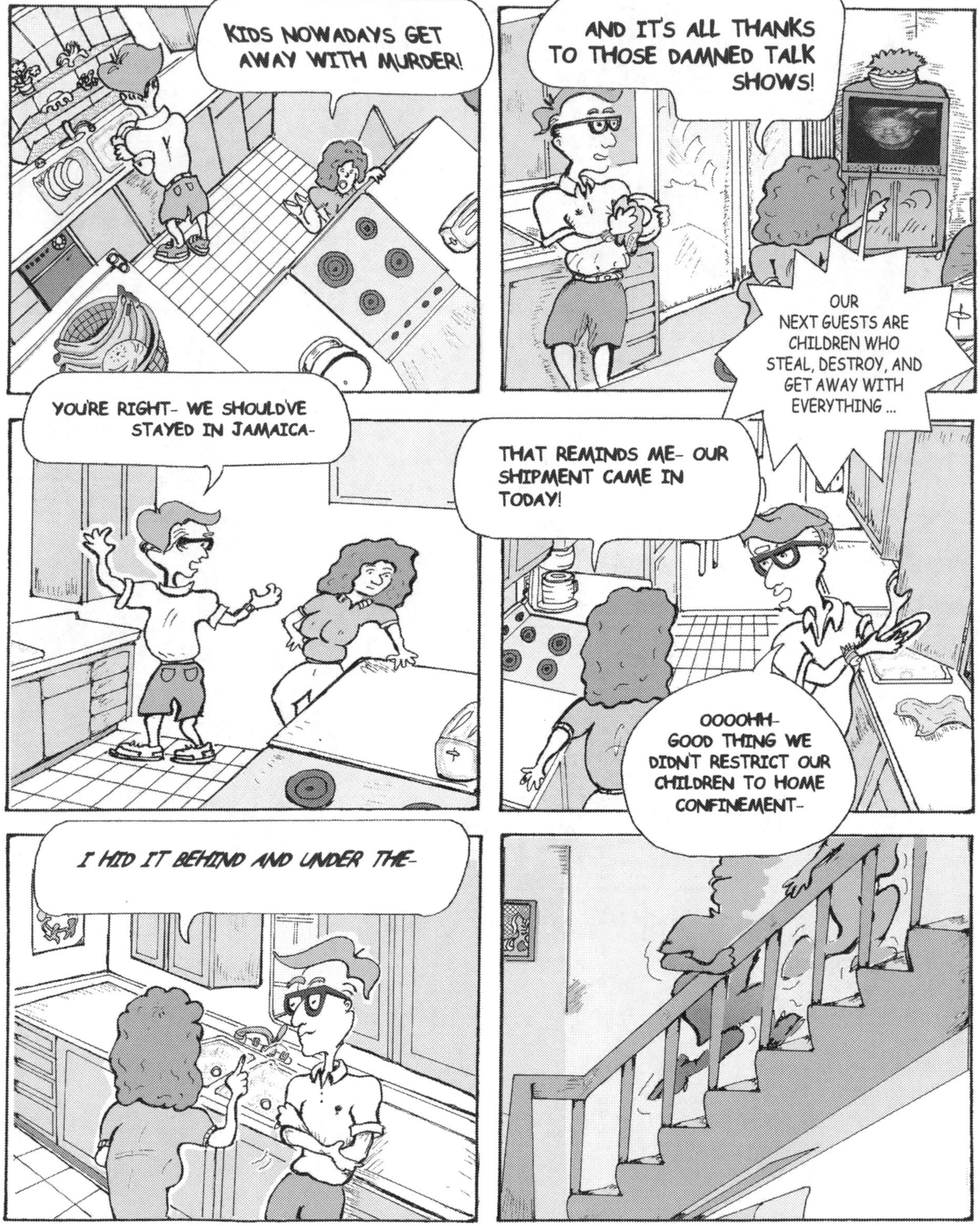
KIDS NOWADAYS GET AWAY WITH MURDER!
AND IT'S ALL THANKS TO THOSE DAMNED TALK SHOWS!
OUR NEXT GUESTS ARE CHILDREN WHO STEAL, DESTROY, AND GET AWAY WITH EVERYTHING ...
YOU'RE RIGHT- WE SHOULD'VE STAYED IN JAMAICA-
THAT REMINDS ME- OUR SHIPMENT CAME IN TODAY!
OOOOHH- GOOD THING WE DIDN'T RESTRICT OUR CHILDREN TO HOME CONFINEMENT-
I HID IT BEHIND AND UNDER THE-

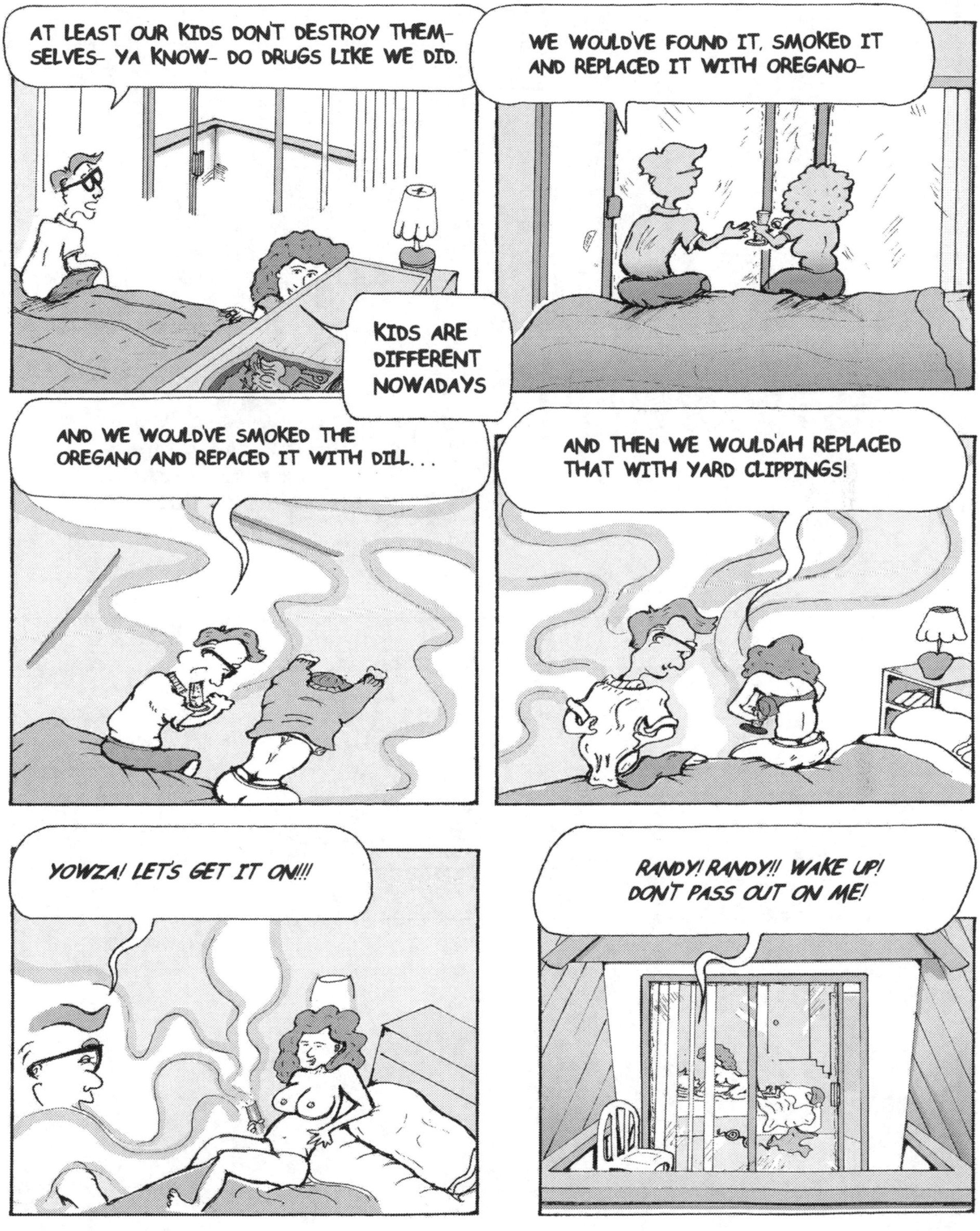
AT LEAST OUR KIDS DON'T DESTROY THEMSELVES- YA KNOW- DO DRUGS LIKE WE DID.
WE WOULD'VE FOUND IT, SMOKED IT AND REPLACED IT WITH OREGANO-
KIDS ARE DIFFERENT NOWADAYS
AND WE WOULD'VE SMOKED THE OREGANO AND REPACED IT WITH DILL...
AND THEN WE WOULD'AH REPLACED THAT WITH YARD CLIPPINGS!
YOWZA! LET'S GET IT ON!!!
RANDY! RANDY!! WAKE UP! DON'T PASS OUT ON ME!

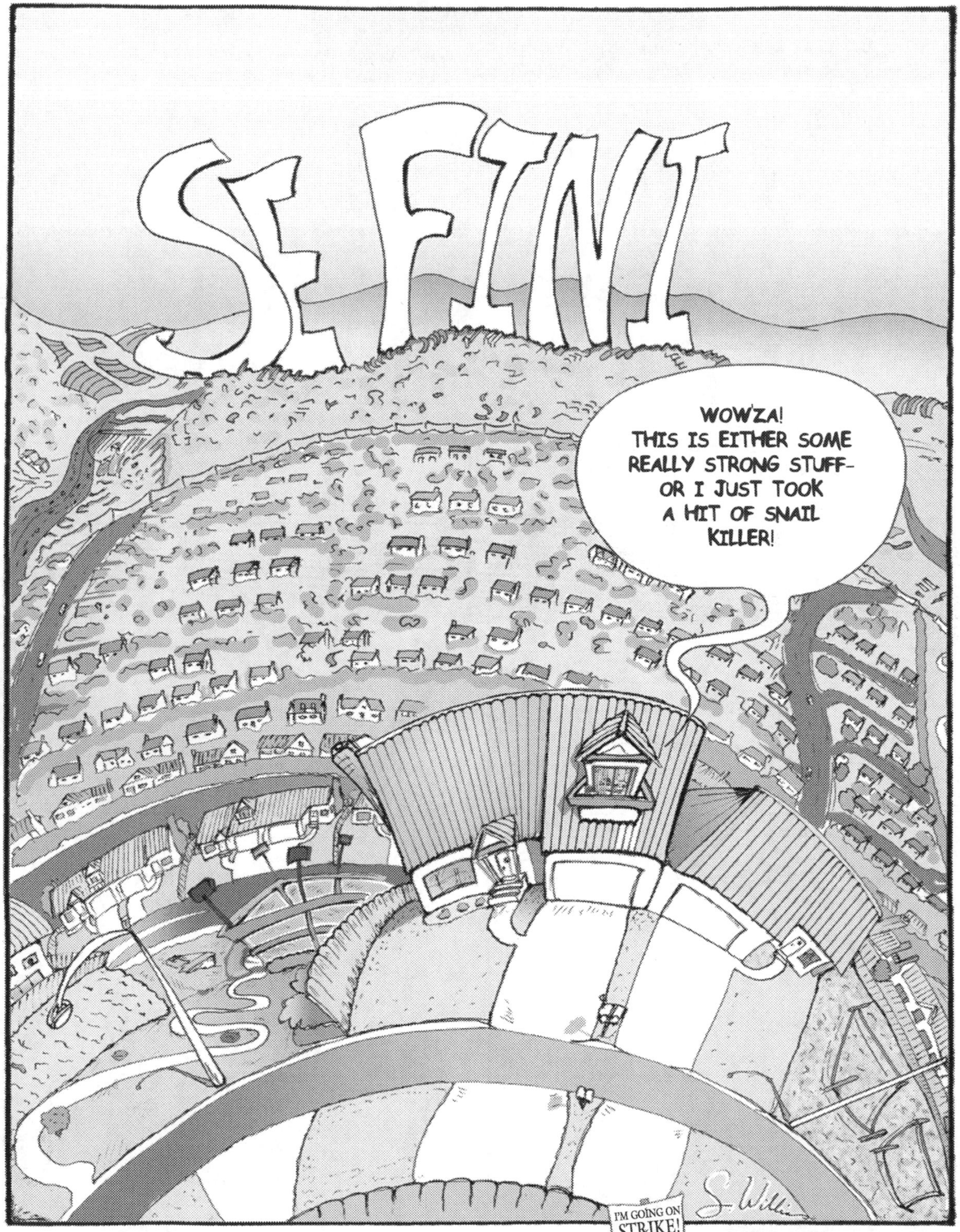
SE FINI
WOW'ZA!
THIS IS EITHER SOME
REALLY STRONG STUFF-
OR I JUST TOOK
A HIT OF SNAIL
KILLER!

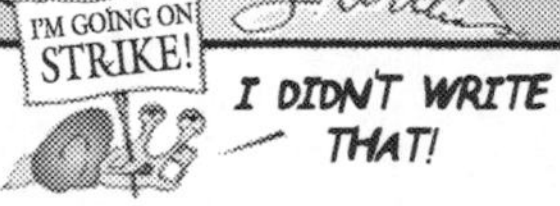
I'M GOING ON
STRIKE!
I DIDN'T WRITE
THAT!